A PEACEFUL REALM

THE RISE AND FALL OF THE INDUS CIVILIZATION

A PEACEFUL REALM

THE RISE AND FALL OF THE INDUS CIVILIZATION

JANE R. McINTOSH

A PETER N. NEVRAUMONT BOOK

WESTVIEW PRESS
A MEMBER OF THE PERSEUS BOOK GROUP

Copyright © 2002 by Jane R. McIntosh
Maps Copyright © 2002 by Nevraumont Publishing Company, Inc.

Westview Press books are available at special discounts for bulk purchases in the United States by corporations, institutions, and other organizations. For more information, please contact the Special Markets Department at The Perseus Books Group, 11 Cambridge Center, Cambridge MA 02142, or call (617) 252-5298.

Published in 2002 in the United States of America by Westview Press, 5500 Central Avenue, Boulder, Colorado 80301–2877, and in the United Kingdom by Westview Press, 12 Hid's Copse Road, Cumnor Hill, Oxford OX2 9JJ

Find us on the World Wide Web at www.westviewpress.com

Library of Congress Cataloging-in-Publication Data
McIntosh, Jane.
    A peaceful realm: the rise and fall of the Indus civilization / Jane R. McIntosh
        p.cm.
    Includes bibliographical references (p.) and index.
    ISBN 0-8133-3532-9 (hc.: alk. paper)
        1. Indus civilization. I. Title
    DS425.M34 2002
    934—dc21   2002017688

The paper used in this publication meets the requirements of the American National Standard for Permanence of Paper for Printed Library Materials Z39.48–1984.

10 9 8 7 6 5 4 3 2 1

Created and produced by
Nevraumont Publishing Company
New York, New York
President: Ann J. Perrini

Jacket and book design by Barbara Balch

CONTENTS

INTRODUCTION

We live in a world that has been civilized for so long that we take its order as the natural state for humanity. In the West and many other areas we are embedded in a way of life in which we are strongly isolated and insulated from nature—where food comes from supermarkets, hygienically wrapped, and there are children who do not know that milk comes from cows—where almost everyone is employed in an activity that is not directly related to creating the means to sustain life and where day and night, summer and winter, rain or shine may almost have no meaning. In other parts of the world, the gap between humanity and nature is less great but we still take for granted the trappings of civilized modern life.

The vast majority of us also know and accept that our distant ancestors were animals whose lives were inextricably bound up with the natural world—and that this was not so long ago either. Relative to the history of our planet, humans appear on the scene almost in the last minute—and out of that minute, only for the blinking of an eye have we been civilized. Of the 5 million years that humans and our earlier ancestors have been around, we have been farmers for only 10,000 years and civilized for less than 6,000.

And yet, how much we have packed into that time. What remarkable changes we have wrought in our lifestyles and what ingenuity has been displayed in thus transforming our lives! In recent times, and in some places less recently, we can actually credit known individuals with these transformations. For the rest of human time we do not know who was responsible—but this does not lessen their achievements.

For as long as I can remember, I have been fascinated by the past, filled with wonder and a desire to know what happened. How did human societies develop into civilizations? What was life like in ancient times? Why did some regions become civilized and others not? I first read of the Indus Civilization in my teens and was filled with a desire to know more. Studying Indian prehistory, I accumulated a great deal of data about this civilization, and about the civilizations that followed later in the subcontinent. But whereas my studies of other civilizations began to give me a clear picture of their how and why and what, the Indus Civilization remained a mystery. Who were these people? How were they organized? Why did they become civilized? Why did they suddenly decline and where did they go to?

I offer here the questions that many people are asking about the Indus Civilization, the clues that they are finding in their attempt to solve the puzzles, and a few of the solutions that seem to emerge—but there is so much still to be found out.

CIVILIZATIONS

Great rivers thundering down from their mountain sources have brought the waters of life to desert lands since time immemorial. Five thousand years ago, three of the world's greatest rivers—the Nile, the Euphrates, and the Indus—had civilizations along their fertile banks. A thousand years later, the lands of the Yellow River also saw the emergence of civilization.

Every schoolchild knows of the ancient civilization of Egypt, the land of the pharaohs, gift of the Nile, where pyramids still stand witness to the aspirations of early kings. Wall paintings and sculptures make us intimately familiar with every detail of their sunlit lives, from the humble peasant in the fields to the queen in her private chamber, while their mummies bring us face-to-face with the very individuals themselves. Hieroglyphic inscriptions and papyrus manuscripts tell us their story—the frank confessions of the tomb robber, the tender words of love between husband and wife, the fears of the deceased as they enter the afterworld, the satisfaction of the successful hunter or warrior.

Mesopotamia, the land between the rivers Tigris and Euphrates, has also impressed itself upon us. The Assyrians and Babylonians, familiar as oppressors in the Bible, have captured the imagination with the magnificence of their palaces, guarded by vast man-headed bulls and lions and decorated with scenes of battle and lion hunts. The Babylonian king Hammurabi is universally revered as the first lawgiver, the father of justice. The Sumerians, their predecessors, were the founders of civilization, the earliest people to use writing, the first to dwell in cities, authors of the first literature in the story of the hero-king Gilgamesh and his doomed quest for eternal life. Their magnificent ziggurats remain in the imagination even as they crumble back into the mud from which they were constructed. And who can fail to be moved by the Royal Cemetery at Ur, filled with the bodies of servants and soldiers who had willingly followed their kings and queens into death, lying alongside exquisite gold jewelry, gaming boards, jars of makeup, clothes, and musical instruments?

But the Indus Civilization has almost vanished into obscurity, although in its day it controlled an area larger than either Egypt or Mesopotamia. Its sailors roamed the known world, its people enjoyed a lifestyle that would be the envy of most today, and the fabric of its cities has well stood the test of time. Nevertheless, unlike Mesopotamia and Egypt, whose civilizations endured for several millennia, within less than a thousand years the Indus Civilization—like a candle—had flared up, burned brightly, and gone out. Why?

CITY DWELLERS

Around 4000 B.C., cities were emerging in the fertile lands watered by the river Euphrates. By 500 B.C., cities were to be found in many areas, in many different forms relevant to local patterns of existence—Greek city-states, Mesoamerican ceremonial centers, Persian and Chinese metropolises. Complex civilized and urbanized societies developed in different parts of the world at different times, and many that were once great later fell, to be replaced by others, often centered in different areas.

It is at this time, when many parts of the world were developing from simple farming communities into complex civilized societies, that the lessons from the past become particularly relevant to our understanding of our own society. We can now begin to see strong parallels between the life of antiquity and that of the modern city dweller. Although the majority of people still engaged in agriculture as their means of livelihood, many inhabitants of early civilized societies earned their living, fully or in part, by other means, as artisans, merchants, priests, porters, ferrymen, laborers, or rulers. It was no longer necessary for every individual to be a primary producer and self-sufficient—specialists could now also be supported by society—a trend that has resulted in many parts of the modern world in a society almost entirely composed of specialists, each forming a tiny cog on an immensely complex wheel.

Cities arose where lavish architecture reflected not only religion but also social status. Although previously there had been some social inequalities, such distinctions had been limited in degree and number. Now, however, societies emerged in which many status differences and levels came into being—high priests, kings and emperors, nobles and bureaucrats, merchants and artisans, soldiers, farmers and herders, serfs and slaves. Different societies were organized in different ways and accorded high and low status to different activities, but all were alike in their complexity. The dwellings of the elite in these societies were often splendid in size and architectural complexity, finely decorated and lavishly furnished, while their burials were often richly endowed with magnificent offerings, reflecting the affluence and far-flung connections of the civilization, and the gulf between ruler and ruled.

Art, often an excellent window on the past, was now frequently supplemented by written sources, so that for the first time we can find out the names and deeds of individuals. We can read the achievements and anxieties of Gilgamesh, the hero king of Uruk, a real historical ruler but a figure around whom legendary tales and myths have accreted. We can learn of the activities of more historically solid rulers such as Menes (Narmer), the unifier of Egypt. And we can also glimpse the daily life of the ordinary person, such as the thousands of peasants who toiled to raise the pyramids or the anxious Roman mother sending underwear to her soldier son on Hadrian's Wall.

The Indus Civilization was no exception. Developing around 2600 B.C., it flourished for hundreds of years. It has left us the remains of fine planned cities and towns of baked brick houses, furnished with bathrooms, toilets, and excellent sanitation [Figure 1]. Here all manner of crafts took place, making polychrome pottery, superb jewelry, fine stone and metal tools, which have come down to us, as well as many fine products that have not survived but of which we have occasionally tantalizing traces—finely woven cotton textiles and woodwork, for instance. The Indus Civilization was a strong trading partner of contemporary Mesopotamia, flourishing at the same time as the first civilization in Egypt. All three civilizations were at their height some centuries before China's first civilization, the Shang, emerged around 1760 B.C.

PAST AND PRESENT

All these four primary civilizations were literate. Fascinating glimpses of elite life in Sumer and Akkad, Old Kingdom Egypt and Shang China have come down to us through their writings—the Sumerian king Shulgi's memories of his schooldays, Egyptian spells to protect the noble dead in the afterlife, Shang divinations about royal health or hunting expeditions. But no such glimpses are available into the lives of people in the enigmatic Indus Civilization, for we are unable to read their writings [*see* Figure 47].

The Indus script, unlike those of the other three civilizations, still defies attempts at decipherment—and is likely to remain largely undeciphered. Not only are the surviving texts (mainly on seals) very brief and restricted in nature, but there are also no clues from later texts. In Mesopotamia, Akkadian cuneiform was the precursor of Babylonian writing, while Sumerian remained the scholarly script and language, as Latin did in medieval Europe. Egyptian hieroglyphic script developed throughout ancient Egyptian history and was still in use in Classical times. The Shang script was the beginning of a writing system that grew into the one in use in China today. But the Indus script vanished with the civilization that created it, almost 4,000 years ago.

This leaves a void in our knowledge and understanding of the civilization, throwing us back on purely archaeological evidence and its interpretation, providing us with no more information than we have about any prehistoric culture. And yet how much there is to know.

Here we have a state (or was it a state? Some people doubt even this), a complex society in which a great diversity of people created a unique way and style of culture—but we know so little about it. We do not even know if the Indus people had rulers, though it seems inconceivable that they should not. Their sophisticated organization is apparent in so many aspects of their material world. How could such a society possibly have functioned without rulers? And if there were rulers, why can we find so few clues to help us identify them?

FIRST CIVILIZATIONS TIMELINE

INDUS	EGYPTIAN	MESOPOTAMIAN	CHINESE
100 B.C	100 B.C Cleopatra, last of Ptolemaic line, commits suicide (30 B.C.); Octavian claims Egypt for Rome	100 B.C. Roman occupation of Palestine	100 B.C. Sima Qian, historian (c. 145–86 B.C.); Emperor Han Wudi (141–87 B.C.) conquers extensive territories, opens Silk Road, and extends the Great Wall
		200 Parthians take Mesopotamia from Seleucids (c. 250 B.C.)	200 Shihuangde unifies China and founds Qin Dynasty (211 B.C.); Foundation of Han Dynasty (c. 202 B.C.–220 A.D.)
300 Alexander the Great reaches the Indus River	300 The satrap of Egypt, Ptolemy, sets up his own dynasty (305 B.C.)	300 Conquest by Alexander the Great (331 B.C.) 400 Cyrus the Great of Persia conquers Babylon; first postal system under Darius I	300 Mencius (Mengzi), philosopher (b. 372 B.C.) 400 Warring States Period (458 B.C.); copper coinage
500 Life of the Buddha (c. 593–483 B.C.)	500 Persian army, under Cambyses, occupies Egypt (525 B.C.)		500 Confucius (Kongfuzi), philosopher (c. 551–479 B.C.); iron casting; coinage begins
	600 Egyptian force defeated by the Babylonians at Carchemish (605 B.C.); Assyrians attack Egypt, sack Thebes, and leave vassal rulers in charge (663 B.C.)	600 Attacks from Iranian Medes and Babylonian Chaldeans cause Assyria to collapse (612 B.C.); Nebuchadnezzar's Hanging Gardens built	600 Laozi, philosopher (c. 604–520 B.C.); iron working
	700 Seizure of power in Egypt by Nubians (c. 715 B.C.)	700 Height of Assyrian Empire, controlling Middle East from Egypt to Persian Gulf (730–650 B.C.); Sennacherib begins to build library	
		800 Assyrian Queen Sammuramat reigns (811–807 B.C.)	
	900 King Sheshonq intervenes in Israel and sacks Jerusalem (925 B.C.); Kings of Libya establish Dynasty 22	900 After fighting Arameaen and Chaldean tribes, Assyria begins to expand again (c. 910 B.C.)	
1000 "Upanishad" tradition, compilation of the *Rigveda;* Aryan invasion of Indus River Valley	1000 New Kingdom ends (c. 1080 B.C.) 1100 Ramesses III successfully defends Egypt against determined assault by the "Sea Peoples" (c. 1182 B.C.)		1000 Overthrow of Shang by Zhou Dynasty (1027 B.C.); introduction of chariots; mature writing and art
	1200 Peace treaty signed between the Egyptians and Hittites (c. 1269 B.C.); Ramesses II narrowly escapes defeat at the hands of the Hittites at the battle of Kadesh (c. 1286 B.C.)	1200 Assyrian armies conquer Babylon (c. 1225 B.C.); Nebuchadnezzar I expels Elamites; Gilgamesh epic is recorded	
	1300 Brief rule of Tutankhamen, whose tomb survived virtually intact until discovery in 1922 (c. 1350 B.C.); Amenhotep III's son Akhenaten breaks with the established religion (c. 1367 B.C.)	1300 Assyrian Empire established	

INDUS

1600
Collapse of Indus civilization

2100
Disintegration of centralized Indus Civilization

2300
Cultural exchange prominent between Indus and Mesopotamian Civilizations; advanced city planning; early scripts

3000
Beginning of Indus Civilization
3200
Urbanization begins

3700
First evidence of weaving (at Mohenjo Daro)

4300
Development of farming communities; early food producing era

EGYPTIAN

1400
Power and prosperity merged to bring Egyptian civilization to highest point under Amenhotep III (c. 1405 B.C.); Queen Hatshepsut becomes only woman to rule Egypt for any length of time (c. 1490 B.C.)
1500
Theban forces complete expulsion of the Hyksos

1600
End of Middle Kingdom; much of Egypt taken over by Asiatic rulers known as the Hyksos (c. 1652 B.C.)
1700
Introduction of the horse and chariot; establishment of the Middle Kingdom by the Theban Mentuhoten; ability to predict flooding of the Nile

2100
Climatic conditions hasten the end of the Old Kingdom (c. 2160 B.C.)

2500
Great Pyramid of Khufu built at Giza (c. 2575 B.C.)
2600
The Step Pyramid, first monumental building in stone, constructed for King Zoser at Saqqara (c. 2650 B.C.)

2800
Pharaoh "Menes" becomes first ruler of unified country; earliest hieroglyphic writing

3900
Development of early writing

4500
Amratian (Naqada 1) Period
5000
Egyptian calendar: 360 days, 12 months of 30 days each; basketry, pottery, weaving, animal hide tanning
6400
Oldest evident of epipaleolithic peoples

MESOPOTAMIAN

1400
Height of Hittite culture

1500
Raid launched by Turkish Hittites brings Babylon down (c. 1595 B.C.); beginning of Kassites control of Babylon (c. 1550 B.C.)

1700
Hammurabi of Babylon (reign c. 1792–1750 B.C.) briefly unites country at end of his reign; Hammurabi's Code written (c. 1790 B.C.)
1800
Advanced mathematical operations
1900
Influxes of Elamites from the east eventually destroy Ur
2000
Horse introduced to western Asia
2100
Sumerian King List written
2200
The Gutians, tribesmen from the eastern hills end Akkadian rule (c. 2218 B.C.)
2300
Sargon, first king of Akkadian dynasty, defeats Lugalzaggisi, creating vast Semitic empire in Mesopotamia (c. 2350–2100 B.C.)

2700
Rule of King Gilgamesh in Uruk (c. 2750 B.C.); Mis-anni-padda, king of Ur, first recorded ruler in Mesopotamia; first Mesopotamian cities; Sumerians use wheeled transportation

3400
Introduction of potter's wheel; Sumerians settle on the site of the city of Babylon

4000
Simple copper artifacts
4300
First use of ceramics

5000
Ubaidians develop first division of labor
6000
Early food producing era
7000
Oldest know permanent settlement in Mesopotamia at Jarmo

CHINESE

1700
Traditional date of Shang dynasty's overthrow of Xia and beginning of Shang rule (c. 1750 B.C.)

2000
First written texts; first of Xia dynasty

2300
Shun dynasty

3000
Silk manufacturing; Longshan culture; first ceramics

5000
Yangshao culture

Figure 1. (opposite)
HIGH WESTERN
MOUND,
MOHENJO-DARO

*The western mound
at Mohenjo Daro
rises more than 11
meters above the
current level of the
Indus plain.
Constructed on a
massive artificial
platform, its summit
held a number of
substantial public
buildings, including
the Great Bath. Its
modern profile is
dominated by the
much later Buddhist
stupa built above its
ancient ruins.*

What *can* we find out? We have substantial material evidence of cities—clues that allow us to build quite a detailed picture of the skills that the Indus people had developed in all manner of craft activities and what they created using these skills. We can reconstruct a great deal of the appearance of the cities and of the material aspects of people's lives—the considerable comfort in which they lived, for instance, and their sophisticated urban use of water.

We know too, from the materials that they used and from the written and other evidence left by their neighbors, that the Indus people traded over a very wide region. We can build up a reasonably detailed picture of their international relations—but at the end of it we come up against an unexpected puzzle: why did they trade so far afield when everything they seem to have needed was available quite close to home?

The spotlight is trained upon the city dwellers of the Indus, on the householders who lived in the baked brick houses, who walked along the cities' sun-drenched streets and spent their time creating miniature masterpieces of stone or shell or terracotta—and upon their compatriots who braved the perils of sea, desert, or mountain to bring home the exotic produce of distant lands. Darkness overshadows all the rest of the civilization—the invisible rulers, the bureaucracy whose only signs are in its results, the priests performing the rites of an almost unknown religion, the peasant farmers and herders whose endeavors supported the entire society but who can hardly yet be glimpsed. What clues can we pick up to enable us to dispel even a fragment of this darkness?

Even with the clues available, we will only have created a static picture of the Indus realms—a snapshot of a society as it went about its business. Deprived of written sources, we can reconstruct no history for this fascinating and apparently exuberant state. History elsewhere so often concerns the rise and fall of dynasties, so very often backed by force or falling victim to it. But far from glimpsing the devastating effects of wars to which we can put no dates or names, as we would expect from experience elsewhere, the clues from the Indus Civilization seem to be showing us a state without violence or conflict. Can this really be so, in defiance of all our experience of the world elsewhere?

Who were these peace-loving people? Where did they come from? How did they come together to create a state? And why did it not endure? Some of the fragments of information that archaeologists have uncovered can begin to answer some of these questions—but there is a lot that is still speculation.

Interest in the Indus Civilization is not mere antiquarian curiosity. Although the civilization itself collapsed, of all the primary civilizations it is actually that of the Indus which seems to have left the most lasting inheritance and which has had the most profound effect on the shape and culture of later society in its area. Strip away a few accretions of recent centuries—recently introduced religions, railways, telephones, electricity—and you are left with a society and a way of life that would not seem unfamiliar to the Indus people. By studying the Indus Civilization we can gain an insight into many aspects of modern South Asian life.

Such a mirror of the present in the past is less apparent elsewhere. On a wider stage, therefore, the Indus Civilization can provide a model of how the past has shaped the present that broadens our understanding of human society. The pace of change in the modern world has been so rapid that it is often hard for people to perceive the links between past and present. Many now deny the relevance of the past to modern life and turn their backs on the study of history. But by denying themselves the knowledge of the past, they turn their backs on all that it can teach—the lessons to be learned from past failures and successes and the fundamental understanding of the human condition of which the present is only a tiny, transient fragment.

FIRST LIGHT ON A LONG-FORGOTTEN CIVILISATION:
NEW DISCOVERIES OF AN UNKNOWN PREHISTORIC PAST IN INDIA.

By SIR JOHN MARSHALL, Kt., C.I.E., Litt. D., Director - General of Archæology in India.

NOT often has it been given to archæologists, as it was given to Schliemann at Tiryns and Mycenæ, or to Stein in the deserts of Turkestan, to light upon the remains of a long-forgotten civilisation. It looks, however, at this moment, as if we were on the threshold of such a discovery in the plains of the Indus.

Up to the present our knowledge of Indian antiquities has carried us back hardly further than the third century before Christ. Of the long ages before the coming of the Greeks and the rise of the Maurya dynasty ; of the birth and growth of civilisation in the great river basins ; of the cultural development of the races who one after another poured into the peninsula from the north and west—of these and other problems relating to that dim and remote past, archæology has given us but the faintest glimmerings ; for almost the only remains of those early times that have come down to us have been rough implements of the Stone and Copper Ages, groups of prehistoric graves in the south of the peninsula, and some rude cyclopean walls at Rajagriha in Bihar. On the other hand, from the third century B.C. onwards, we have, on the whole, a fairly clear idea of man's handiwork in general : of his religious and domestic architecture, of his formative arts, of his weapons and utensils, of his personal ornaments and his jewellery, his coins and gems, and of the scripts which he used in his writing. And whenever it happens that new antiquities come to light—no matter to what race or religion they may belong—it is invariably possible to assign them with confidence and within relatively narrow limits to their respective age or class.

Now, however, there has unexpectedly been unearthed, in the south of the Panjab and in Sind, an entirely new class of objects which have nothing in common with those previously known to us, and which are unaccompanied by any data that might have helped to establish their age and origin.

The two sites where these somewhat startling remains have been discovered are some 400 miles apart— the one being at Harappa in the Montgomery District of the Panjab ; the other at Mohenjo - Daro, in the Larkana District of Sind. At both these places there is a vast expanse of artificial mounds, evidently covering the remains of once flourishing cities, which, to judge from the mass of accumulated débris, rising as high as 60 ft. above the level of the plain, must have been in existence for many hundreds of years. Such groups of mounds abound in the plains of the Indus, just as they do in Mesopotamia and the valley of the Nile ; and they are specially conspicuous along the banks of the old, dried-up beds of the main stream and its tributaries, not only in Sind, but in Bahawalpur State and in the Panjab.

The opportunities for excavation, therefore, in this part of India may be regarded as almost limitless ; and, when it can be carried out on thorough and systematic lines, there is no doubt that the field will prove a peculiarly fertile one. Up to date, however, the meagre resources at the disposal of the Archæological Department have permitted it to undertake little more than preliminary trial-digging on these two sites : and it goes without saying that the remains disclosed are correspondingly limited. Yet, such as they are, they are full of promise.

At Mohenjo-Daro, the main street of the old city can still be discerned as a broad highway running from the south bank of the river towards the southeast, with houses fringing it on either side. What is surmised by the discoverer, Mr. Banerji, to have been the royal palace, stood at the point where this road emerged on to the quays of the river side. Opposite to it, in the now dry bed of the river, are several islands from which rose the principal shrines of the city, the highest and, no doubt, the chief of them all, being a massive Buddhist stupa raised on a high oblong platform, and surrounded by subsidiary shrines and monastic quarters. These remains belong to about the second century A.D., when the Kushans were paramount in the north-west of India ; and, judging by the finds already made—particularly the urn burials, remnants of painted frescoes

inscribed in Brahmi and Kharoshthi characters, new types of coins and other novel objects—there can be no doubt that their further exploration will result in welcome light being thrown on this very obscure period of Indian history.

Valuable, however, as these remains are likely to prove, it is not in them that the real interest of Mohenjo-Daro centres at the moment. Deep down below the Buddhist monuments described above, or at other parts of the site appearing close to the surface itself, there are at least two other strata of buildings belonging to much earlier epochs, and containing a variety of brick structures—the character and antiquity of which can at present only be surmised. Among these older structures one group is especially worthy of mention. Besides various halls and passages and chambers, it includes a massive structure—apparently a shrine—with walls seven or eight feet thick, pierced by several conduits which, in the opinion of the excavator, served for carrying

UNEARTHED DEEP DOWN BELOW THE BUDDHIST MONUMENTS OF THE SECOND CENTURY AT MOHENJO-DARO: MUCH EARLIER REMAINS—A STAIRCASE OUTSIDE A SHRINE, WITH A CONDUIT COVERED BY MARBLE SLABS (IN THE FOREGROUND).
Photograph by the Archæological Survey of India, Western Circle. By Courtesy of Sir John Marshall.

off the lustral water when the shrine or image within it was washed. In another part of the same group is what appears to be an altar built of small glazed bricks, and provided with a drain of similar brickwork. Some idea of the appearance of these early buildings, and of their present state of preservation, is afforded by two of the photographs reproduced, the one (on this page) showing a staircase to the south-west of the shrine referred to, with a conduit in the foreground from which the covering of marble slabs has been removed ; the other (on page 529), illustrating the glazed-brick flooring in a bay on the western façade of the same shrine.

At Harappa, Mr. Daya Ram Sahni's excavations disclosed as many as seven or eight successive levels, demonstrating the long and continuous occupation of the site during many hundreds of years prior to the third century B.C. ; and throughout most, if not all, of this long period, burnt brick of a good quality was used for building purposes. The site at Harappa, however, has suffered much from the depredations of railway contractors and others, and the structures brought to light are in a more fragmentary condition than at Mohenjo-Daro. On the other hand, the smaller antiquities are generally identical in character with those from Mohenjo-Daro, and some of them even are better preserved. These smaller antiquities from the two sites comprise new varieties of potteries both painted and plain, some fashioned by hand and some turned on the wheel ; terra-

cottas ; toys ; bangles of blue glass, paste and shell ; new types of coins or tokens ; knives and cores of chert ; dice and chessmen ; a remarkable series of stone rings ; and, most important of all, a number of engraved and inscribed seals. Iron does not occur at all, except in the latest deposits, and metal objects of any kind are scarce, particularly at Harappa.

Of all these antiquities the most valuable are the stone seals, not only because they are inscribed with legends in an unknown pictographic script, but because the figures engraved on them, and the style of the engraving, are different from anything of the kind hitherto met with in Indian art. Some of them are of steatite, others of ivory, and others of stone and paste. In shape most are square, and provided at the back with a boss pierced with a small hole for suspension. The animals engraved on them are in some instances bulls ; in others, unicorns ; but it is to be observed that neither the Indian humped bull nor the water-buffalo occurs among them.

As to the strange pictographs which do duty for letters, three points are worthy of remark : first, that the marks (apparently vowel signs) attached to many of the pictographs indicate a relatively high stage of development ; secondly, that some of the inscriptions from Mohenjo-Daro betray a later stage in the evolution of this script than those from Harappa ; thirdly, that they bear no resemblance whatever to any ancient Indian alphabet known to us ; but, on the other hand, they do bear a certain general affinity to pictographs of the Mycenæan age in the Mediterranean area, though it is not possible to point to any of the symbols as being actually identical.

Examples of this pictographic writing are found not only on the seal dies, but also (at Mohenjo-Daro) on certain oblong bars of copper which their discoverer assumes to have been coins, since they are similar in shape to the early Indian oblong coins known as "punch-marked," though they do not correspond in weight with any recognised standards used in ancient India. Should this assumption of Mr. Banerji's prove correct, it would mean that these coins may turn out to be the earliest in existence, since the first coins hitherto known to have been struck in any other country are the Lydian pieces of the seventh century B.C.

Notwithstanding that the curious ring stones mentioned above have been found in large numbers on both sites, the purpose to which they were put has hitherto quite baffled the ingenuity of the excavators ; though, for reasons into which it would take too long to enter here, Mr. Banerji believes that they were in some way connected with the *Bhartaris*, or shrines of eternal fire. They are of all sizes, from that of a small napkin ring up to fifty pounds in weight, and are made of various coloured stones or marble ; but what is particularly curious about them is that in many specimens the upper and lower surfaces are undulating.

Another remarkable and significant feature at the Mohenjo-Daro site is the character of the burial customs. In the earliest period the practice was to bury the body in a hunched position in a brick tomb, generally of square or oblong form. Later on (it may be very much later), the custom obtained of burning the body, as is commonly done in India to-day, and depositing the ashes in a small urn, which, along with two or three others, was placed inside a larger round jar, accompanied by several miniature vessels containing food, raiment, and so on.

To what age and to what people do these novel antiquities belong ? Those are the two questions which will naturally occur to the reader, and to which a score of different answers may perhaps suggest themselves. As to the first question, all that can be said at present is that the period during which this culture flourished in the Indus valley must have extended over many centuries, and that it came to an end before the rise of the Maurya power in the third century B.C. So much may be inferred, on the one hand, from the many successive strata of habitation, particularly on the Harappa site ; on the other, from the presence of copper weapons, and

Continued on page 548.

CHAPTER ONE

LOST CIVILIZATIONS

SPLENDORS OF ANTIQUITY

People have been fascinated by the civilization of ancient Egypt since the days of the Classical Greek writer Herodotus, who breathlessly recounted tales of its legendary and mysterious past. This fascination never completely died out in medieval times, and in the 16th century, explorers and travelers began again to visit Egypt's monuments. The pyramids, one of the most enduring survivors of antiquity, caught the imagination of scholars and public alike and the dissection of looted mummies provided a popular entertainment. Napoleon's Egyptian expedition in 1798, its military army accompanied by an army of scholars, greatly increased popular interest in and awareness of ancient Egypt. Its most significant find was the Rosetta Stone, a discovery that led directly to the decipherment of the Egyptian hieroglyphic script. By the 19th century, explorers and antiquarians were plundering the magnificent painted tombs of the ancient Egyptians for papyri and the mummified bodies of pharaohs, nobles, and sacred animals, and investigating the imposing temples and pyramids.

Similar interest was being shown in the relics that survived in Mesopotamia. French and British scholars competed ruthlessly to uncover the splendid palaces of early Mesopotamian kings, their great temples, and their spectacular burials. Biblical connections with Mesopotamia fueled popular interest in this land, the cradle of civilization, and Austen Layard's books describing his excavations in the magnificent cities of Nimrud and Nineveh became best-sellers.

Many of these ancient societies had been known from their echoes in later literature: Biblical accounts of the Exodus from Egypt and Belshazzar's Feast, Homer's *Iliad* and *Odyssey*, Roman legends of their early history and their city's foundation. At Troy and Mycenae, Heinrich Schliemann had demonstrated the historical validity of the Homeric tales of the Mycenaean Civilization. A fragment of cuneiform tablet from Nineveh, found in 1872, mentions the Great Flood, and Britain held its breath while an expedition was mounted to search (successfully) for the rest of the text, which showed that the Sumerians had also had a legend

Figure 2.

ILLUSTRATED LONDON NEWS, MARSHALL'S DISCOVERY

This is a reproduction of the actual front page of the September 20, 1924 Illustrated London News *announcing Sir John Marshall's unexpected discovery of the long lost civilization of the Indus.*

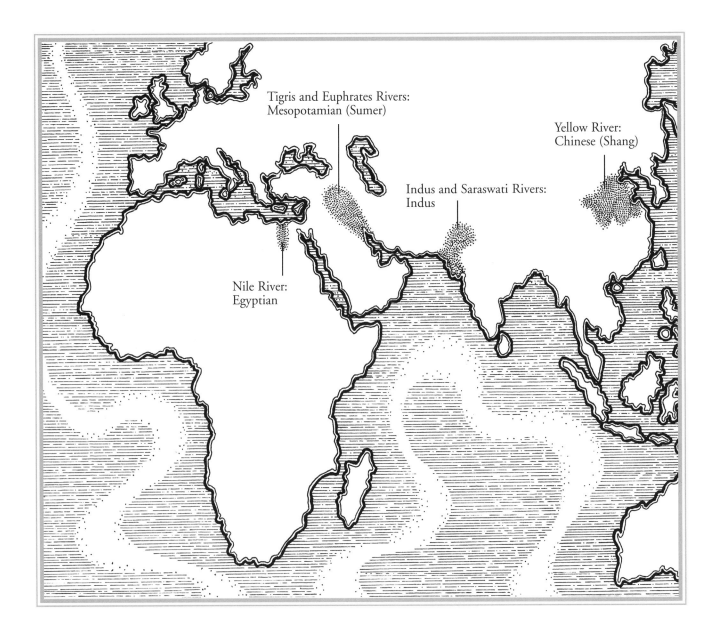

Tigris and Euphrates Rivers:
Mesopotamian (Sumer)

Yellow River:
Chinese (Shang)

Indus and Saraswati Rivers:
Indus

Nile River:
Egyptian

Map 1.

LOCATION OF
THE FOUR
"FIRST"
CIVILIZATIONS

*The Indus remains
the most enigmatic
of the primary
civilizations.*

that the gods sent a deluge to destroy humanity. Almost sixty years later, Sir Leonard Woolley excavating at Ur believed that he had found physical evidence of the flood that had inspired this legend. Many excavations of the 19th and early 20th centuries similarly uncovered remains that supported and fleshed out the stories preserved in literature [Map 1].

SECRETS OF INDIA'S PAST

In India, exploration in the 19th century and before had been just as intense. Literary echoes of the early past existed in the *Vedas* and other sacred texts transmitted orally. By the close of the 1st millennium B.C., there were

CUNNINGHAM'S WORK AT HARAPPA

In the 1850s, Sir Alexander Cunningham visited the ruins of Harappa. He recognized that the mounds were not natural but man-made, the ruins of a vast accumulation of brick structures, but seems to have accepted a view expressed by other visitors that the site was a castle of no very great age.

"The people," he noted, "refer the ruin of Harapa to the wickedness of a Raja named Har Pal, or Hara Pala, who was in the habit of claiming the sovereign's rights at every bridal. At last, in the exercise of this royal privilege, he committed incest with a near relative. The girl prayed to heaven for vengeance and then the city of Harapa was instantly destroyed. Some say that an invader suddenly appeared, and the city was taken by storm, and the Raja killed. The period of its destruction is vaguely said to be 1,200 or 1,300 years ago. I am inclined to put some faith in this belief of the people, as they tell the same story of all the ruined cities in the plains of the Punjab, as if they had all suffered at the same time from some sudden and common catastrophe. . . ."

Cunningham collected a small quantity of Indus material from the mounds, but he was far from suspecting its significance, nor did he guess the part the site was later to play in revealing South Asia's past.

"I made several excavations at Harapa, but the whole surface had been so completely cleared out by the Railway contractors that I found very little worth preserving. The most curious object discovered at Harapa is a seal, belonging to Major Clark. The seal is a smooth black stone without polish. On it is engraved very deeply a bull, without hump, looking to the right, with two stars under the neck. Above the bull there is an inscription in six characters, which are quite unknown to me. They are certainly not Indian letters; and as the bull which accompanies them is without a hump, I conclude that the seal is foreign to India."

Cunningham
Archaeological Survey of India: Report for the Years 1872–3, 1875, pp. 105–108

many written sources to provide information on India's flourishing civilization, centered in the Ganges Valley—for example, Buddhist, Jain, and Hindu sacred literature. The accounts of foreign visitors devoted much time to investigating sites associated with the Buddha, while many others explored the fabulous rock-cut temples and monasteries of the Deccan. Beyond the range of historical texts, however, India's past was illuminated by fragmentary clues—a few stone tools and the enigmatic megaliths of the south. These structures intrigued scholars of the 18th and 19th centuries because they bore strong similarities to the imposing megalithic monuments of western Europe.

Archaeology and tradition combined to suggest that the development of civilization in India had been relatively late, in the mid 1st millennium B.C. Urban society was thought to have emerged in the Ganges Valley around the time of the Buddha (563–463 B.C.), its antecedents being the heroic but barbarous petty kingdoms whose conflicts have been immortalized in the great Indian epic, the Mahabharata. Sir Alexander Cunningham actually discovered some material belonging to the Indus Civilization while excavating at Harappa in the 1850s but did not recognize its significance—how could he have, given the knowledge available at the time?

MARSHALL]

On September 20, 1924, Sir John Marshall announced his discoveries in the *Illustrated London News:*

"Not often has it been given to archaeologists, as it was given to Schliemann at Tiryns and Mycenae, or to Stein in the deserts of Turkestan, to light upon the remains of a long-forgotten civilization. It looks, however, at this moment, as if we were on the threshold of such a discovery in the plains of the Indus.

"Up to the present our knowledge of Indian antiquities has carried us back hardly further than the third century before Christ. Of the long ages before the coming of the Greeks and the rise of the Maurya dynasty; of the birth and growth of civilization in the great river basins; of the cultural development of the races who one after another have poured into the peninsula from the north and west— of these and other problems relating to that dim and remote past, archaeology has given us but the faintest glimmerings; for almost the only remains of those early times that have come down to us have been rough implements of the Stone and Copper Ages, groups of prehistoric graves in the south of the peninsula, and some rude cyclopean walls at Rajagriha in Bihar.

"Now, however, there has unexpectedly been unearthed, in the south of the Panjab and in Sind, an entirely new class of objects which have nothing in common with those previously known to us, and which are unaccompanied by any data that might have helped us to establish their age and origin. . . .

"To what age and to what people do these novel antiquities belong?"

It was therefore a tremendous and amazing discovery in the 1920s when excavations beneath the much later Buddhist stupa at Mohenjo Daro revealed the remains of substantial brick-built structures, associated with seals, pottery, and other material in a hitherto unknown style [Figure 3]. At the same time, excavations in the ruined mounds at Harappa were uncovering similar material. The quality of this material and the sophistication of the urban architecture astounded the excavators. Here was something new and completely unsuspected—a civilized society of which not the slightest hint had survived.

A FORGOTTEN CIVILIZATION

When had this civilization flourished? Clearly it was earlier than the historically known Mauryan Empire of the 3rd century B.C. Sir John Marshall, director-general of the Archaeological Survey at the time of these discoveries, was to be a leading figure in the investigations. Marshall amassed clues that showed the Indus cities to be earlier also than the literate Ganges Civilization of the later 1st millennium B.C.: the stratigraphy of the sites, with Indus deposits well below those

of the historical period, the use of copper but not iron, the seals with their mysterious writing that was clearly unrelated to the Brahmi script of the later centuries B.C. Marshall put a tentative date of around 1000 B.C. on these puzzling remains.

Marshall published his first account of these finds in the *Illustrated London News* on September 20, 1924 [Figure 2]. Within just a few days, Mesopotamian scholars were writing in to point out general similarities between the Indus material and finds from Susa, the great Elamite city in western Iran, and from Ur and other Sumerian sites. Once this link between the Indus region and 3rd millennium B.C. Mesopotamia had been spotted, many more examples of similar material, particularly seals and beads of "etched" carnelian and other materials, were noticed. Not only did these provide clues to the age of the Indus Civilization but they also revealed its well-established trade links with the world of the first Mesopotamian Civilization.

The historical Ganges Civilization was built on foundations laid by the Indo-Aryans, a nomadic people who had invaded the sub-

Figure 3.

EARLY EXCAVATION

The British archaeologist Ernest McKay excavated at Mohenjo Daro from 1927 to 1931. This photograph documents a pathway, lined with the mudbricks with which all Indus settlements are constructed.

RIGVEDA ON PURA

The *Rigveda*, the earliest collection of Indo-Aryans' hymns, described their struggles against the fortified strongholds of their enemies, the dark-skinned Dasas, who were tentatively identified as the Indus people.

"With all-outstripping chariot-wheel, O Indra, thou
 far-famed, hast overthrown the twice ten kings of men
With sixty thousand nine and ninety followers.
 Thou goest on from fight to fight intrepidly,
 destroying castle after castle here with strength."

Rigveda I, 53, quoted in
Piggott 1950, p. 261

continent at some time before 1000 B.C. and who were well-known from their religious literature, the *Vedas*. These hymns were composed in the 2nd and early 1st millennia B.C. and handed down orally until they were committed to writing in medieval times. The earliest of these collections of hymns, the *Rigveda*, describes the advent of the warlike Aryan people and their destruction of the forts or cities (*pura*) of their enemies. Could it be that the "cities" they sacked were those of the Indus Civilization? By the time that Marshall published his definitive report on the Mohenjo Daro excavations and the Indus Civilization in 1931, this idea had taken firm hold.

The cities of Mohenjo Daro and Harappa were nearly 400 miles apart. Comparable mounds of ruined buildings were to be seen throughout the plains. These sites offered, as

Marshall lamented, almost limitless scope for investigation, if only the resources were available. Despite their straitened circumstances, by the mid-1930s, the staff of the Archaeological Survey had undertaken excavations and survey work that uncovered Indus sites as far afield as Rangpur in Kathiawar and Kotla Nihang Khan in east Punjab. Already it was clear that the Indus Civilization was considerably larger in extent than the only other two states that existed at this time—Old Kingdom Egypt and the Akkadian Empire.

Other fieldwork revealed the antecedents of the Indus Civilization. The intrepid explorer of Central Asia, Sir Marc Aurel Stein, had conducted surveys that located many earlier sites, such as Mehi and Kulli, in Baluchistan. At Amri in Sindh, N. G. Majumdar, a distinguished officer of the Archaeological Survey, excavated the first town in the Indus plains that belonged to the period before the development of the civilization. The first of many American-funded Indus excavations took place at Chanhu Daro under Ernest Mackay, a veteran of Near Eastern archaeology who had also directed the Archaeological Survey's excavations at Mohenjo Daro in the late 1920s. Here he uncovered the remains of a small Indus town and its workshops.

In 1944, Sir Mortimer Wheeler, who had already had a distinguished career in British archaeology, was seconded to India as director-general of the Archaeological Survey. The Survey had become run-down in the Depression years of the 1930s and the succeeding Second World War. One of his principal aims during his four years in office was to train the rising generation of archaeologists in the field methods that he had perfected in Britain. He therefore ran a number of training excavations at key sites, choosing places that could be expected to further the understanding of India's past. These included the great historical city of Taxila; the Roman trading post at Arikamedu in the south; the megalithic tombs and town of Brahmagiri, spanning the periods from the Neolithic into historical times; and the two major Indus cities, Mohenjo Daro and Harappa.

Despite his fulminations against other scholars for failing to publish their excavation results, Wheeler himself never produced a full report on his work at either site, contenting himself with an interim report on Harappa published in 1947 in *Ancient India,* the new journal that he founded; various articles in the *Illustrated London News;* and discussion of both sites in his various books on India's past and on the Indus Civilization in particular, published in the 1950s and 1960s.

A clearer picture of these cities and of the civilization as a whole was now emerging as a result of Wheeler's work and that undertaken in the 1930s. Mohenjo Daro was divided into two main sections, the "citadel" in the west, containing public buildings, and in the east a residential lower town. The streets of Mohenjo Daro were constructed in a checkerboard layout oriented north-south and east-west, reminiscent of the much later cities and towns of the Greek and Hellenistic world. Excavations at Harappa and the smaller town of Chanhu Daro confirmed the impression that the Indus cities were constructed to a standard plan. Highly competent and well-maintained drains and sanitation were standard features of these cities. Standardization was apparent in the Indus artifacts, too, such as the finely made pottery, stone, and metal tools and beads.

Marshall 2

Marshall continued to share news of his finds with the readers of the *Illustrated London News.* On February 27, 1926, he wrote:

"At the moment of writing I am starting on the systematic excavation of Mohenjo-daro with 800 laborers, five officers besides myself, and an adequate number of technical assistants. Later on, our operations will be extended over the Panjab, Western Rajputana, and Baluchistan, and this will embrace a general survey of the remains of this remarkable civilization.

"To the archaeologist the site of Mohenjo-daro is one of the most fascinating that can well be imagined.

"The existence of roomy and well-built houses, and the relatively high degree of luxury denoted by their elaborate system of drainage, as well as by the character of many of the smaller antiquities found within, seem to betoken a social condition of the people far in advance of what was then prevailing in Mesopotamia and Egypt."

WHEELER AND THE ARYANS

Wheeler, with characteristic vigor, seized enthusiastically on the theory that the Indo-Aryans were largely responsible for the end of Indus Civilization.

"The Aryan invasion of the Land of the Seven Rivers, the Punjab and its environs, constantly assumes the form of an onslaught upon the walled cities of the aborigines. For these cities the term used in the Rigveda is pur, meaning a 'rampart,' 'fort' or 'stronghold.'

Indra, the Aryan war-god, is puramdara, 'fort-destroyer.' He shatters 'ninety forts' for his Aryan protégé, Divodasa. The same forts are doubtless referred to where in other hymns he demolishes variously ninety-nine and a hundred 'ancient castles' of the aboriginal leader Sambara. In brief, he 'rends forts as age consumes a garment.'

"Where are—or were—these citadels? It has in the past been supposed that they were mythical, or were they 'merely places of refuge against attack, ramparts of hardened earth with palisades and a ditch.' The recent excavation of Harappa may be thought to have changed the picture. Here we have a highly evolved civilization of essentially non-Aryan type, now known to have employed massive fortification, and known also to have dominated the river-system of north-western India at a time not distant from the likely period of the earlier Aryan invasions of that region. What destroyed this firmly settled civilization? Climatic, economic, political deterioration may have weakened it, but its ultimate extinction is more likely to have been completed by deliberate and large-scale destruction. It may be no mere chance that at a late period of Mohenjo Daro men, women and children appear to have been massacred there. On circumstantial evidence, Indra stands accused."

Wheeler, R.E.M.
Ancient India, No. 3, 1947

The distinguished archaeologist Stuart Piggott was unfavorably impressed by the Indus material and, writing in 1950, characterized it as exhibiting "competent dullness . . . a dead level of bourgeois mediocrity in almost every branch of the visual arts and crafts." Shortly after, however, Wheeler commented favorably on the technical achievements of the Indus people and the aesthetic qualities of some of their work, including their charming figurines [Figure 5]. The impression generally emerging was of a civilization in which great technical competence and a high standard of living were offset by cultural stagnation and the stifling effects of rigid bureaucracy and an authoritarian regime, continuing unchanged for nearly a millennium.

How did the Indus Civilization compare with its contemporaries in Egypt and Mesopotamia and with other civilizations that were by now well known? Wheeler and other early investigators looked for the features that were familiar to them from these other civilizations: monumental public architecture such as temples, defensive works and weaponry, royal burials, and palaces. They thought they had found some of these. In the earliest days of the excavations at Mohenjo Daro, Marshall had identified the Great Bath as a shrine. Other structures on the citadel mounds could also reasonably be interpreted as public and religious buildings, including, Wheeler suggested, state granaries. Wheeler, arriving in India straight from the battlefields of North Africa, enthusiastically identified and excavated massive walls and impressive gateways around the citadels of Mohenjo Daro and Harappa [Figure 4].

These structures fitted the notion of defenses and fortifications. Artifacts that might have been weapons, such as spearheads, daggers, arrowheads, and axes, were identified, but, as Wheeler noted, "a majority may have been used equally by the soldier, the huntsman, the craftsman, or even by the ordinary householder [*see* Figures 55 and 57]." Other familiar features of the early civilizations were absent, however—no palaces or royal graves had been discovered, for example, and thus it was already clear that the Indus Civilization was significantly different from Egypt and Sumer and was therefore not established by culturally superior colonists from either region. Wheeler nevertheless still argued that

Figure 4.
HARAPPA GATEWAY, ARTIST'S RENDITION
This is what the settlement of Harappa might have looked like in its heyday.

the Indus people had adopted the idea of civilization from the Sumerians, along with significant features such as the use of writing. How this would have worked in practice was difficult to grasp at the time he suggested it. In the decades that followed, changes in our understanding of the way that cultural groups interact and cultures evolve have made this suggestion untenable.

SHEDDING FURTHER LIGHT ON THE INDUS PEOPLE

In 1947, the British government bowed to many years of unrest and agitation and granted independence to India, partitioning the country into mainly Muslim Pakistan and mainly Hindu India. To Pakistan fell the lands of the northwest—and suddenly India found itself deprived of virtually all the region of the Indus Civilization. This spurred Indian investigations in the remaining areas, resulting in the discovery of many sites in Gujurat and Kutch and in the northern Ganges-Yamuna region. A number of the newly discovered sites were excavated, most notably the "port" town of Lothal in Gujarat. This important town housed a concentration of craft workshops, producing a wealth of typical Indus material, and also an enigmatic large stone basin, interpreted initially as a dock and still not understood. Excavations in the surrounding area also uncovered a number of burials, relatively rare finds from the Indus Civilization.

Intensive field surveys were now undertaken on both sides of the new international border. Marshall, who had a masterly grasp of the broad picture of India's past, had already observed in 1924 that ancient mounds clustered particularly on dried-up riverbeds in Punjab and Sindh. Officers of the Archaeological Survey had explored some of these areas in the 1920s and 1930s, recording a number of sites. In 1974 the Pakistan Archaeology Department under Rafique Mughal began a major program of exploration in one of these areas, along the now dry river valleys in the Cholistan desert of Bahawalpur state. This work revealed an incredibly dense concentration of sites, along the dried-up course of a river that could be identified as the "Saraswati," a sacred river that was drying up when the Indo-Aryans first entered this region in the 2nd millennium B.C. In Indus times the river had flowed through this now desert area, to debouch into the Indian Ocean in Kutch. Suddenly it became apparent that the "Indus" Civilization was a misnomer—although the Indus had played a major role in the rise and development of the civilization, the "lost Saraswati" River, judging by the density of settlement along its banks, had contributed an equal or greater part to its prosperity. Many people today refer to this early state as the "Indus-Saraswati Civilization" and continuing references to the "Indus Civilization" should be seen as an abbreviation in which the "Saraswati" is implied.

Archaeologists had spent a great deal of their time in the first half of the 20th century attempting to establish chronologies for the developments in the regions that they studied,

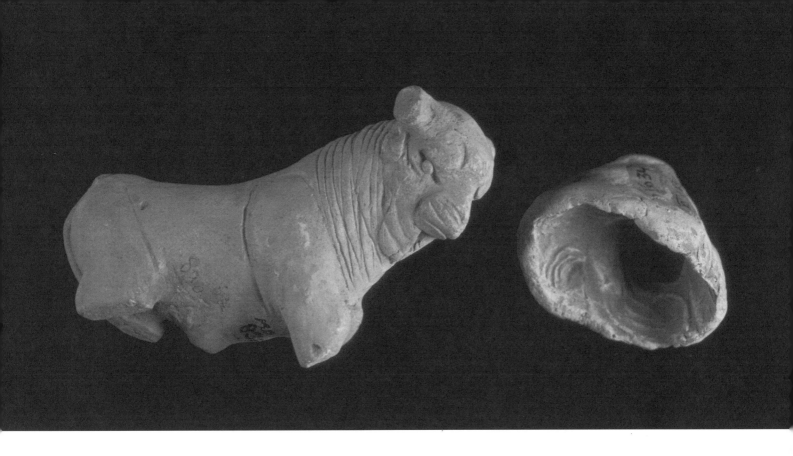

and the Indus-Saraswati region was no exception. The links with historically dated empires in Mesopotamia had provided a firm anchor for the Indus Civilization at its height—the Mature Indus Period—showing it to have been flourishing between 2500 and 2000 B.C. How much earlier the civilization began and how much later it continued were a bit vague. Those who blamed the Indo-Aryans for the Indus demise put a figure of 1500 B.C. on this supposed cataclysm—but this date was itself only guesswork. Early Indus material was being found in deposits predating the Mature Indus levels at sites like Kalibangan, an important town excavated in the post-Partition era. Dates for this period were tentatively assigned to the early 3rd millennium B.C. Investigations in the highland regions that bordered the Indus Valley to the north and west, where the origins of the civilization might be expected to lie, continued to reveal sites that were clearly earlier than the Mature Indus Period—but how much earlier were they? There was no way of telling—as indeed there was no way of determining how early agricultural communities had developed anywhere in Western Asia or in the world at large.

In 1949 the physicist Professor Willard Libby invented radiocarbon dating—a tool that was to spark a revolution in archaeology. This discovery permitted surviving organic materials, such as bone, wood, and shell, to be dated directly, instead of relying on indirect or contextual methods such as stratigraphy and association or comparison with dated artifacts. Suddenly it became possible actually to date cultures individually and to build up a clear picture of how cultures related to each other in time. Applying this new and

Figure 5.

BULL FIGURINE, MOHENJO DARO

Bulls feature prominently among the figurines found in Indus settlements, which also included birds and rabbits, rams, and even unicorns. The head of this bull was shaped in a mould (right) while the body was modeled by hand.

exciting tool to the farming settlements in the Indo-Iranian borderlands, it was revealed that they were established there at a date by the 5th millennium B.C. and that they gave rise to towns in some areas during the 4th millennium. Dates could be assigned to the periods of the Indus Civilization too, and it is now generally agreed that the Early Indus settlers had colonized the Indus Valley toward the end of the 4th millennium, that the Mature Indus Civilization emerged between 2700 and 2600 B.C., and that by 1800 B.C. the Indus Civilization was collapsing, giving rise to a number of Late Indus regional groups. The establishment of this firm chronological framework allowed scholars working in the Indus-Saraswati region thankfully to turn their attentions to other aspects of the civilization—such as the fascinating questions of the identity of the Indus people and the cause of the emergence of the Indus Civilization.

The identity of the Indus people was closely bound up with the question of when and how farming developed in the subcontinent. Radiocarbon dating revealed that farming had begun in the Fertile Crescent—

a great arc of land in the Near East—as early as 9000 B.C. Had it spread from there to the borders of India? A discovery in the 1970s threw new light upon this question—although it still has not completely been answered. Excavations on a large settlement site at Mehrgarh on the Bolan River in Pakistan revealed the remains of a farming village that proved to date back as far as the early 7th millennium B.C. The remains showed that farming developed in this area at much the same time as in northern Mesopotamia and not much later than the earliest farming communities in West Asia.

THE INDUS CIVILIZATION TODAY

Since the days of the first discovery of the civilization, knowledge of its political geography has been dominated by Mohenjo Daro and Harappa, for decades known as the "twin capitals." Other sites of almost comparable size have also been discovered in the intervening years. One, Ganweriwala,

A BALLOON OVER MOHENJO DARO

When Michael Jansen and his team, the German Research Project on Mohenjo Daro at the Technical University of Aachen, began work on documenting and reassessing the city of Mohenjo Daro, they were faced with the monumental task of recording details of around 100,000 m² of ruins, containing the remains of more than 300 houses. To succeed they needed to be able to make a photographic record of the whole site in detail using low-level vertical aerial photographs. They therefore designed and constructed a special hot-air balloon from which they suspended a camera. With this device they were able to take hundreds of photographs that form a complete mosaic picture of the remains of the city [*see* Figure 26].

was found in the heart of the dense settlement cluster in the Cholistan Desert—its location makes it extremely intriguing and its excavation is awaited with bated breath. While we curb our impatience to find out about this city, our curiosity has been satisfied about another—the excavation of the great city of Dholavira in Gujurat began in 1990. The results from this metropolis have been fascinating and in many ways surprising. Unlike Mohenjo Daro and Harappa, its citadel is not a separate mound set apart from the residential area, but a high area within the city, the innermost of a series of walled compounds. Here too has been found a unique artifact—a series of enormous letters that are believed to have been written on a wooden signboard hung over a gateway to the citadel [*see* Figure 27]. And Dholavira has also solved a nagging puzzle that goes back to the first excavations at Mohenjo Daro: what purpose was served by the great carved "ringstones"? At Dholavira, at last, they have been found in

situ doing their job—as the base for wooden columns.

Early work in the Indus Valley had revealed cities, and subsequently towns were also uncovered. But what of the country dwellers, the farmers who must have constituted the bulk of the population? Glimpses of their existence and way of life could be seen in terracotta figurines of domestic animals and bullock carts, and in the surprising discovery of the remains of a ploughed field in the Early Indus deposits at Kalibangan, but nothing had been done to trace and investigate these rural dwellers [*see* Figure 11 and Color Plate 5]. In recent years considerable work has been undertaken to redress the balance and investigate the rural setting of the Indus Civilization. Several villages and herdsmen's camps have been found and excavated. Large-scale regional surveys have been undertaken that provide a general picture of the distribution of Indus sites and their relationship to the landscape. For example,

Greg Possehl studied the patterns of settlement in Saurashtra (in the southwest) during the 3rd and 2nd millennia B.C., not only revealing the changing pattern of farming settlement in this region, where the end of the Indus Civilization saw a great increase in population, but also focusing attention on anomalies in the previously known pattern of settlement elsewhere in the Indus Civilization, thus sparking future research. Other surveys showed that Harappa was virtually the only substantial Indus site in its region: this discovery focused attention on Harappa's major importance in trade, particularly in Himalayan timber. It also highlighted the vital role of pastoral nomads in connecting and integrating the different communities within Indus society. Then as now, nomads provided a link between settled communities and acted as carriers in local trade [Figure 6].

Continuing work along the course of the "lost Saraswati River" system added further data to the picture that had already emerged of the Saraswati as the civilization's breadbasket. The now-dry Hakra River forms part of this river system. Surveys along its dry bed revealed that this was one of the most densely settled areas of the 3rd millennium, the agricultural heartland of the civilization, although it is now virtually desert. The 19th-century geographer R. D. Oldham had already painstakingly surveyed and mapped the dry river courses along much of the Saraswati system. His work has been reassessed over recent years, using modern scientific aids such as satellite photography, and the sequence and timing of

the gradual drying up of this river system, caused by tectonic activity, is being worked out. As a result a powerful new explanation has been formulated for the demise of the Indus Civilization: that the progressive desiccation of this region played a significant part in the decline of Indus Civilization by drastically reducing agricultural output in the heartland.

From the first days after the discovery of the Indus Civilization had been announced to the world, its links with Mesopotamia were spotted and publicly debated. The intervening years have seen a great deal of flesh put on the bare bones of this connection and on the other international relations of the Indus Civilization. A full-fledged Indus settlement has been discovered and excavated at Shortugai in Central Asia, 1,000 km from the Indus, a trading outpost controlling the nearby lapis mines. The Indus people seem likely to have founded Shortugai to enable them to monopolize the supply of lapis from Badakhshan in Central Asia. Until about five years ago, this was believed to have been the only source of lapis known to the people of the ancient Near East, but another source has now been discovered in the Chagai Hills of Baluchistan, an area much closer to the Indus people's homeland and one from which they obtained other raw materials—so they probably knew of this lapis source too, although it is quite likely that they concealed the information from their neighbors.

Sumerian texts name Mesopotamia's foreign trading partners as the lands of Dilmun, Magan, and Meluhha. Naturally it has been of great interest to identify these places. After many decades of study scholars are now confident that the Indus Civilization was the land of Meluhha. Expeditions to the countries of the Persian Gulf have also slowly unraveled the secrets of Dilmun and Magan, the sea-trading cultures that occupied the intervening lands. Dilmun has been located on and around Bahrain, whereas Oman seems likely to have been known as Magan.

The excavations of Marshall and his colleagues at Harappa and Mohenjo Daro in the 1920s and 1930s were mammoth undertakings, executed at a time when field archaeology was a relatively young discipline. It is small wonder that the excavations are found wanting by more recent standards and that they leave unanswered a host of questions that are now seen as important. Currently work is being undertaken at Mohenjo Daro and Harappa aimed at reassessing the evidence from these early excavations, with seventy years of hindsight and all the most up-to-date equipment, technology, and techniques. At Mohenjo Daro a joint team from the Technical University at Aachen, led by Michael Jansen, and from IsMEO, the Italian Institute of the Middle and Far East (Istituto del Medio e Estremo Oriente), have been studying the original excavation photographs and records, making their own complete photographic and documentary record of remaining architecture, and investigating craft activity areas and other previously exposed remains.

At Harappa the American HARP (Harappa Archaeological Research Project), initially under George Dales and since his death by his able successors Jonathan Mark Kenoyer and Richard Meadow, has been undertaking some excavation, teasing out new information from the scanty ruins that survived the 19th-century railway builders' depredations. They have been extending their understanding of these remains by conducting many experiments, such as constructing and firing replicas of Indus kilns, and by studying the abundant ethnographic evidence, such as the craft techniques of traditional potters and shellworkers. From the work of these teams we are gaining a far clearer understanding of the layout of these cities and how they operated. Although many other cities and towns have been laid bare in the years since the civilization was discovered, Mohenjo Daro and Harappa still seem to have been outstandingly important, holding the key to much that we would like to know about life in the Indus Valley 5,000 years ago.

And yet there is still much to be found out. Who were the rulers of this vast area and why have they left so little trace of themselves? How was cultural unity imposed within such a huge realm and what forces held it together? Are we right in believing that military force played no part in its internal organization? Why did it suddenly collapse? What secrets lie within its undeciphered texts? These and many other questions are still to be answered, making the Indus the most intriguing of the world's first civilizations.

CHAPTER TWO

BEFORE THE INDUS CIVILIZATION

A LAND OF CONTRASTS AND DRAMATIC CHANGE

The Indian subcontinent is a region of contrasts: from the snows of the Himalayas to the tropical heat of Sri Lanka, from the jungles of the interior to the beaches of the extensive coastline, from the flooded expanses of the Ganges Delta to the aridity of the Great Indian Desert. Within these diverse and contrasting environments, groups of people have adapted to these myriad terrains. Changes have taken place as new ways of obtaining food have evolved or been introduced, but traditional ways of dealing with drawbacks in the local environment and of making the most of the opportunities offered by it have endured.

The northwest region of the subcontinent is dominated by the great Indus River, originating in the heights of the Himalayas along with its major tributaries, the Jhelum, the Sutlej, the Ravi, the Beas, and the Chenab, which together water the Punjab, the Land of the Five Rivers. The Punjab is a region of forests—in antiquity the forest cover was considerably denser. South of the confluence of the five rivers, the now mighty Indus flows through extensive and fertile alluvial plains until it debouches into the Arabian Sea and the Ranns of Kutch. To the north, the plain is enfolded by the foothills of the Indo-Iranian borderlands, a mountainous and often semidesert region dissected by valleys leading down to the arid and inhospitable coast of the Makran. In the south, much of the plain is bordered by the exceptionally arid Great Indian Desert, relieved by the waters of Lake Sambhar and the Luni River flowing south from it. The desert itself is fringed to the south by the range of the Aravalli Hills, also arid but rich in minerals. In contrast, farther to the southwest lies the swampy terrain of the Ranns of Kutch, separating the well-watered lands of Saurashtra from the solid mainland of the Indian subcontinent.

Despite the strong thread of continuity running through Indian history and prehistory, the environment of the northwest has experienced massive changes. Most dramatically, the

Figure 7.

ROCK PAINTING

At Bhimbetka in Central India there are over 130 rock-shelters, some of which have been occupied for 100,000 years. On the walls of some are paintings contemporary with those that decorate the famous Ice Age caves of northern Spain and southern France. This painting of a hunter was rendered about 7,000 years ago.

Himalayan mountain range is still a region of tectonic uplift, which can bring about major changes in the landscape, environment, and climate for hundreds of miles beyond. At the time of the Indus Civilization, two major rivers flowed westward to the Arabian Sea, the Indus itself and a parallel system, the Saraswati, to its south. Between them they framed a huge and fertile plain between the foothills of the Indo-Iranian borderlands and the arid wastes of the Great Indian (Thar) Desert. By the mid–1st millennium B.C., the Saraswati had vanished, the tributaries that supplied its waters captured by other major rivers, the Indus and the Yamuna. Where once the Saraswati flowed, its banks dense with settlements and fields, today there remains only desert.

The rivers themselves are also subject to change. The massive Indus, meandering through its great floodplain, has changed its course many times as the huge volume of silt it carries has been deposited and has built up the alluvial plain. Meanders have become oxbow lakes and have been left stranded as the river has cut itself a new course, causing settlements on its banks to be abandoned. On a wider scale, the river as a whole has gradually been shifting westward. At the river's mouth, the deposition of silt has formed a great delta, extending the coastline out far beyond that of 5,000 years ago. The Saraswati of the past and another ancient river, a fragment of which survives as the Luni, have added their silt to that from the Indus to create the swampy Ranns of Kutch: 5,000 years ago this was open water, separating mainland South Asia from a large island

that is now Kutch and making neighboring Kathiawar a peninsula.

EARLY INHABITANTS

The story of settlement in South Asia stretches back to the common ancestors of apes and humans in the Miocene, 10 to 14 million years ago. Within a (relatively speaking) short space of time, by 1.8 million years ago, the first humans had spread across Asia as far as China, Indonesia, and Java. Few in number, these early humans have been hard to trace and only small numbers of their bones have been found [Figure 8]. Their stone tools, on the other hand, have preserved well and can be used to reconstruct something of the lifestyle of their makers.

India and Pakistan have the stones but not the bones, so we can see a little of what people were up to but not who they were. The story may begin around 2 million years ago, with a simple stone tool found at Riwat in the Potwar Plateau in the Punjab—a pebble with a cutting edge made by striking a few flakes off the longest side. The tool bears some similarity to the earliest stone tools in Africa (known as Oldowan tools), although tools of this simple form were also in use considerably later. If this tool is dated correctly, we may need to perhaps broaden the area where humans are thought to have evolved to include South Asia as well as Africa. However, the tool was not found in a primary context, but on the lip of a small

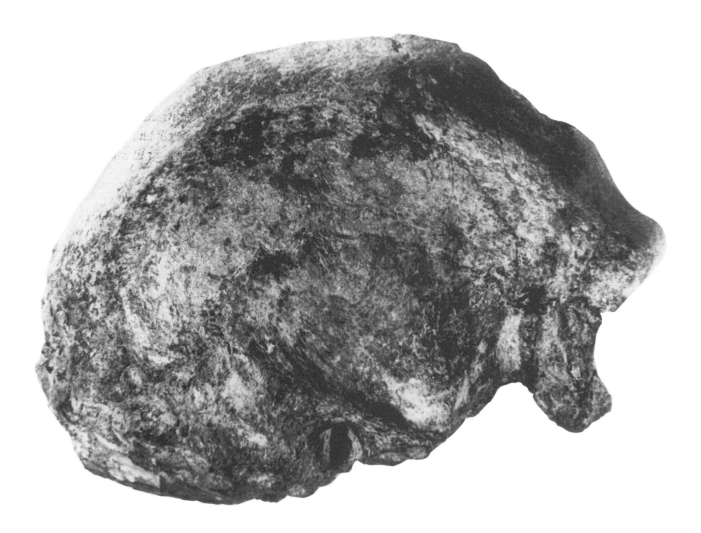

waterfall, eroded from a deposit whose date we cannot know. At present, the Riwat pebble tool remains as a question mark hanging over the constantly revised story of early humanity.

Sometimes the homes of the earliest South Asians have also been found—places in caves and rock shelters or in the open air where people camped for a time, perhaps returning there every year. Simple one-edged choppers like the Riwat pebble were being made and used by people in the Potwar Plateau more than a million years ago. By half a million years ago early people in South Asia were also making more com-plex shapes like the multipurpose hand axe, a popular tool used across a vast area from western Europe and Africa into Asia, although not found in East Asia. The rock shelters at Bhimbetkar and other sites in Central India were home to such people, whose remains have also been found in the south and in the northwest, particularly the Potwar Plateau.

From around 30,000 years ago, however, the evidence from the Indian subcontinent becomes much more abundant and varied, giving us a much fuller picture of the way of life of the inhabitants of South Asia. Their tools were now made from fine long stone

Figure 8.

FOSSIL SKULL

Discovered in north central India, the Narmada skull is dated to 300,000 years ago. It is associated with Acheulean stone tools, and thus with the second wave of humans who left Africa 600,000 to 500,000 years ago.

blades struck from a core, sometimes using an unusual technique, inverse indirect percussion, that continued in use not only right into Indus times but even up to the present day. Stoneworking debris at the great factory site of the Rohri Hills bears witness to the use of these techniques.

HUNTERS, GATHERERS, AND FISHERS

Bones and other food remains, along with hunting tools, knives and grindstones, and other tools used to obtain and process foods, show that the people of the subcontinent were hunting game such as antelope, goat, and cattle. They were also collecting shellfish and various plant foods, including some cereals. Some changes in the nature and distribution of these resources took place after about 10,000 B.C. as the icesheets retreated in northern parts of the globe and rainfall increased worldwide, but many of the economic patterns established during the previous 20,000 years endured.

Seasonal movement to exploit plant foods as they become available and to follow the herds of animals as they move between seasonal pastures is a common pattern in hunter-gatherer life. Evidence shows that this was the normal pattern in many parts of South Asia. In the northwest, the availability of vegetation was influenced by marked differences between very hot summer and very cold winter temperatures, with associated aridity. It is therefore probable that many

groups moved seasonally, spending the winter on the Indus plains and the summer in the mountains of Baluchistan. These seasonal constraints continue to dictate the pattern of life, despite major changes in global temperature, environment, and human economies. The same pattern still holds good among some groups up to the present day.

Similar seasonal movements occurred elsewhere in the subcontinent, between upland and lowland regions and between coastal and inland locations. It is possible that in some tropical areas local resource abundance and the relative lack of seasonal extremes of temperature made it possible for some hunter-gatherer communities to occupy permanent or semipermanent settlements. In the Ganges Valley, for example, resources were available year-round and there is evidence of considerable population increase through time. Tools made of stone from the nearby Vindhyan Hills, however, indicate that the people of the Central Ganges region either traveled to the uplands at certain times of year or were in contact with communities who lived there.

PICTURES OF THE PAST

One fascinating development that took place in the period from around 30,000 B.C. was the beginning of art. Best known from the spectacularly decorated caves of southern France and northern Spain, and the magnificent figurines from Russia and other parts of Europe, the creation of art was actually a global phenomenon. Some of the earliest works may be the geometric designs engraved on rocks in Australia, although their date is still debated. South Asia's contribution can be seen in caves such as those at Bhimbetkar in Central India, where elegant green paintings of animals are found among the abundant paintings of later times [Figure 7].

By 10,000 B.C. the global climate was warmer and wetter than in the preceding Ice Age. The Indian subcontinent, like other parts of the world, was home to many hunter-gatherer groups, who exploited a range of different environments. The rock paintings executed by Central Indian groups give us a superb picture of their everyday life, which is an important supplement to the material remains uncovered by archaeologists. As in other parts of the world, people in this era manufactured mainly tiny stone tool components, called microliths. These were combined to create a variety of tools—a row of blades set in a wooden handle to form a sickle, for example, or individual microliths hafted on the end of wooden shafts to form arrows. The paintings show many scenes of people using such tools—men brandishing a fistful of arrows, shooting them from a bow or hotly pursuing game with a many-barbed spear. Other scenes, however, show us tools of which there are no surviving traces, because they were made of perishable material. Here we see women fishing with nets or digging small creatures out of their burrows with wooden digging sticks, men and women carrying home game or fruit in bags slung from their heads, others climbing trees with bags or bas-

kets to collect honey or fruit, and the whole family sitting down to eat within a tent.

Life had its exciting side too. As depicted in the paintings, there were great dances where men, dressed in loincloths and often wearing bangles on their legs and arms and streamers on their heads, moved together in a long line or executed complicated individual steps, accompanying themselves with a song or accompanied by musicians. Some late scenes even show the dangerous sport of bull-leaping, in which contestants perhaps used domestic cattle acquired from neighboring farming communities.

TRACING THE BEGINNINGS OF FARMING

In the late millennia of the last glacial period, hunter-gatherers in areas of Western Asia (known as the "Fertile Crescent") exploited a range of wild foods including cereals and nuts. These foodstuffs could be stored against lean seasons and years, and so the people were able to establish permanent settlements occupied year-round. What pushed these groups into planting cereals rather than just harvesting them is still much debated. For many decades it was believed that farming was better as a way of life and began when the appropriate techniques were discovered. This viewpoint was abandoned as it became clear that hunter-gatherers do not lack the knowledge to practice farming—

on the contrary they are intimately familiar with the plants and animals upon which they depend. Farming is not an easier way of life than hunting and gathering: although farming greatly increases the productivity of an area from a human perspective, in general the effort required to produce food is greater than that required to gather or hunt. People who began farming must have had good reason to do so. One possible explanation is that farming began as a way of supporting a growing population. Nomadic people space their children at around four-year intervals so that generally at any one time there is only one child in a family so young that it needs to be carried around. Settled communities are not constrained in this way, so they can have larger families much more closely spaced—as a result, the population grows. The small step from gathering to planting and tending desirable food plants may have been taken as a way of feeding a growing number of mouths.

Another explanation relates to short-term climatic fluctuations that occurred around 9000 B.C. in the Near East. The warmer and wetter postglacial environment underwent a temporary return to a drier regime that endured approximately 1,000 years. During this time many communities turned again to seasonal movement to ensure adequate food supplies. Some, however, living in settlements beside permanent water sources, such as lakes and springs, began to plant cereals rather than merely harvesting them—this was the case at the famous settlement of Jericho, for example. As conditions improved with increasing rainfall after around 8000 B.C., it became possible for communities now well established as farmers, and the crops and farming techniques that they had developed, to spread out into other areas, such as Anatolia and northern Mesopotamia. Although human population had been steadily growing worldwide, the population of sedentary farming communities grew much faster, and so they rapidly spread—sometimes they displaced hunter-gatherers living in the regions that they colonized, sometimes the hunter-gatherers themselves adopted farming as part of their way of life, and sometimes there was no conflict of interests between hunter-gatherers and farmers as each exploited different parts of a varied environment.

As farming became the dominant way of life in the Near East, there was also a change in the exploitation of livestock. A range of species—particularly gazelle in the Levant, cattle and pigs elsewhere, and sheep and goats in many regions—had formerly been hunted. Now it became expedient or desirable to herd some of these species, particularly sheep and goats. These wild species evolved into domestic species dependent upon people. There was an explosion in the number of communities whose economy was at least in part dependent on agriculture, embracing much of Anatolia, northern Mesopotamia, western Iran, and pockets of southwest Central Asia by 7000 B.C. The regions that border the Iranian plateau share many features of environment and climate. Contacts were maintained between the communities that inhabited these regions, and similar developments took place throughout the Iranian plateau at much the same time. And so the eastern margins of the region, in Baluchistan, were also involved by 7000 B.C., in particular, a small community on the very edge of the Indus plains in Pakistan, the place now known as Mehrgarh.

MEHRGARH AND THE FIRST INDIAN FARMERS

The Bolan River flows from the mountains of central Baluchistan across the alluvial Kachi Plain, a triangular extension into the mountain foothills from the plains of the Indus River. Approximately 9,000 years ago, the Kachi Plain lay much lower than now—in the intervening period many meters of alluvium have been deposited by the Bolan River, often in major episodes of flooding. More recently, however, the river changed its course and has been cutting down through these deposits accumulated over the millennia, to form a steep cliff near the modern town of Dadhar. In the 1970s, a French team was excavating the exposed remains of a settlement here, dating from the 5th and 4th millennia B.C., on the alluvial plateau above the river at Mehrgarh. Their investigations of the strata below this village, visible in the section cut by the river, dramatically revealed traces of a much earlier settlement.

Excavations after 1976 have uncovered a sequence of villages going back to about

7000 B.C. And right from the start the people of the Mehrgarh village were farmers—a discovery that answered the question of when farming began in this region of South Asia. The find also posed a new question: Did farming develop here or was it introduced (and if so, by whom)?

Many specialists have been focusing their attentions on the site of Mehrgarh—it is one of the best-known villages in the Indian subcontinent. The abundance of evidence from Mehrgarh goes some way to compensate for its uniqueness. Even today, more than twenty years later, Mehrgarh is still the only agricultural site of this date known from either India or Pakistan. Other sites, presumably, still lie buried beneath comparable alluvial deposits, or have been destroyed by river downcutting and floods (as is the case with a part of the Mehrgarh site) or are hidden beneath later settlements. How typical Mehrgarh is of its time we do not yet know—nor do we know where its earliest inhabitants lived during the summer months when Mehrgarh may have been deserted, given the extreme summer temperatures of the area—often above 100° F (38° C) during the coolest part of day. At the least some of Mehrgarh's villagers will have taken their herds into Baluchistan to find summer grazing—probably in the Quetta region where modern pastoralists from the Kachi Plain take their animals during the summer.

In the time of the earliest settlement at Mehrgarh—around 7000 B.C.—the people of the village hunted game and raised domestic goats, and grew barley and wheat. Careful studies of the plant remains and animal bones show that the goats and wheat must have been introduced from the western end of the Iranian plateau where they were staples of the developing farming communities.

This does not yet answer the question of how farming came about here. Were the inhabitants of Mehrgarh indigenous people who had taken up farming alongside their traditional hunting and gathering way of life, at first using imported crops and animals? Or were they immigrants ultimately from Western Asia, settling here along with their Western Asiatic domestic animals and plants?

Burials provide some clues toward answering this question. The people of Mehrgarh buried their dead with their stone tools, their jewelry of beads and shells, and sometimes with baby goats. The eminent physical anthropologist K.A.R. Kennedy has studied the bones from these burials as well as other early South Asian skeletons and has found no more differences among them than one would expect within a population. This suggests that the people of Mehrgarh were probably locals—but the question is by no means settled yet.

What other clues do we have? The presence of wheat and goats that must derive ultimately from Western Asia makes it clear that farming did not develop at Mehrgarh entirely as an indigenous phenomenon, independent of outside influence. Some scholars point to the established pattern of agricultural dispersal from the early centers of agriculture in the Near East into adjacent regions that came about because the farming population was increasing far more rapidly than that of the contemporary hunter-gatherers. They suggest that the earliest farmers in the Indo-Iranian borderlands were colonists who had gradually spread there from the Zagros Mountains of western Iran. Once farmers were established in the region, local groups of hunter-gatherers were likely also to have adopted farming from them. In the earliest village at Mehrgarh, agriculture and hunting and gathering were practiced side by side, agriculture only becoming the main way of life in later periods. So this scenario is possible.

On the other hand, many scholars argue that farming developed independently in the Indo-Iranian borderlands—that local hunter-gatherers domesticated indigenous crops and animals. Barley, the main crop of the settlement at this time, may or may not have been locally domesticated—there is disagreement on whether wild barley was available locally. A local plant that probably grew as a weed in the fields of Mehrgarh, goats-face grass *(Aegilops squarrosa)*, seems to have hybridized with the cultivated emmer wheat, producing free-threshing wheat *(Triticum aestivum)*, which was to become the breadwheat of the eastern part of the farming region that stretched from West Asia to India. The people of Mehrgarh also began cultivating the cotton plant—the earliest evidence for this—so presumably they were beginning to make cotton garments.

Similarly, there is considerable debate about the origins of the sheep kept at Mehrgarh. All modern domestic sheep derive from one wild ancestor, the Asiatic moufflon, which is not native to this eastern area of the Iranian plateau but is confined to the west. It is difficult to match sheep and goat bones to specific species, so it is possible that the early Mehrgarh sheep were domesticated from the local wild sheep, the urial, later being replaced by moufflon-descended stock from the west. Domestic sheep became increasingly important as time went by [Figure 9].

Less in doubt is the domestication of the local wild cattle, *Bos namadicus*, and their development into the zebu cattle, *Bos indicus*, that are so characteristic of the Indian subcontinent. Studies of the bones of cattle from Mehrgarh show the progressive diminution in size that is a characteristic of domestication in many species. As time went on, cattle became progressively more important in the economy of Mehrgarh's inhabitants.

Wheat and goats could have reached this region through trade across the Iranian plateau. Evidence demonstrates the existence of trade networks across this vast area, stretching from the Zagros Mountains in the west through the southwest regions of Central Asia, and into Baluchistan. Domestic animals and plants could have been transmitted from west to east in the same way. New ideas and innovations could also be transmitted through these exchange networks. So a mechanism existed by which Western Asiatic domestic plants and animals could have reached Mehrgarh and its region. If agriculture developed independently in the Indo-Iranian borderlands, this requires an explanation: What could have pushed people into adopting a more labor-intensive way of life in this region? Why cultivate and herd if hunting and gathering provides an adequate food

supply? On balance the introduction of agriculture by colonists ultimately from Western Asia still seems more plausible—but, as with so many archaeological questions, we just don't know. What we do know is that agriculture did not develop anywhere else in the Indian subcontinent until much later.

Whether agriculture began as an independent development at Mehrgarh (and the other sites that haven't yet been found but which must have existed) or was introduced,

Figure 9.

MODERN SHEEP

Sheep have been kept in the Indian subcontinent for more than 8,000 years. Today sheep provide sacrifices for important occasions and may have been similarly used in Indus times.

it rapidly took off, soon becoming the main way of life of the region. By around 5000 B.C., the people of Mehrgarh had come to rely mainly on domestic cattle, sheep, and goats for their meat.

A BROADENING PICTURE

Other changes had taken place by this time. The earliest settlers at Mehrgarh had lived in mudbrick houses with flat thatched roofs. By 6000 B.C. they were also building granaries, compartmented buildings without doors, in which they stored large quantities of grain—a clear indication of the strengthening importance of agriculture to the village's inhabitants. The earliest settlers had used baskets as containers, lined with bitumen to make them watertight. By about 5000 B.C., however, they were beginning to make pottery vessels. At first this pottery was coarse and crude; within a few hundred years, however, the people of Mehrgarh were turning out fine painted vessels decorated with geometric designs or with stylized figures, as well as a few terracotta figurines, later to be an extremely common product of the borderlands [Figure 10]. They were also burying their dead in more elaborate graves: chambers excavated in the side of a burial pit and closed by a brick wall.

From our point of view, another major change by this time is that Mehrgarh no longer provides all our evidence—other farming settlements of the period from 5000 to 4500 B.C. have been found, such as Kili Gul Mohammed near modern Quetta, Anjira farther to the south, and Mundigak to the northeast. Differences in the styles of pottery from these sites suggest the existence of regional groups, but there are also strong similarities between them, as well as continuing evidence of contacts over vast areas, bringing mother of pearl from Arabia, and lapis and turquoise from Turkmenia. Long-distance trade, flourishing in the west as the emerging cities of Mesopotamia sought essential raw materials and desirable luxuries, began to extend across the Iranian plateau. By the mid–4th millennium, towns were appearing in this area at important nodes in the long-distance trade routes and in areas where important raw materials were to be found. These formed a network that conducted trade in local products (such as chlorite vessels made at Shahr-i Sokhta) and in exotic materials from further afield (such as lapis lazuli from Badakhshan).

In the borderland towns of Baluchistan we can see the flowering of craft traditions, already foreshadowed at earlier Mehrgarh, where finely crafted steatite (soapstone) and turquoise objects were made. The craftsmen of these towns produced fine painted pottery, charming figurines, and elaborate jewelry including tiny beads. Some sites developed as specialist centers—for example, Lewan, a village in the Bannu basin in northern Baluchistan, specialized in the production of stone tools, including querns, axes, and hammers, which were traded over a wide area. Mehrgarh itself had become a center of craft production by the early 4th millennium.

Figure 10.

POLYCHROME POTTERY SHERDS *These beautifully colored pieces of pottery are from the 3rd-millennium B.C. Baluchistan site at Niai Buthi, which was discovered in 1943 by Hungarian archaeologist Sir Aurel Stein. One sherd has a geometric pattern that ringed the lip of the vessel. The other depicts a stylized fish, a popular motif as fish were a ready source of food for the Indus people.*

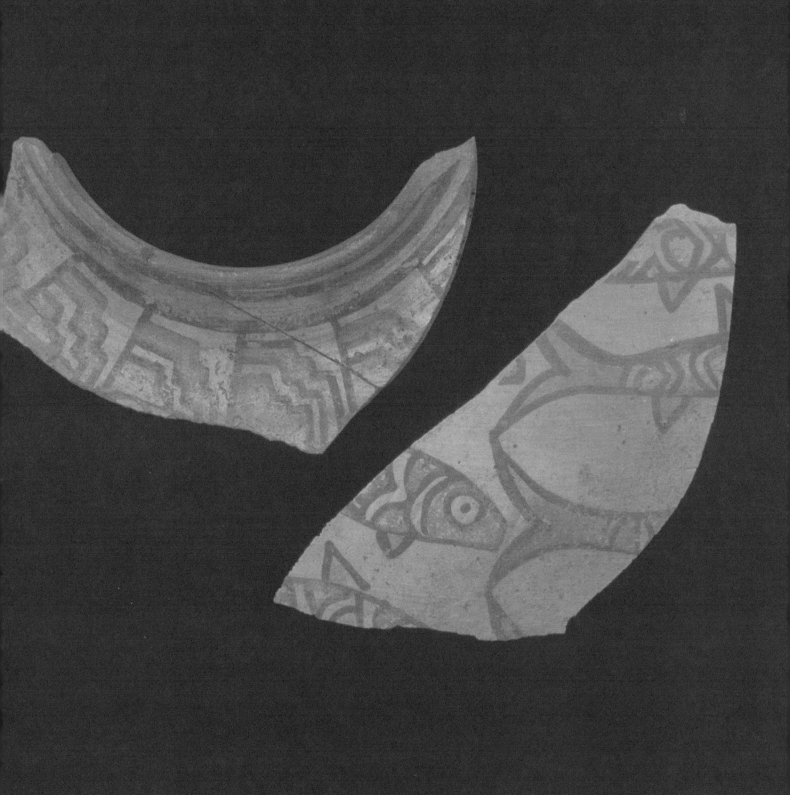

The people of the Indo-Iranian border-lands had also now mastered the complex technology needed to work metal. As in Western Asia and Europe, the first metal objects must have been cold-hammered from native copper—a copper bead has been found in the early period at Mehrgarh. True metallurgy, involving the smelting of metal ores and the production of cast-metal objects, came later. The development of kilns used to fire pottery at high temperatures taught the people of Baluchistan skills in controlling firing temperatures, and these then allowed them to smelt copper and gold ores. By the middle of the 4th millennium, the people of the region were making a range of copper and bronze jewelry, such as beads and pins, as well as some tools. By the end of the millennium, they were also manufacturing larger, more complex metal shapes, such as shaft hole axes.

Much of the Indo-Iranian borderlands are semidesert, although the region enjoys summer monsoon rains as well as winter rainfall. Settlements grew where there was a reliable source of water, such as rivers, springs, and perennial wells. The size to which a settlement could grow was determined to a considerable degree by the extent of arable land around it. Over much of the region sheep and goat pastoralism was extremely important, as it is today, because perennial vegetation suitable for grazing was available, watered by the summer and winter rains. By the late 4th and early 3rd millennia, substantial towns were emerging in some favored locations, such as Mundigak on a tributary of the Arghandab River in southeast Afghanistan or Rahman

Dheri on the Gomal plain. Here the mud-brick architecture began to include large structures like the "palace" at Mundigak, and massive defensive walls with bastions were constructed around the settlements. Whether these were truly defensive, built against outside threats, or whether they were designed merely to impress is not clear. Although there were stone and bronze objects that could be interpreted as weapons, they could all have had other functions, such as hunting weapons. There is no unequivocal evidence of warfare, and in view of what was to follow in the Indus Civilization, an entirely peaceful realm, this seems significant.

In this arid region, dry farming was only possible in river valley bottoms and water conservation was vital for high agricultural productivity. Many settlements built tanks (reservoirs) with earth or stone embankments to store rainwater for irrigation. Taking advantage of the annual flooding caused by the melting of highland snows, people also began building dams to impound runoff water, in order to use it for irrigation later in the year when temperatures rose and the ground became parched. As population increased, this technological expertise aided the settlement of new regions. Competition for the limited arable land was also a factor in the move to new regions. In addition, the importance of cattle in the economy put pressure on arable land. In the later centuries of the 4th millennium B.C., pastoralists began to penetrate the lowlands in search of additional grazing. Farmers eventually followed in their wake and began to settle the Indus plains, a region where it was necessary not only to conserve water but also to control its excess. At first their settlements were confined to rocky salients and other land raised above the plains themselves. It was only later, in the early 3rd millennium B.C., that they took up the challenge of the Indus plains. Settlers also spread into the adjacent valley of the Saraswati River, eventually reaching as far east as the Ganges River though they did not penetrate the lands beyond it. Pastoralists probably moved into Gujurat in the early 3rd millennium although it is still not certain when farmers also settled in the region. At the same time, it is likely that some of these pioneering farmers continued to move southward, settling in the Deccan and South India, where they established villages relying particularly on cattlekeeping.

THE BEGINNING OF INDIAN AGRICULTURE

It is clear that the first farmers in the subcontinent were confined for millennia to the northwest, where agricultural villages, beginning with Mehrgarh around 7000 B.C., grew eventually into substantial towns.

These were in the eastern margin of the Western Asiatic "interaction sphere" in which sheep, goats and cattle, wheat, barley, and pulses such as lentils were the main domestic plants and animals. From this region, farmers spread in the 4th millennium onto the plains of the Indus and Saraswati Rivers, many settling there but some gradually moving farther south into the peninsula where cattle herding became the mainstay of the economy. During the 3rd and early 2nd millennia B.C., there were also contacts between parts of the subcontinent and its neighbors in both East and Southeast Asia, and many things, including plants, animals, and agricultural know-how, were being exchanged between the people of these regions. It also seems apparent that the people of the eastern part of the subcontinent were not farmers until 3000 B.C. at the earliest and generally it was not until sometime after 2000 B.C. that agriculture really took off here. In the 3rd millennium B.C., therefore, at the time of the Indus Civilization, farming was almost entirely confined to the northwest of the subcontinent, and the remaining regions were home mainly to hunter-gatherer groups.

CHAPTER THREE

FARMERS OF THE INDUS

PIONEERS ON THE INDUS PLAINS

The pioneer farmers who settled in the Indus and Saraswati River Valleys in the later 4th millennium B.C. moved into a land previously inhabited only by hunter-gatherers and fishing communities. A community excavated at Jalilpur, on the Ravi River in the Punjab, gives a glimpse of the lives of one such indigenous group. As shown by the terracotta netsinkers (weights to ensure that the net would sink into the water), fishing was important for the people of Jalilpur—but domestic sheep, goats, and cattle also played an important role. The presence of domestic animals in what was otherwise a hunter-gatherer community probably reflects contacts that already existed between the people of the Indus-Saraswati plains and the hills of Baluchistan before the arrival of agricultural settlers on the plains.

Much of Asia, from Mesopotamia across the Iranian plateau via Turkmenia to Baluchistan, and from the Caucasus through the steppes into northern China, was linked into an "interaction sphere" in which innovations and ideas as well as actual commodities circulated freely. The Indus plains are unlikely to have been entirely outside this network of contacts even before farmers from the Indo-Iranian borderlands began to settle there. So although the Indus-Saraswati region presented huge challenges as well as huge opportunities to the arriving settlers, it cannot have been entirely unfamiliar or unknown.

The Indus floodplains enjoy an environmental regime that in many ways is ideal for the farmer. In the Punjab to the north the monsoon rains water winter-grown crops, while farther south in Sindh the rich alluvium deposited by two annual inundations can allow crops to be raised both in summer and winter. Vegetation in the areas between the rivers of the Punjab provides rich grazing for domestic animals. In the 4th millennium B.C., dense forests probably grew widely along the course of the rivers beyond their immediate banks. South of the Indus another equally productive—if not more productive—river system, the Saraswati, flowed in this period. Unlike the mountainous region of Baluchistan, where arable land was

Figure 11.

PLOWED FIELD AT KALIBAGNAN *This field belonged to the Early Indus Period, and at present is the earliest plowed field known in the world. The field was tilled with the same technique used in the region today. The tools and equipment used by the Indus farmers, such as plows and solid-wheeled carts drawn by bullocks, are also still in use today.*

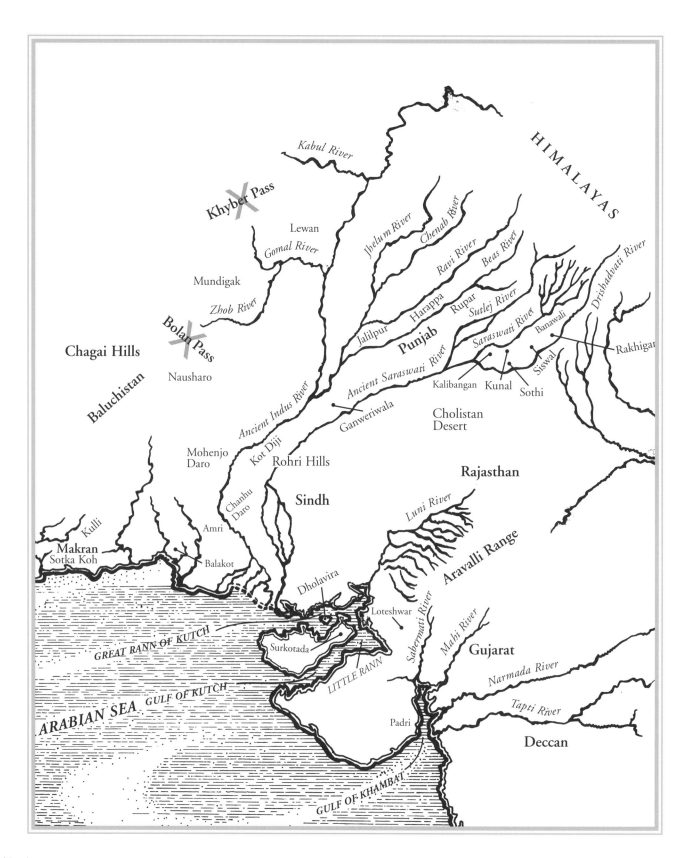

severely limited, the Indus, the Saraswati, and their associated river systems were capable of supporting a huge population [Map 2].

Riverine environments, though agriculturally rich, often are deficient in other resources considered essential by their inhabitants—raw materials such as stone and metal ores for manufacturing tools, and luxury commodities like precious stones for making objects to enhance personal status or to offer to the gods. The Indus-Saraswati region, however, was more favorably situated than many others: for instance, it had timber from forests along the rivers and in the adjacent hills, a substantial outcrop of exceptionally good flint in the middle Indus Valley, gemstones and metal ores in the surrounding hills—a bountiful supply of nature's riches.

But the region had significant drawbacks. Mosquitoes brought malaria and other fevers to the plains. The impact of malaria, long suspected to have been rife in the Indus-Saraswati region, has recently been demonstrated by studies of the pathology of some of the skeletons from Indus burials. The forest housed not only game such as gazelle and jungle fowl but also deadly predators and dangerous wild animals—tigers, wild boar, snakes, and the formidable elephant [Color Plates 7, 8, and 9]. The instability of the Indus was also a major problem, with frequent floods and changes in the river's course. And beyond the area of annual inundation, much of the region was desert, requiring irrigation to enable it to produce any usable vegetation. In the long term, irrigation would have caused salination, as in southern

Mesopotamia, though this was not of immediate consequence. Taken as a whole, however, the advantages of the Indus and Saraswati Valleys greatly outweighed the disadvantages.

Regional styles of pottery and of other artifacts suggest that the borderlands were home to a number of distinct, though culturally related, groups, their distinctiveness determined to a considerable extent by the topography of this mountainous region. Similarities between the material from early settlements in the Indus Valley and parts of the borderlands indicate that the Indus plains were colonized by groups from different regions, as one might have expected. In the south, Balakot was established as a coastal village by about 4000 B.C. Its inhabitants were affiliated to those of the adjacent regions of southern Baluchistan. Farther north, Amri, a settlement that was established in the earlier 4th millennium B.C., relates to the Kalat region of central Baluchistan. Kot Diji, in the central Indus Valley, a region dominated later by the great city of Mohenjo Daro, was culturally affiliated to the region leading up from Mehrgarh into northern Baluchistan. Harappa in the Punjab and Kalibangan to its east on the Saraswati are linked to towns and villages in the north of the borderlands. The people of the borderlands gradually colonized adjacent regions of the Indus plains. The access routes onto the plains, such as the Bolan and Gomal passes, acted as funnels through which groups first entered the plains and from which they spread out like fans. Regions farther from the borderlands, such as the eastern portion of

Map 2.

EARLY INDUS SITES

Cities of the Indus c.3000 B.C.

the Saraswati system where it borders on the Ganges Valley, tended to be settled later than those immediately adjacent to the borderlands, so there were pioneering settlements still being established in the east after the Mature Indus Civilization had emerged in the Indus-Saraswati plains, around 2700–2600 B.C.

SETTLING DOWN

After the initial settlement of these regions, the distinctions between these small groups began to break down. The material at Balakot, for example, by 2900 B.C. resembles that from Amri. People native to the plains also became caught up in this growing cultural homogenization: in the fishing village of Jalilpur the artifacts increasingly were of types known from sites of the Kot Diji sphere of influence. During the earlier 3rd millennium B.C., three major traditions seem to have emerged in the greater Indus region and extended back into the borderlands from which they had first come, named after important sites: the Amri (or Amri-Nal), Kot Diji, and Sothi (or Sothi-Siswal) traditions, respectively, in the south, center/north, and east.

Among the fine objects being produced at this time one may single out two types as worthy of further comment. Figurines display great liveliness and imagination. Many depict women, scantily clad but generally well endowed with jewelry and head ornaments [Figure 12]. These have frequently been labeled mother goddesses. Other figurines depict animals, with cattle prominent

among them [*see* Figure 34]. Goddesses and cattle are important in the folk religion of the subcontinent today and in historical times, providing good evidence of cultural continuity, so we may see these models as representations that had some religious significance. Stamp seals made of steatite also begin to appear at this time, indicating a development in the organization of society, probably reflecting the need of rulers or people of power and standing in the community to mark their control over the movement of commodities [*see* Figure 48]. The trade network that had linked Baluchistan to areas to the north and west of the Iranian plateau now extended to encompass the Indus region too.

This was a period when towns were developing out of the smaller settlements in the borderlands. Those on the plains were generally similar. All were bounded by a massive defensive wall that, whatever its purpose in the hills, served here as vital protection against river flooding. Houses were constructed of mudbrick and were generally distributed in a haphazard arrangement within the settlement walls, although the highland town of Rahman Dheri shows a certain degree of planning.

DRAMATIC CHANGES

Many of these highland and lowland towns were destroyed by fire or razed around 2700–2600 B.C. Until recently this was seen as a single, sudden and deliberate phenomenon, perhaps the work of a charismatic

Figure 12. (opposite)
FEMALE
FIGURINES,
HARAPPA AND
NAUSHARO
The vast majority of terracotta figurines of people represent women, who were rarely depicted in the more sophisticated stone or metal sculptures. These simple but charming models give a fascinating insight into the variety of headgear and personal ornaments worn by Indus women, including turbans, bangles, and necklaces.

leader. But doubts have now been cast on this picture. The destruction levels may have occurred at different dates at different sites, given the imprecise nature of our dating methods. Not all sites were destroyed and the causes may be many and varied, from deliberate razing of settlements to devastating accidental fires. The timescale of change now seems longer than previously supposed. As a result, one may no longer argue for a sudden transformation.

But the region's transformation was still dramatic, even if it took place over more than a century instead of a few years and even if there is no causal link between the destruction of individual settlements. Many new features appeared during this time, reflecting major developments in the organization of society—features that we associate with civilization.

In this crucial century between 2700 and 2600 B.C., the haphazard settlements of the Early Indus people disappeared. Above their ruins were built the planned cities and towns of the Mature Indus Civilization, with their set pattern of citadel and lower town. Mudbrick architecture now gave way in many settlements to construction largely in baked brick. Public buildings appeared, along with an efficient network of public drains [Color Plate 15].

Many craft activities now became the preserve of specialists rather than the occasional activities of people who spent most of their time farming, and craftsmanship attained new heights. There is evidence for the emergence of different classes. Writing, which greatly facilitates the organization and administration of society, now began to be used.

And whatever the cause of the destruction of the Early Indus settlements, there seems likely to have been a cohesive force behind the pattern of reconstruction. The settlements that now developed were planned in their layout, whether they were constructed above the leveled remains of an earlier settlement or built on entirely new foundations. The layout of the cities was planned along the cardinal directions, the streets running north-south and east-west. The streets conform to a series of set proportions, main streets being twice the width of minor streets, for example [Color Plate 16]. Within the blocks delineated by these streets, houses were laid out in an orderly fashion. They were generally constructed to one of a series of modular designs; bricks were made to a standard size. These regularities in town planning and architecture cannot have arisen by chance.

A similar transformation took place in the objects used by people in the Indus Valley. Whereas previously there had been a number of regional styles in such things as pottery, now there was considerable stylistic uniformity throughout the Indus realms. These features indicate that throughout the Indus region there had developed a cohesive and uniform culture, within which some standardization of design was imposed. It seems likely that this was dictated by some universally recognized authority.

The nature of this authority and of the unifying principle is still elusive, however, although it is only a part of the great cloud of unknowns that still hangs over the civilization. We can only speculate about what took place over the critical period. Do the razed or burnt towns represent the stirrings of interregional conflict that horrified the Indus people into adopting a policy of nonviolence that lasted for almost a millennium? We have the example of the Mauryan emperor, Ashoka, who followed just this path a little over 2,000 years later, when his horror at the destruction wrought in his war against Kalinga led him to espouse and proselytize Buddhism, giving its creed of nonviolence the backing of the law. In Indus times, too, religion is likely to have played a central role in the organization and maintenance of authority, so perhaps we should be looking for some religious inspiration behind the planning and standardization of the Indus cities. The cardinal orientation of the streets probably reflects an intimate knowledge of astronomy, closely bound up with religion. Tradition may also have played a major part in enforcing a pattern once it was established, giving the weight of custom to practices that may originally have been imposed by authority.

What factors underlie the major transformations from small-scale societies to states—the emergence of civilization—in other parts of the world? Are they the same as those that operated in the Indus-Saraswati region? Many "prime movers" have been suggested by archaeologists as an explanation for the emergence of civilization, and many factors have been proposed as being essential prerequisites for the development of civilization. The first civilizations appeared in areas of high agricultural productivity where large and dense populations could be supported. They had strong religions and often constructed immense religious monuments. They had cities and specialist craftsmen, producing goods that were widely distributed. They were strongly organized, with a marked social hierarchy, often headed by kings. The authorities often used writing in their administration. Many civilizations had armies and engaged in warfare against their neighbors. Trade with adjacent regions was of great importance.

Before we can actually attempt to answer the vital questions of what caused the Indus Civilization to emerge, how it functioned, and why it disappeared, it is necessary to examine the evidence in detail to see how the Indus Civilization measures up to these theories— to see which factors might be relevant here. This is a difficult task, because the Indus Civilization still withholds the answer to many of the vital questions. A good starting point in our search for the clues to unraveling these factors is an examination of the agricultural potential of the Indus region and the responses that the Indus people made to these opportunities.

INTENSIVE AGRICULTURE— THE UNDERPINNING OF CIVILIZATION

There is general agreement that civilizations emerged only in areas with the potential to support dense populations. Although there are a variety of ways in which this might be achieved, intensive agriculture seems to have been the most common and it

THE SARASWATI IN THE RIGVEDA

The Saraswati River, though reduced in Rigvedic times (later 2nd millennium B.C.), was still a mighty river. This is how the Rigvedic Aryans described it:

"Foremost mother, foremost of rivers, foremost of goddesses, Sarasvati. In thee, Sarasvati, divine, all genera-tions have their stars.

"Yea, this divine Sarasvati, terrible with her golden path, foeslayer, claims our eulogy. Whose limitless, unbroken flood, swift-moving with a rapid rush, comes onward with tempestuous roar. She hath spread us beyond all foe, beyond her Sisters, Holy One.

As Surya spendeth out the days. Yea, she most dear amid dear streams, Seven-sistered, graciously inclined. Sarasvati hath earned our praise. Guard us from hate Sarasvati, she who hath filled the realms of earth. And that wide tract, the firmament! Seven-sistered, sprung from three-fold source,

Five Tribes prosper, she must be invoked in every deed of might."

Rigveda Book II Hymn 41, verses 16-17, Book VI Hymn 61, verses 7–12—modified after Griffith 1896—quoted in Possehl 1999 p. 362

---

underlay the prosperity of the earliest civilizations in Egypt, Mesopotamia, and China—so what about the Indus?

This is not an easy question to answer. Although the origins and development of farming in the region in earlier times have been intensively studied, in the Indus Period the massive cities and towns with their highly visible remains have tended to attract most archaeological attention, along with related subjects, such as craft production and trade. Few studies have concentrated on rural life and the subsistence economy that underpinned the whole civilization. In recent decades this situation has been partially rectified although the picture is still skewed in favor of the urban settlements. And although much can be surmised about the farming and other economic practices of the Indus people, a great deal of this is based on a common

sense interpretation of the potential of the region at the time rather than on concrete data from excavation. So we must still say "this is how it was likely to have been" rather than "this is how it was."

THE LOST SARASWATI

At its height, the Indus Civilization was an extremely prosperous land, composed of a number of different regions, each with its own economic opportunities and problems: In the northwest was the highland region— the Indo-Iranian borderlands—where agriculture and pastoralism began many millennia before the time of the Indus Civilization and where cultivation was possible only in certain favored areas. The extensive and fertile floodplains of the Indus, in contrast, provided bountiful harvests over the years, although the river was prone to flood excessively and often changed its course without warning. To the north lay the Punjab, watered by other rivers besides the Indus, an area of forests and grassland where cultivation was confined to the relatively restricted strips along the rivers themselves. In the south, Gujurat presented a similar situation. These regions have suffered since Indus times from considerable deforestation and other man-made changes, such as the destruction of much of the indigenous fauna, but studies of the environment and climate based on such evidence as pollen in lake sediments indicate that rainfall, temperature, and other climatic features were basically the same in the Indus Period as they are today.

One very significant change has taken place because of the tectonic instability of the region. Although imperceptible on our own timescale, what was in geological time a dramatic event took place here hundreds of millions of years ago when the Indian peninsula crashed into the Asian plate, causing the land to buckle. The Himalayas were pushed up—an ongoing process that occasionally produces dramatic changes in the pattern of rivers flowing down from their higher slopes. One such transformation that took place in the 2nd millennium B.C. means that part of the Indus region as we know it today is very different from how it was in the time of the Indus people.

For the Indus people did not rely on the Indus and its tributaries alone for sustenance. During the 3rd millennium B.C. (and earlier times) another major perennial river

lay to the south of the Indus, running roughly parallel with it. This river system, often called the Saraswati, was even more productive than that of the Indus itself, to judge by the density of settlement along its course. In the Bahawalpur region, in the central portion of the river, settlement density far exceeds that elsewhere in the civilization.

Several sizeable cities lie within this dense concentration, including the metropolis of Ganweriwala. This intriguing city is one of the five largest in the Indus realms and might well have been as important as Mohenjo Daro, given its central location and fertile, densely populated hinterland—but for some reason it has never been excavated and so we know virtually nothing about it. Indus settlements are also densely concentrated along other parts of the river's course—there are some fifty sites known along the Indus whereas the Saraswati has almost 1,000. This is actually a misleading figure because erosion and alluviation have between them destroyed or deeply buried the greater part of settlements in the Indus Valley itself, but there can be no doubt that the Saraswati system did yield a high proportion of the Indus people's agricultural produce.

This region today is desert. Portions of the river and its tributaries survive as the modern Saraswati—now a small stream: the Chautang, Naiwal, Ghaggar, Sotra, Hakra, and Nara, rivers that flow along parts of its ancient course. But in Indus times, the Saraswati was a mighty river.

Since the 19th century, geologists, geographers, and archaeologists have been attempting to trace the course of the ancient river systems in the Punjab and adjacent regions. Recently they have employed satellite photography but the results of earlier times, obtained by the hard slog of mapping dry watercourses on the ground, are still highly regarded for their accuracy and comprehensiveness. The perennial rivers of this area depend for their water mainly on snow melt-waters and rainfall in the Himalayas, which feed a number of substantial rivers including the Yamuna and Sutlej. Today the Sutlej is a tributary of the Indus, but formerly it flowed into the bed of what is now the Hakra, joining it at a point that moved as time went on. Another major river, known to the Indo-Aryans as the Drishadvati, flowed along what is now the bed of the Chautang, forming a major tributary of the ancient Saraswati. Later its waters were captured by the Yamuna, which in Indus times was a very minor east-ward-flowing river. The combined waters of the Sutlej, Saraswati, and Drishadvati created a vast river system giving life to a huge alluvial plain.

The full course of the Saraswati has still not been confidently established. Recent work has uncovered evidence of a possible inland delta around Fort Derawar, and it has been suggested that the Saraswati ended here. For a stretch of around 150 miles no ancient channels of the river can be traced, but what may well be its further continuation reappears as two rivers flowing through the Thar desert, the Raini Nullah and the Wahinda. These probably joined the Eastern Nara, to debouch into the Ranns of Kutch. Certainly the eastern Nara flowed through this southern region—but the question is whether it was fed by the Indus or the Saraswati. Ancient river courses can often be traced but dating them is a nightmare, and often relies on external clues, such as the date of settlements along them. Establishing the course of the rivers of the region during the 4th to 2nd millennia B.C. is clearly of great interest—but it is extremely complicated and it is likely to be a long time before final agreement is reached. Within this 2,000-year period there were probably many changes, some only of local relevance but some of national importance to the Indus people [*see* Map 11 on page 184].

PASTORALISTS

A study of the distribution of Indus settlements shows significant clusters of towns and villages in some regions, particularly on the Saraswati River, separated by large tracts in which few or no settlements have been located, despite intensive fieldwork. Pastoralists, and perhaps also hunter-gatherers, moved within these tracts, grazing their cattle, sheep, and goats and providing the vital links that held together the civilization. A few settlements have been found that can be linked to these people, although they are hard to find given their ephemeral nature. One such settlement was found at Nesadi (Valabhi) in Gujarat. Here pastoralists dwelt in circular huts with rammed-earth floors, occupying the settlement during the winter months, as their successors do today. At this time of year there was abundant lush grazing in the region, which not only provided fodder

for the domestic cattle of the inhabitants but also attracted wild game such as deer. In the summer, this campsite and probably many others in the region were under seasonal (monsoon) floods and the pastoralists had moved away to higher ground.

A symbiotic relationship existed between the pastoralists and the settled farmers in the regions that they visited, each providing the other with their produce. The farmers supplied grain, vegetables, and fruits, as well as stubble grazing when the fields had been harvested, while the pastoralists provided meat, leather, wool, and goat hair, as well as dung to fertilize the fields and perhaps milk products like ghee, cheese, and yogurt. The farmers also probably kept small numbers of domestic animals, dogs, water buffaloes for milk, chickens (domesticated from the Indian jungle fowl) for meat and eggs, possibly rabbits for

meat, and bullocks for drawing plows and carts [Figure 13]. Transport over short distances relied on these bullock carts, enabling farmers to bring their offerings to their nearest town [*see* Color Plate 5]. Pastoralists provided longer distance connections, as did boats on the rivers.

FARMERS, THE BACKBONE OF INDUS SOCIETY

"Land, everything you have will increase." Thus ordained the Sumerian god Enki when he spoke of Meluhha (the Indus Civilization) in the Mesopotamian poem describing the Creation.

Figure 13.

DOG FIGURINE, HARAPPA

In contrast to the finely and elaborately carved stone sculptures, most representations of animals were made of clay modeled and pinched, often roughly, into simple shapes. This little dog figurine is wearing a collar. The collar is yet more evidence that the people of the Indus Civilization kept domesticated animals.

Indus farmers raised wheat and barley, pulses, fruits, and vegetables, as well as cotton for cloth, as their ancestors had done for thousands of years. Farming was undoubtedly the main occupation of the majority of the Indus population and the foundation upon which the civilization was based, even though so few farming settlements have actually been excavated. One of these few was the 6 ha (hectare) village at Kanewal in Gujurat, a settlement surrounded by fine arable black cotton soil. The village contained circular huts with rammed-earth floors, built of wooden posts, wattle, and daub. The people of Kanewal had fine pottery and copper ornaments as well as the more everyday objects like beads, figurines, and cooking pots.

Extensive surveys have mapped the distribution of surface traces of Indus settlement, such as broken pieces of Indus pottery. From this we are beginning to piece together a picture of the layout of the Indus Civilization. Settlement was concentrated along the banks of major rivers and their tributaries, taking advantage of the strip of land that was flooded annually in August-September and which was therefore free of trees. As the flood waters receded, they deposited fertile silt in which crops could be sown—in some areas, such as on the "self-plowing" black cotton soils of Gujurat, the seed was simply broadcast, whereas in others the ground was first prepared by plowing. A model plow made of terracotta was found at Banawali and at Kalibangan a plowed field was uncovered [Figure 11]. This belonged to the Early Indus Period and at present is the earliest

plowed field known in the world. It was plowed in two directions, a practice still in use in the region today. In modern times, narrow strips are first plowed in one direction and these are sown with horsegram (a type of pulse). More widely spaced strips plowed at right angles to the first furrows are sown with mustard seed. Although we do not know what crops were grown in the Kalibangan field, they are likely to have been something similar.

The floods filled numerous small seasonal watercourses that for some months acted as a reservoir from which to draw water to irrigate the crops. These were supplemented by artificial channels that served also to drain water from the fields after the floods. The Indus people probably used shadufs to raise water from the streams and channels—one piece of Indus pottery bears a scratched picture of a shaduf. A simple T-shaped device consisting of an upright and a horizontal pole with a bucket on one side and a counterweight on the other, the shaduf is known to have been used in Mesopotamia around the time of the Indus Civilization and was later introduced to Egypt.

A certain amount of rain also fell during winter storms, watering the mountains and foothills of the Indo-Iranian borderlands and Punjab and increasing the water carried by the perennial rivers during January and February. Wells could also be used to provide water for the growing crops, although this required a considerable input of labor. Almost all the crops grown by the Indus people were sown in the autumn and harvested in the spring—wheat and barley were the main staples, along with a variety of pulses such as lentils and chickpeas, and probably vegetables and fruits like the jujube.

SPREADING THE RISK

Although in good years the summer floods and winter rains allowed the Indus and Saraswati plain to produce abundant crops, the risks of failure were high. Excessive monsoon storms and floods could wreak terrible damage; inadequate or late monsoon or winter rainfall could cause the crops to fail for lack of moisture; and the rivers and streams frequently changed their course, leaving fields dry. The unreliability of the agricultural water supply was a powerful encouragement to the development of alternative strategies. Such strategies probably included the maintenance of kinship ties over long distances, so that if your crops failed you could call on your cousins elsewhere in the greater Indus region to bail you out. Producing a surplus of grain in good years and storing it against bad years was another way of coping, and it is probable that this was organized by the authorities in each community. Indeed, the need to organize the storage and redistribution of the agricultural surplus may be one of the fundamental reasons for the development of the civilization, as it was in a number of early civilizations such as Mesopotamia.

Economic diversification was another mechanism that helped deal with the unreliability of the agricultural yield. One way of doing this was by storage on the hoof. In good years when crop yields were high, grazing would also be good. The number of animals that were kept could be increased, using surplus agricultural produce as fodder if the grazing ran out. In lean years, when grazing was limited, the additional animals could either be killed for food or used to obtain other foodstuffs, for example, by trading with pastoralists, by sending the animals as gifts to distant kin in expectation of useful return gifts, or by paying them in to the central authorities in exchange for grain.

Wild creatures were another useful source of supplementary food supplies. The scrub and jungle away from the cultivated area were home to a host of wild animals, many of which made good eating, and some species were bold enough to raid the farmers' fields. In some modern Indian communities, hunter-gatherers are employed to guard crops and deal with marauding wild animals, a role they could have had in the Indus realms as well. The bones discarded in farming settlements like Kanewal in Gujurat show that the farmers were eating a wide range of the game locally available, including wild pigs, various kinds of deer and antelope, and even lizards. They probably hunted many of these themselves but could also have obtained them from hunter-gatherers. When farmers first moved into the Indus-Saraswati plains in the 4th millennium B.C., all the indigenous groups that they encountered still lived by hunting, fishing, and gathering wild resources. Although the farmers must have absorbed or displaced the hunter-gatherers who lived in the regions that they began to cultivate, particularly along the courses of rivers, hunter-gatherer groups remained in possession of many other areas. For example, the Indus people never colonized the north Gujurat plain, because, it is thought, of its well-established hunter-gatherer population; and the Indus people traded with hunter-gatherer communities such as those in Gujurat and fishing groups in the Aravalli Hills such as the inhabitants of Jodpura.

FISHERS

Fish were also a ready source of food for the Indus people. In coastal areas, sea fish were caught, probably by professional fishermen. Many fish bones were found at the coastal settlement of Balakot, where there was also a major industry processing shellfish to make shell bangles and other objects. Freshwater fish such as carp and catfish were caught particularly during the winter and spring in the backwaters and smaller channels where water flow was slow. Nets were used here, as is vividly depicted on one sherd of pottery from Harappa. The bottoms of the nets were weighted down with net-sinkers—these have been found in many Indus settlements, from the mighty city of Harappa to the small village of Kanewal. During the period immediately after the monsoon floods when the rivers were still high and turbulent, fish could also be caught in the shallower areas along the riverbanks, using hook and line. Many copper fishhooks have been found in Indus houses, showing that fishing was a common activity. Fresh fish would have been a welcome addition to the diet, but fish were also dried

so they could be eaten at a later date. Many bones of marine fish at Harappa show that dried fish from the coast was transported even this far inland, in considerable quantities—this reinforces the very strong picture we have of the Indus Civilization as an organized and integrated society.

NEW CROPS

One last means the Indus farmers had of spreading the risk inherent in their productive but unreliable environment was to cultivate more than one crop a year. Throughout the Indus Period, the main crops cultivated in the Indus and Saraswati plains were sown in the winter and harvested in the spring—a system known in India today as "rabi" cultivation. Rabi cultivation characterized the agriculture of the whole Western Asiatic-European domain, of which the Indus region was the easternmost end. A few Indus crops would not have prospered in the rabi regime, as they can be damaged by frost—these included both cotton and the important oilseed sesame. They belong to a complex of crops, which also includes rice and various millets, that are sown today in the spring or summer and harvested in the summer or autumn—these are known as "kharif" crops. However, the monsoon period sees widespread flooding of fields. Although this may suit rice it is not suitable for other kharif crops. Cotton was probably grown on the well-drained fringes of the Indus plain.

Rice and millets, however, were not grown in the Indus-Saraswati plains during the Indus Period. But by the end of the 3rd millennium B.C. and probably earlier, they were being grown in the east and west extremes of the civilization, in Gujurat and the Indo-Gangetic divide. Rice is native to the subcontinent, growing wild in the central and lower reaches of the Ganges Valley and along part of the east coast. It may also have occurred as a wild plant in Gujurat though the evidence is uncertain. Villagers in the lower Ganges region and eastern India were cultivating rice by 2000 B.C. or perhaps earlier. Rice cultivation also began in the northeast around the same time, in the Swat region and in the eastern part of the Indus realms. It is not clear yet how rice was introduced into these regions and what prompted the eastern Indus people to begin the cultivation of what was to prove a revolutionary crop, but it was not long before it was being grown on the southwest margin, in Gujurat, as well.

Several genera of what are confusingly all called "millet" in English were introduced to the Indus realms around the same time—sorghum *(Sorghum bicolor)*, locally known as jowar; finger millet *(Eleusine coracana)*, known as ragi; and bulrush millet *(Pennisetum typhoideum)*, known as bajra. Ultimately these are supposed to have come from Africa but were under cultivation in Arabia during the 4th millennium B.C., and recently it has been suggested that they may also have been part of the original flora of the Yemen and taken into cultivation there. The Indus people acquired these new crops through trade with the Oman peninsula. Other millets may have

had a local origin—these include common millet *(Panicum miliaceum)*, which may have been cultivated in the lower Ganges region by this time; Job's tears *(Pennisetum lacrimae jobi);* and foxtail millet *(Setaria italica).*

Millets can be sown immediately after the summer floods on the margins of the Indus plains, in areas like the Kachi Plain, but are generally grown without irrigation in regions where rainfall is adequate, conditions that pertained in Gujurat and the Indo-Gangetic divide on the eastern margin, and rice can also be raised in these conditions though it can also be grown on land too wet for other cereals. In many areas, such as the Kachi Plain, rice growing requires irrigation. It is not surprising that, when the opportunity arose, rice and millets were taken into cultivation in appropriate parts of the Indus realms. These crops are the staples of most of the subcontinent today, and the beginning of their cultivation had a revolutionary effect that ultimately transformed both the Indus Civilization and the course of Indian prehistory.

The Indus Civilization was undoubtedly founded on the rich agricultural and pastoral productivity offered by its region—without this basis, civilization could not have emerged here when it did. But this alone does not explain the dramatic coalescing of the region into a unified state. It is now necessary to examine in turn the other factors that may have played a part, such as craft specialization, religion, population, social evolution, and trade.

CHAPTER FOUR

CRAFTS OF THE INDUS

THE FIRST SPECIALISTS

In small-scale societies of hunter-gatherers or subsistence farmers, men and women may make different contributions to the daily activities of obtaining and preparing food and making the necessities of life such as shelters and clothing. The old and young may also have their own specified tasks. Apart from these gender and age differences, however, there are generally no divisions of labor—everyone is involved in the range of basic activities. As societies become more complex and more organized, however, some activities become the special concern of certain individuals, who in return are exempted from the everyday tasks of food production. Looking at the development of ancient societies we see that often the first such specialist to be supported by the community is the person responsible for their supernatural well-being—their priest, shaman, wise-woman, or medicine-man. In other societies, a secular leader may have emerged at a similar time—an individual capable of organizing activities of benefit to the community, such as trade, defense or aggression, land improvements, or the construction of monuments.

Although those with certain skills may at times have been called upon to practice these for the benefit of the community, it is not until the emergence of civilizations that we see the development of other full-time specialists, such as craftsmen and women, entirely supported by the agricultural produce of the rest of society.

How does the Indus Civilization fit into this picture? In the previous chapter, I discussed the agricultural basis of the Indus Civilization. There is evidence that there were full-time pastoralists, fishers, and hunter-gatherers among the Indus people as well as farmers who also hunted and fished a bit and kept some domestic animals. But in a civilization, we would expect to find a far greater range of specialists. So what does the Indus have to show?

In pre-Indus times, craft objects were locally made and varied both in style and in quality. In contrast, craft specialists produced most of the everyday objects used by the Indus people,

Figure 14.

FEMALE FIGURINE, HARAPPA

This early Indus figurine of a woman in a long skirt was found at Harappa. The design on her skirt may represent the pattern in which it was woven or dyed. Around her neck, a necklace has been painted with strands of beads hanging from it.

Figure 15.

MODERN POTTERS
AT HARAPPA

As part of the current investigations at Harappa, the expertise of modern potters has been enlisted to study and reproduce (center and right) some of the handmade pottery of the earliest settlers here, such as the bowl-on-stand held by the potter on the left.

and these objects were both standardized and of high quality. The degree of standardization depended on the nature of the products and the complexity of the technology involved in their production: those that were made of local materials using simple technology were least standardized, while those that required nonlocal materials and complex technology meant greater skills were employed and therefore greater standardization was achieved.

Some objects were still produced within each home—textiles for everyday use, for instance. Others were made by specialist craftsmen, residing generally in the towns and cities but sometimes in specialist villages, and these were supplied not only to the townsfolk but also to the rest of the inhabitants of the surrounding region—pottery for normal domestic use fell into this category, as did a

variety of personal ornaments. Some objects, however, were made only in a few of the cities and were produced by highly skilled individuals who specialized in producing particularly complex and unusual artifacts, whose distribution was restricted—stoneware bangles, for example.

POTTERS

Since its invention more than 12,000 years ago, pottery has been used by most sedentary societies for many domestic purposes, particularly cooking, eating, and storage [Figure 15]. Many goods were also transported in pots, such as oil and wine. Fine pottery was often a highly valued and prestigious luxury. Fired clay was also used to make other objects, from fine figurines to building materials like bricks and tiles. The Indus range of ceramic objects included a number whose use is entirely unknown, such as terracotta cakes and cones [Color Plate 18]. Pottery was made in the Indo-Iranian borderlands from about 5000 B.C. and ranged from plain everyday wares to fine painted vessels decorated with a range of distinctive geometric, animal, and plant designs.

Pottery for everyday use was probably manufactured in every Indus settlement and certainly in all the towns and cities. Clay was readily available locally in most areas and was used to make plain reddish orange wares. The range of these locally made pots included round-base cooking pots with a substantial turned-over rim to made them easy to lift when hot, storage vessels, plates, bowls, and cups. Some pots were modeled by hand but the majority were made on a wheel.

The wheel consisted of a turntable on which the clay was thrown, attached by an axle to a lower flywheel that was set in a pit and turned with the foot. After drying, the pots were probably fired in a simple bonfire kiln—these are still in use in the subcontinent and had been for millennia by the time of the Indus people. Fuel is spread over a level open piece of ground and the pots are stacked above it. Particularly fragile pieces were protected by being placed inside a pottery firing-box of heavy clay. The pottery stack is covered with more fuel, with a central smoke hole and other holes at ground level to allow the fuel to be ignited. After lighting the bonfire kiln is left for about ten days—about three days for the firing and another week or so to allow the pots to cool. We have excellent evidence of this process because one bonfire firing of pottery at Mehrgarh, a few hundred years before the Indus Period, went disastrously wrong, destroying all the pottery within it. The kiln site was abandoned—no attempt was made to clear up the mess—and so it was preserved until discovered by archaeologists in the 1970s.

The highly organized nature of the Indus Civilization is clear from the fact that even these simple straightforward wares were manufactured in pottery workshops by specialized potters, rather than being made in the home by every family. One such workshop has been found in the town of Nausharo. It consists of a small structure with several rooms, with a pillared verandah on one side open on to a lane. The pots were made in the

Figure 16.

Dish-on-stand, Harappa

This vessel from the late period (after 1900 B.C.) Cemetery H at Harappa is one version of the uncommon but characteristic pedestaled vessels found in Indus sites from the period of first settlement in the Indus region.

Figure 17.

TERRACOTTA
BANGLES,
MOHENJO DARO

*Terracotta was used
as an everyday
material for making
bangles, the item
of jewelry most
commonly worn by
Indus women. Many
discarded broken
terracotta bangles
have been found
as well as intact
examples like these.*

center of the workshop, where flint blades used for turning and scraping the vessels had been left when the workshop was, for some reason, abandoned. The potters had also left shelves of finished pots—once dry these would have been decorated and then fired in the adjoining yard.

Although there were many features shared by the pottery throughout Indus Civilization, these local wares were more variable and show regional or local styles. In contrast, special wares made in the major centers were extremely uniform—these included black-slipped storage vessels that were made at Harappa (and possibly only there) and that were also used in trade with Magan (Oman).

These more specialized wares were manufactured only in the towns and cities, and often individual workshops specialized in particular types such as pointed goblets in several of the Mohenjo Daro workshops. These pots included more complex shapes that required a high level of skill to produce. For example, the large storage jars began by having their lower portion thrown on the wheel. The upper portion was then built up using slabs. After forming, these vessels often had cords wrapped around them to ensure that they kept their shape while drying.

Other specialist wares included a range of less common shapes, such as the dish- or bowl-on-stand, fine pedestaled vessels that

may have been used for making offerings or some other special purpose [Figure 16]. The finer vessels were often coated in a red slip and many were painted with animal motifs or geometric designs, such as a distinctive fish-scale pattern [Color Plates 21 and 23]. The complete symmetry of the geometric designs shows that those who decorated them had used compasses and other instruments to mark out the designs before painting them. These finer wares were fired in kilns built of clay, sometimes used and renewed over centuries. The majority of these kilns were of the updraft type, in which the fuel chamber was at the bottom and the pots were stacked on a perforated platform supported above it on a pillar of bricks. A temporary domed roof would be constructed over this for each firing and removed afterward. Some kilns, however, were probably of the horizontal type, in which the fuel chamber and firing chamber lay side by side. Several specialized kilns at Mohenjo Daro and Harappa were used to produce the fine stoneware bangles. These were one of the most elaborate products of the Indus Civilization. Within these kilns the bangles were encased in a series of containers, the ensemble being supported on piles of terracotta bangles [Figure 17].

Terracotta figurines were another widely made pottery product. Many are in the form of animals, particularly bulls but covering a great range of other creatures such as rabbits, birds [Figure 18], elephants, and dogs [Figure 19]. Some are jointed, with a movable head, and are likely to have been toys. Numerous figurines depict people, especially women [Figure 14]. Those at Harappa have recently

been studied in detail and have revealed some surprising features. One is that many of them were made in two pieces—left side and right side—and then joined together. Usually the joint is invisible but sometimes it can be made out. Others were made as a basic torso and bits were added on later, perhaps customized for individual customers—not just such things as clothing and jewelry but also arms and thicker shoulders. If these figurines represent mother goddesses, it may be that the additions represented particular attributes of the deity that an individual might wish to emphasize or select.

Figure 18.

BIRD FIGURINE, HARAPPA

Terracotta figurines such as this delightful little bird were likely to have been toys. Although this bird's wings have been broken off, we can imagine they were outstretched to represent a bird in flight.

FLINT KNAPPERS

Flint blades were among the tools used by potters in shaping their vessels and in fact the majority of tools used by the Indus people were of stone. Almost all the workshops at Mohenjo Daro had a selection of flint tools for working with. Many of these tools were of types that had been in use for several thousand years. Although copper and bronze objects had been manufactured in this region for about a thousand years, here as in many parts of the world, stone continued to be used for tools. Stone was generally more readily available than metal ores, particularly tin, and also, a freshly knapped flint edge was sharper than a metal edge, although it would blunt more quickly. Only with the beginning of iron metallurgy (which was unknown worldwide until the 2nd millennium B.C. and which did not become widespread until the 1st millennium B.C.) did metal tools largely supplant those of stone.

The earlier stone tools in the Indo-Iranian borderlands and Indus-Saraswati plains were generally made of local flint in each region. Those of the Indus people, however, were made almost exclusively from the very high quality brownish gray flint that was available in the Rohri Hills on the middle Indus. This substantial outcrop of fine quality flint had been quarried since Paleolithic times. The Indus stoneworkers swept the debris of earlier flint knappers aside to make cleared areas where they sat cross-legged to work the flint cores into tool blanks. Debris from their activities—waste flint, discarded cores and blades—still lies there, defining their working areas. The initial working of the flint took place here. First a suitable core was prepared by flaking off the outer cortex (a "rind" of weathered stone on the nodule) and roughly shaping it, using a hammerstone. The core was then worked into a shape suitable for striking blades, using a copper-tipped punch to remove flakes from its sides. (The use of such a tool can be deduced from the nature of the impact marks on the butt of these flakes.) At this stage, some cores were taken to Indus settlements where blades could be struck from them. In other cases the blades were manufactured in the Rohri Hills factory site itself. The majority of Indus tools were made on long regular blades that were struck using a tool with a copper point that was pressed against the top of the core using the weight of the body. Alternatively, inverse indirect percussion may have been used, a technique that is peculiar to South Asia. The flint core was held against a stake tipped with copper or antler and was struck with a soft hammer made of wood, antler or horn, detaching a long blade.

These blades could function as cutting tools as they were or they could be used as blanks on which to make other types of tools. Some were worked into drills for boring beads, scrapers for turning pottery, and saws for incising shell. Other blades were snapped into small segments and set into wooden handles or shafts to make sickles and arrows. Leaf-shaped arrowheads were also made by retouching blade segments (shaping them by removing small flakes of stone). Cores were also shaped into cubical weights and into stone celts that were probably ploughshares [Color Plate 19].

Although the vast majority of Indus stone tools were made with Rohri Hills flint, there were some exceptions. In particular, an extremely hard stone called Ernestite was used to make drill bits for perforating small beads. This was not a naturally occurring stone but one that the Indus people produced artificially by heating a rare type of fine-grained metamorphic rock until a change in its crystalline structure occurred, giving it exceptional hardness.

METALWORKERS

Flint tools were suitable for many purposes but not all. They were used for engraving shell, for instance, but not for cutting it—this was done with metal saws. The copper saws used by the Indus shell workers were apparently as efficient as the steel saws in use today for cutting shells and presumably for other tasks such as working wood. Although some saws had a straight row of teeth, others were of the more effective variety used today, with the teeth bent alternately left and right.

Copper was used for many small everyday objects such as knives, arrowheads, and fishhooks, more prestigious versions of the tools that were generally made in stone. Most of these were of a very simple form that could be cast in a one- or two-piece mold or created by hammering and chiseling.

Many people have commented unfavorably on this technological simplicity in Indus metal tools, pointing out, for example, that the Indus metalworkers were still making simple flat axes even though they were aware of the technically more advanced shafthole variety of axe made by some of their contemporaries. However, a close look at Indus metallurgy makes it clear that the production of such simple artifacts was not the consequence of lack of technical knowledge and expertise. In addition to these simple forms, the Indus metalworkers produced a range of sophisticated and complex products. Like the fine pottery, these were made in specialist workshops in the big cities while the production of everyday objects was more widespread.

A few metal figurines, including a girl clad in bangles and holding out a bowl, found at Mohenjo Daro, and a variety of animals, show that the Indus people were masters of complex casting using the *cire perdue* (lost wax) technique [Color Plate 1]. They also created fine copper or bronze bowls by beating a piece of metal over a bronze anvil like the one identified recently at Chanhu Daro. This was found in metalworking workshop along with several of the bowls that would have been raised on it and a number of other metal objects. In addition there was a set of scale pans for weighing the metal. Collections of metalwork like this were the stock-in-trade of metalworkers—a mixture of tools for working metal, finished and unfinished objects, and old and broken objects for recycling.

The Indus metalworkers also made various alloys of copper and other metals, carefully matching these to the purpose of each artifact. Unalloyed copper was used to make objects that did not have to stand up to hard use, but those, like knives, axes, and chisels, that were intended to work against hard surfaces were made from an alloy of copper and up to 13 percent tin—conventional bronze. Other alloys were also made for particular purposes, using arsenic, lead, or much higher levels of tin, to improve the ease of casting complex shapes, to make surfaces that would take a high polish for mirrors or beautiful vessels, and to produce an attractive color resembling gold.

Gold itself was also worked, particularly to make jewelry such as pendants and spacer beads (beads with a number of perfo-rations that kept several strings of beads together but apart) [Color Plate 25]. Silver, on the other hand, was used mainly for vessels such as elegant jars. The two metals were also combined as electrum, although this may have occurred naturally. Gold from Karnataka in South India has a natural admixture of silver, so electrum objects may indicate that gold from this region was being imported and worked by the Indus people—this is a much debated and intriguing possibility.

The metals used by the Indus craftsmen were almost certainly all smelted at source rather than imported as ore. Copper was made into bun-shaped ingots and probably came from a number of sources. Of these sources, the most important was probably the Aravalli Hills—spectrographic analysis has shown that many Indus artifacts were made of Aravalli copper. Magan (Oman) was also likely to have been important, and there were a number of different sources in the mountains to the north and west, including the Chagai Hills from which lapis was also available; the Kandahar region, source also of tin, lead, and silver; and the upper reaches of the Jhelum River, where gold was also to be found. The copperworking furnaces so far found at Mohenjo Daro and Harappa were used for melting the metal for casting rather than for smelting although silver and lead may possibly have been smelted in the cities. On the other hand, one would expect such heavy and polluting industrial activity as smelting to have taken place on the outskirts of the city or beyond, so they may still lie there undiscovered.

BRICKMAKERS

Other industrial activities must also have been located outside the city, for example, brickmaking. This would have been a major activity in Indus times, given the volume of fired bricks used in building the cities. It used to be suggested that the climate and environment of the Indus Valley 5,000 years ago must have been different from today, with more rainfall supporting dense riverine forests whose timbers were needed to fire the great quantity of bricks used by the Indus people—but more recently it has been shown that this need not be the case. The scrubby natural vegetation that still grows in the region would have provided perfectly adequate fuel, in both quality and quantity.

Modern brickmaking takes place well away from towns and cities, but within a reasonable distance for transport. Although no evidence of brickmaking areas has been uncovered in the Indus cities, the techniques used are unlikely to be very different from those of today. Bricks would have been made in molds, probably of wood. Houses used cuboid bricks of 7 × 14 × 28 cm—these might either be sundried or fired—whereas baked bricks were used in building the walls surrounding the towns and cities. Wedge-shaped bricks were also made in molds for building the numerous wells. After the bricks had set, the molds would be removed and the bricks left to dry. Mudbricks were now ready for use, but for a more durable product, many were stacked, covered with fuel, and fired. The stack would burn for days, sending off foul fumes.

SHELLWORKERS

A foul stench also greeted the visitor to another industrial area set apart from the main city—the place where chank shells were cleaned. Although the main body of the shellfish was removed and probably eaten by the fishermen who gathered them, the soft parts in the inaccessible apex of the shell were left to rot. Later the apex was chipped away and the foul-smelling black putrefied mess removed. Segregated areas for this unpleasant task have been uncovered not only in the specialist shellworking settlement of Nageshwar in Gujurat but also in an isolated quarter in the northeast part of Mohenjo Daro itself.

Nageshwar is situated on a freshwater lake with easy access to extensive shallow bays in the sheltered waters of the Gulf of Kutch from which abundant supplies of *Turbinella pyrum* (chank) and *Chicoreus ramosus* (spiny murex) shells could be obtained. Although these could be gathered in the shallow coastal waters, the fishermen of Nageshwar seem generally to have gone into deeper water on rafts or small boats to obtain shells that were free from the boring activities of Cliona sponges and other marine organisms to which those near the shore were prey. Farther north, the shellfish collectors of Balakot and other settlements on the coast of Sindh and the Makran had to brave the open sea, where they might encounter hazards such as moray eels, Portuguese man-of-wars and other jellyfish, and poisonous sea snakes and fishes. In addition to chank and spiny murex, these regions yielded *Lambis truncata sebae* (spider conch) and *Fasciolaria trapezium* (tulip conch) shells,

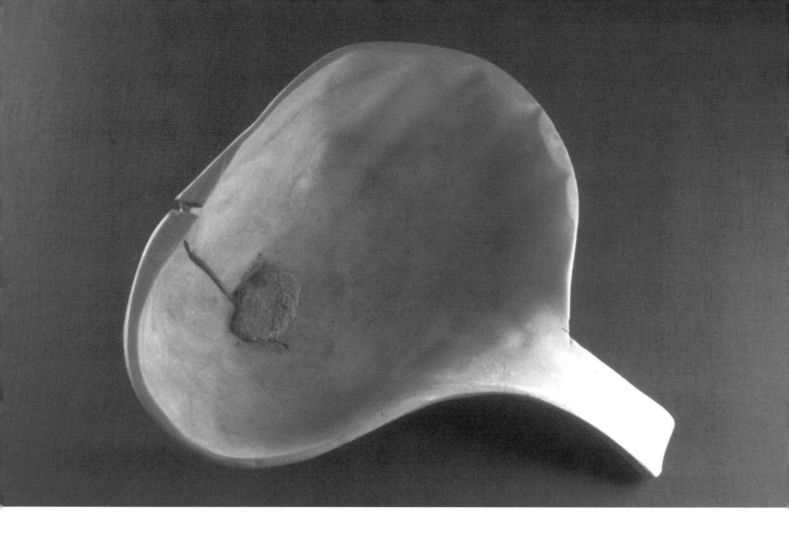

Figure 20.

SHELL LADLE, HARAPPA

This ladle fabricated from a spiny murex shell was found in a disturbed burial at Harappa—it probably served a ritual purpose for pouring libations. A hole, probably produced by the boring of a marine creature, has been stopped up with lead to make the ladle watertight.

all used for making objects found throughout the Indus realms, as well as various species whose circulation was more restricted. Clam shells *(Tivela damaoides)* were worked at Balakot to make shell bangles similar to those made from chank shells, using simpler technology, and these were worn by people in the local area and at other sites along the Makran coast but not further afield.

The making of clam shell bangles was laborious but required only stone tools. The shell was chipped with a hammerstone, ground using wet sand as an abrasive and filed with a stone rasp until the central portion of the shell was worn away and the edges were smoothed to produce an almost circular bangle.

Each shell produced only one such bangle. A number of rather more symmetrical bangles could be made from a single chank shell, but this required bronze tools and a higher level of skill. The shellworkers would chip off the apex of the shell with a stone or bronze hammer and remove the columella using a metal punch. They would then saw the shell into rings using a bronze saw and finish them by grinding them on an abrasive surface. The debris in workshops at Mohenjo Daro and Nageshwar shows that each stage in the process might be undertaken by different workers working in separate locations.

The various shells available to the Indus people each had their own particular use.

The spiny murex was occasionally made into bangles but its main use was as the only type of shell used for making ladles, objects that seem likely to have been employed in a ritual context, probably for pouring libations [Figure 20]. The spines were sawn off and the shell sawn vertically to make two ladles, one smaller than the other. These were then trimmed and ground. The spiny murex is particularly susceptible to marine boring organisms and so frequently these ladles had holes in them that their makers must have stopped up. One ladle found at Harappa had a mend made out of lead. Chank shells were sometimes, with great difficulty, hollowed out and made into a vessel for pouring libations [Color Plate 20]. Similar vessels are still used for this purpose in India and were also used in the ancient Near East although they were made there from a different kind of shell.

Spider and tulip conch shells were cut up into pieces that were probably used as inlays to decorate wooden furniture. They often bore incised designs, and sometimes traces remain of red and black pigment along their edges or within the incised lines. Small objects like lids, gaming pieces, and figurines were also made from these shells and from material, such as the chank columellas, left from the manufacture of bangles and other shell objects. Nothing was wasted—small pieces of shell were made into beads and debris was burnt to make lime-gypsum plaster.

LAPIDARIES

Indus men and women wore a considerable amount of jewelry, which probably gave

MAKING FAIENCE

Indus faience was made by a technique different from that used in contemporary Mesopotamia and Egypt, giving a stronger material. The Indus people manufactured their faience in two stages. First they ground rock crystal to a powder and mixed it with a flux and with the appropriate color, of which they employed a considerable range, producing not only blue but also red, buff and brown faience. They melted the mixture at a temperature over 1,000°C, producing a glassy material that they again ground to a powder. They combined this fine powder with a flux and some water to form a paste that they could shape by hand or put into a mold to make not only beads but also other pieces of jewelry such as ear studs and bangles, and charming little figurines that included monkeys and squirrels. Tiny faience pots were made by molding the paste around the outside of a small bag filled with sand. Once the pot was formed, the sand was poured out and the bag removed. The faience objects were fired a second time at a high temperature, to produce the finished glazed objects.

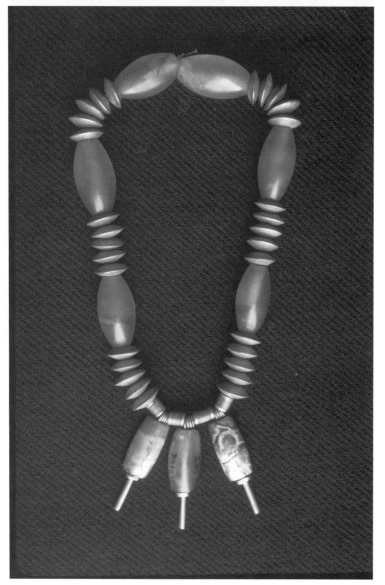

steatite. They rarely used lapis lazuli or turquoise, beautiful blue stones that had been valued in the region and traded in from early times. Instead they preferred stones like agate, chalcedony, jasper, and carnelian that were harder to work but that retained a high polish, unlike the softer lapis and turquoise, which soon became dull. But they also made beads of faience that they colored to resemble lapis lazuli or turquoise.

Some of the hard stones used for bead-making were obtained from the upland regions to the northwest but their main source was in the region lying south and east of the Indus settlements in Gujurat. The mines at Rajpipla were a particularly important and valued source of carnelian. Many of the Indus settlements in Gujurat and Sindh operated substantial beadmaking industries to process this raw material. Beads were also manufactured in the workshops of cities like Mohenjo Daro, using stone imported in the raw state. Often beadmaking took place alongside other craft activities, in small individual workshops. Larger complexes also operated, such as the beadmaking factory at Lothal, where a courtyard was the scene of the main manufacturing activities while accommodation and storage were provided by eleven small rooms that opened from it.

Various types of beads were made, using a variety of techniques related to the different materials and end products. Banded agate was particularly prized and was worked so as to expose symmetrical patterns of bands around the body of the bead or longitudinally, making eye patterns that may have had some significance in popular superstition, such as

information about their social standing from the quantity, the materials used, and the quality of the workmanship. Shell, terracotta, and metal bangles were commonly worn, but even more ubiquitous were beads, made into necklaces, belts, headdresses and other ornaments [Figure 21]. Indus beads were also much prized by other societies and were among the exotic materials found in Mesopotamian graves.

The Indus people were particularly fine lapidaries, making beads from a wide variety of semiprecious stones as well as from gold, silver, copper, shell, ivory, terracotta, and

SECRETS OF INDUS BEAD TECHNOLOGY

The Indus beadmakers produced beautiful white microbeads of talcose steatite (soapstone) only a millimeter across and 1 to 3 mm long. How were they made? This question has baffled archaeologists for decades. Some clues enabled three investigators, Hegde, Karanth, and Sychanthavong, to reconstruct a possible method. They concluded that the raw material, which is quite soft, was ground into a fine powder and mixed with water to make a paste. This was then extruded and cut into lengths. They suggest a possible device for doing this, consisting of a perforated copper disk with a fine copper wire soldered to pass centrally through each hole. A bag fastened to the upper surface of the disk would be filled with the paste and squeezed out. A very fine cutting device, such as a horsehair, would be passed across under the disk to cut the extruded tubes into short lengths. A tray of ash underneath would catch the beads as they were cut off and prevent them sticking to each other or getting damaged. Then the beads were then fired at a high temperature, around 900° C, converting them from the soft steatite paste to the extremely hard white material of the beads as we know them [*see* Figure 42].

for warding off the Evil Eye. The first action of the lapidary on starting work on a bead would be to remove a few flakes from the raw nodule to assess the quality and condition of the stone underneath. From this he could determine how best to work it so as to achieve the most pleasing design of bead. Once this was decided the lapidary sawed or chipped the stone into a rough cube or cuboid shape. Often pieces were rejected at this stage as being, after all, unsatisfactory, but if the block seemed promising, it was then ground down into a bead shape by rubbing it against the abrasive surface of a sandstone or quartzite block. Next, a central perforation was made in short beads by chipping from both ends, giving an hourglass shaped hole. Longer beads, however, were perforated using a micro-drill whose head was made of hardened copper or of phtanite, a type of chert containing iron oxide. Often there was a tiny depression in the tip of the drill to take a fine abrasive used with water to improve the drill's performance. The drill bit was mounted on a wooden rod that was rotated using a bow. A disk of stone or shell on the top of the wooden shaft acted as a cap, allowing the beadmaker to exert pressure on the drill to keep it seated in the bead without injuring himself. After drilling, more grinding put the finishing touches to the bead, before it was polished, probably by being tumbled in a bag with other beads and some fine abrasive.

Red stone, like chalcedony and carnelian, was often heated before work started on roughing out the bead, because this intensified the red color. It also made the stone easier to work, and so other stones like agate were also often heat-treated. Carnelian beads were frequently decorated with designs in white or sometimes black. The designs often imitated the banded agate stripes and eyes but also included trefoils like those on the "priest king's" garment as well as other geometric patterns [*see* Figure 31]. Although these are frequently referred to as "etched" carnelian beads, they were not in fact decorated by etching a design with acid, as this would imply. The designs were painted on with a solution of calcium carbonate. Then the beads were heated, bleaching the surface where the paint had been applied. Over the millennia since the beads were made, the bleached area, which is weaker than the rest of the bead, has often eroded away, giving the impression of etching. Sometimes the whole bead was whitened in this way and designs were then painted on in black, possibly using a solution of copper nitrate or metallic oxide.

Indus beads ranged from microscopic disk beads only a millimeter wide to elegant biconical specimens as long as 13 centimeters [*see* Figure 42]. The microbeads were worn in long strings that each contained several hundred beads. A cache of them found in the late Indus settlement of Zekda in Gujarat numbered around 34,000 beads, stored in two small pots. The sophisticated techniques involved in producing Indus beads have been worked out by experiment and by observing modern beadmakers. These studies have revealed the amazing lengths of time and effort as well as the skill that were involved. The exceptionally long, slender biconical beads were a staggering technical achievement. A special drill tipped with "Ernestite" was needed to create the long perforation down the center. They could take as much as two weeks each to produce—a whole necklace could represent the entire output of a craftsman for one year. Such a necklace would have been an extremely valuable object, destined for someone in a position of great power, status, or authority.

SEAL MAKERS

Among the materials used for beadmaking was steatite, sometimes coated in a blue glaze made of a mixture of copper, lime, and clay. There were many sources from which the Indus people could obtain steatite, both in central India and in the Indo-Iranian borderlands, and these had been exploited for many thousands of years. Steatite had been used to make beads by the peoples of the borderlands since the early days at Mehrgarh in the 7th millennium B.C., and the technique of glazing them was developed by the late 4th millennium.

Steatite was also used as the main material for making the distinctive Indus seals [Figure 22]. Some of the sealmaking techniques were the same as those used by the lapidaries, and one workshop at Chanhu Daro seems to have been engaged in the production of beads and seals side by side. The seal maker first sawed a block of steatite into the required square or rectangular shape, but quite thick to allow for a boss on the back. This boss he then shaped using a knife, forming a hemisphere with a central groove over the outside from top to bottom

and a perforation through the center from side to side. This was the weakest point on the seal and was liable to break if the owner was unlucky.

The front of the seal was then carefully carved to produce an incised design, so that when it was pressed into clay it would leave a design in relief. The seal maker used a burin, a sharp instrument with an angled blade a bit similar to a modern scalpel. The design had two elements: an animal or scene on the lower portion and a short inscription across the top [see Figure 22]. Given the importance of the design and the restricted knowledge of literacy in the Indus Civilization, we can surmise that the design was drawn and probably also engraved by a specialist who was part of the ruling class, very likely a priest.

When he had completed this stage, the seal was returned to the workshop where it was fired to harden and whiten it.

IVORY CARVERS

Engraving skills were also required of those who worked ivory, producing a wide range of small personal objects that were common in Indus towns. These included kohl sticks for applying eye makeup, combs and pins, beads, and amulets. Ivory was also made into carved cylinders. Mesopotamian sources mention small birds made of ivory, which they imported from the Indus people.

Board games seem to have been popular with the Indus people. Most of the boards

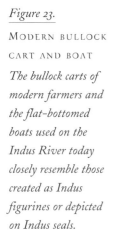

Figure 23.

MODERN BULLOCK CART AND BOAT

The bullock carts of modern farmers and the flat-bottomed boats used on the Indus River today closely resemble those created as Indus figurines or depicted on Indus seals.

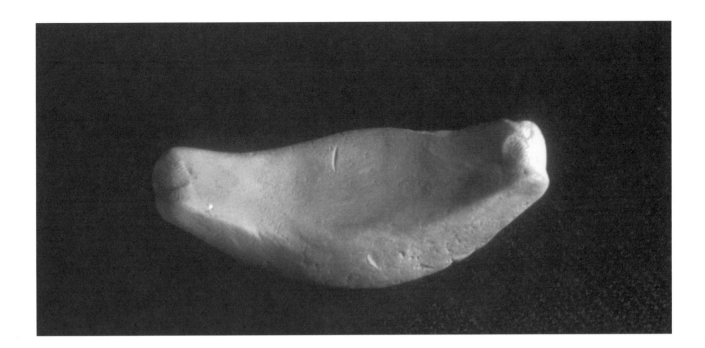

were probably made of embroidered cloth, as they are today, and have therefore disappeared, but some that have been found were made of pottery or engraved on bricks. Gaming counters and dice for use in these games were made of a variety of materials such as pottery, bone, and shell, those of ivory being the finest. The counters were thin rectangular rods engraved with dots and lines, their tops often carved in the shape of animals or birds.

Workshops where ivory objects were carved have been found in a number of Indus towns and cities, including Harappa and Lothal. These two were located close to sources of supply, in Gujurat and the eastern Punjab, where elephants could be hunted either by Indus hunters or by independent local hunter-gatherers with whom the Indus people enjoyed trade relations. The skill of hunting these large and dangerous animals was one of long standing in the subcontinent, because ivory tusks were being used even by the people of early Mehrgarh, thousands of years before the Indus Period. It is possible, however, that the Indus people had succeeded in domesticating elephants. A number of Indus seals show an elephant covered by a cloth, suggesting that they were tame, and a figurine from Harappa depicting an elephant with a painted face points the same way [see Color Plates 8 and 9]. Elephant bones were found in a number of Indus settlements.

WOODWORKING

Many other crafts were undoubtedly practiced by the Indus people, but we know far fewer details of these because the objects themselves have disappeared. Instead we have various indirect clues that help us to determine what was made and how—traces left on other objects, tools, surviving elements in other materials, and a wealth of modern ethnographic information that assists us in

Figure 24.

TERRACOTTA TOY BOAT, HARAPPA

Our knowledge of Indus boats is quite limited, so even tiny clues, like this toy boat from Harappa, provide welcome pieces of information. Although simple, this model gives the impression of having a shallow draught, a high prow, and a flat stern, similar to the boats still used on the Indus.

Figure 25.

TEXTILE

IMPRESSIONS,

HARAPPA

*Evidence of Indus
textiles is quite
limited, although
the textiles them-
selves must have
been in common use.
A toy bed found at
Harappa bore this
imprint of a piece of
tightly woven cloth
made from finely
spun thread.*

reconstructing a picture from such evidence as we have.

Timber was a major export from the Indus people to Mesopotamia. Some rare surviving fragments show that wood was used in the construction of Indus houses—for doors and their jambs, for beams to support the flat roofs, and for pillars. Sometimes entire structures might be built of timber. Fragments of house models show that Indus houses had windows with a lattice grill and these were probably also of wood.

Shell inlay pieces are believed to have been used to decorate wooden furniture, such as the low stools that are sometimes depicted on the Indus seals. Beds made of a wooden frame strung with a rope lattice in use today may have had their counterpart in Indus times—at least one seal shows a deity seated on a long divan or bed.

Terracotta models provide a clear picture of the wooden carts that were widely used for land transport [*see* Color Plate 5]. These are virtually identical to those of modern farmers of the Indus region [Figure 23]. Some simply have a solid wooden platform above the axle, others had an open framework. The platform might have permanent side pieces or just holes into which pieces of wood could be slotted when required to give some side support to a load. The solid wooden wheels were probably fastened to the axle so that they turned together. These carts were drawn by oxen or bullocks, of which there are also models. A different style of cart, with a roof and high sides, was probably a vehicle in which people traveled. A small platform in front of the cab provided a seat for the driver.

The surviving model boats are less easy to reconstruct, but two illustrations on a seal and a tablet show that the Indus people built flat-bottomed wooden boats like the house-boats still used on the Indus today [Color Plate 12 and Figures 23 and 24]. Larger, stronger vessels would have been needed for seagoing voyages, but we have no evidence that could allow us to reconstruct their form.

TEXTILES

Most of the crafts we have looked at so far were practiced by specialists who worked either full- or part-time on producing goods for wider distribution. Textiles, on the other hand, were probably produced in every home to meet the family's needs. A single piece of cloth has been found at Mohenjo Daro, made from cotton, a plant that had been cultivated in the subcontinent since the 5th millennium B.C. There are many traces of Indus textiles—the impressions of fabric on the inside of faience vessels that had been molded on a sand-filled bag, the imprint of rougher cloth on the reverse of sealings that had been fastened on sacks, traces of threads corroded on silver vessels or wrapped around the handles of copper objects, and marks on the base of pottery vessels that had stood on cloth to dry before firing [Figure 25]. These show that the Indus people were making cotton cloth of various grades, including very fine fabrics closely woven from thread spun on a spinning wheel. Loomweights show that some households used large upright looms to weave cloth. Hand-spun thread woven into

cloth on a small backstrap loom was probably the most common product. Judging by the exuberant polychrome decoration on some of the pottery, we would expect the cloth to have been brightly patterned. At present our only clue is that the cloth fragment from Mohenjo Daro had been dyed red with madder. Several Indus cities, however, have buildings with what were probably brick dye-vats set in their floors, so it is likely that cloth or thread was dyed to various colors.

Cotton was certainly used for making cloth but we are not so sure about the other possible materials. Wool and goat hair must surely have been used as the Indus people kept sheep and goats. Flax was probably used too but at present the earliest evidence of its use in India comes substantially later than the Indus Period. Silk is also a possibility. Although Chinese silk from the domestic silkworm was not traded to the west until considerably later, India has several of its own wild species of moth whose pupae produce silk. It is inferior to Chinese silk but it was extensively used in India in historical times. Like many forest products, the cocoons of these wild silkworms were collected in recent times by hunter-gatherers who traded them with settled people. It is therefore quite probable that the Indus people could have obtained supplies of raw silk from the hunter-gatherers with whom they traded various commodities. Currently the earliest evidence of silk in India is from the mid 2nd millennium B.C. but it is not unlikely that the Indus people also used silk.

Mats made from reeds and grasses and woven baskets have also left an impression on clay objects set down upon them and on the clay floors on which they were placed. We do not know whether the floors or walls were sometimes covered with carpets, but Jonathan Mark Kenoyer, a leading authority, has pointed out the similarity between a type of small curved knife made by the Indus people and knives used today to cut the pile of carpets—suggestive evidence.

THE ORGANIZATION OF CRAFT ACTIVITIES

The distribution of craft-working debris, such as dumps of overfired pottery and vitrified kiln linings, discarded pieces of raw materials, and broken manufacturing tools, provides important and interesting insights into the organization of Indus craft production. The distribution of such material in the great city of Mohenjo Daro has recently been intensively mapped by the international team working under the auspices of Aachen Technical University and the Italian Oriental Institute IsMEO. This has revealed that small workshops were scattered throughout the city, each probably operated by a single family. Different crafts were often located side by side, rather than in quarters dedicated to particular crafts. But there were also a few larger scale operations—factories rather than domestic workshops. However, as the known and excavated portion of Mohenjo Daro is only the center of a far larger city, it could well be that this pattern is not typical and that in the suburbs there were far more craft production areas on the factory scale.

It is clear that craft production was highly organized. Taking the example of shellworking, the distribution of different activities both within settlements and across the civilization shows that many different specialists were involved in the manufacture of shell objects. The shells were gathered by fishermen and divers who probably removed and ate the meaty part of the shellfish. Further cleaning of the shells took place in an area set apart because of the smell—either close to the marine source area or in a segregated area within a major settlement.

Individual workshops within both small, specialized settlements and major centers concentrated on producing particular products from particular shell types—ladles in one workshop, chank shell bangles in another, inlay pieces in a third. Generally the debris from each manufacturing process was then passed on to other specialists, to be made into smaller objects such as beads and gaming pieces. The products of individual workshops would then be distributed, the distance they traveled depending on their nature. Ladles and fine bangles were distributed over a wide area—even Shortugai on the distant Oxus had such bangles—but the inferior bangles of clam shells made at Balakot were for purely local consumption.

A similar pattern of a high degree of specialization and segregation of production and variable distribution of different products is to be seen in other industries, such as pottery manufacture. Returning to the question posed at the beginning of the chapter, it is clear that the Indus Civilization, like other societies to which the term has been applied, was marked by a very high degree of occupational specialization, in which some individuals not only devoted their lives to the practice of a particular craft but even probably confined their activities to a particular branch of that craft. Some of the objects they produced were very specialized products indeed, like the carnelian necklaces that took a craftsman a whole year to make. Clearly a society that supported this degree of specialization must have been highly organized and stratified.

CHAPTER FIVE

THE URBAN REVOLUTION

VILLAGES, TOWNS, AND CITIES

The development of civilization is often referred to as the "urban revolution"—cities are virtually synonymous with civilization. So what makes cities different from towns and towns from villages? Why, for instance, do archaeologists regard the massive (13 hectares[ha]) 7th-millennium B.C. settlement of Çatalhöyük in Anatolia, with its population of perhaps as many as 6,000 people, as a village rather than a town?

There are two aspects involved in answering this question—the internal organization and differentiation of the settlement, and the relationship of the settlement to others. A village, regardless of its size, is a collection of houses and virtually nothing else. It may have a few communal facilities, such as a well or pond for water, a community hall for social gatherings, or a shrine for the performance of religious duties. It may also have the beginnings of social hierarchy, with a headman's hut that is larger than those of other members of the village, perhaps surrounded by the smaller huts of his dependents. Although one village may be considerably larger than neighboring villages, it does not differ from them in function, because they are all independent and self-sufficient communities.

A town, in contrast, serves as a focus for the surrounding villages and rural settlements. Although it is likely to be larger than the villages it serves, the crucial difference lies not in its size but in its function. Towns are the center of an area's administration, home of the local chief or lord, the place in which the area's chief shrine is located, and a center of craft production and trade, providing a market or storage center for the agricultural surplus produced by the area's farmers and the source of other goods they cannot themselves produce. Within the town there are distinct areas—the mansions of the elite, the houses and workshops of artisans, in some cases the huts of the local peasants, public buildings including temples or shrines, perhaps a mint after coinage had been invented, and other features related to administration. Towns emerged when larger political units were coming into existence, uniting a number of

Figure 26.

AERIAL VIEW, MOHENJO DARO

This aerial view shows the entire excavation at Mohenjo Daro. The citadel carefully placed on its separate mound can be seen in the center-right of the photograph. There is a clear separation between the public buildings, like the citadel, and the private or residential sectors. Occupied between 2600 and 1900 B.C., Mohenjo Daro is 250 hectares in area.

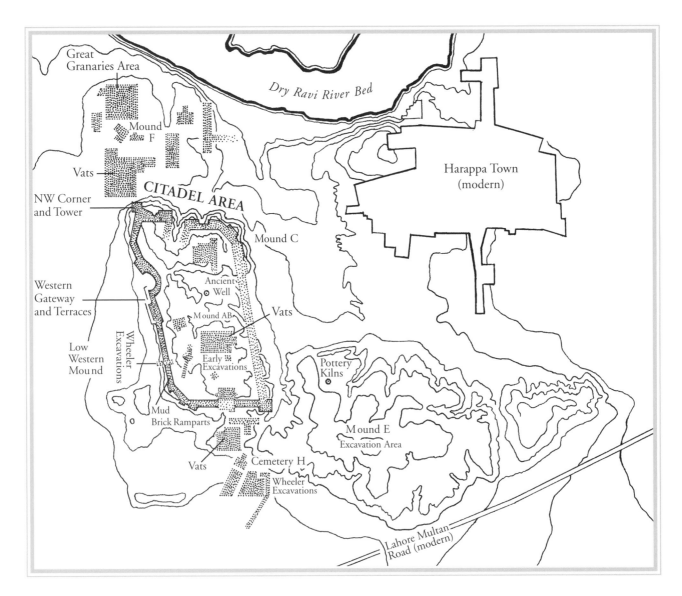

Map 3.

HARAPPA

CITY PLAN

Harappa lies on an old bed of the Ravi River. The latest research has revealed at least five mounds. Harappa provided the first clues to the Indus Civilization.

food-producing communities under the authority of a religious or secular leader.

Cities are to towns as towns are to villages, providing a third tier in the settlement hierarchy. The city is the center of government for the whole region, to which the local administration in the towns is subordinate. It houses the ruler and his family, the chief priest and his subordinates, the principal shrine and place of pilgrimage, the government warehouses and records offices, a great variety of industries, the headquarters of native merchants and the establishments of foreign traders, the places of education, and so on. Often they are stoutly defended, with walls and moats and the barracks of soldiers or guards. Here dwells the whole spectrum of society, from the king in his palace to the beggar in his hovel, from those dedicated to the pure service of the gods down to the most despicable thieves. The presence of cities reflects the existence of a

UNCOVERING INDUS SETTLEMENTS

state or states—a hierarchical society in which a central authority exercises control over a large area in which there are not only farming communities but a variety of specialists not involved in food production, including some working in service industries.

Looking at the settlements of the Indus Civilization, do they fit this pattern? Is there a recognizable hierarchy of villages, towns, and cities, and do the settlements thus labeled match up to the theoretical picture of what each would be expected to be like? And most centrally, the question that has been posed by so many people studying the region: was the Indus Civilization a unified state or merely a collection of smaller entities, united by a shared cultural heritage but politically independent?

Λ considerable amount of evidence has been assembled that sheds light on the nature of the Indus settlements, but there are also significant gaps in our knowledge. The huge settlements of Mohenjo Daro and Harappa have been extensively excavated, although a lot of work is now needed to unravel the findings of the early excavations here [Figure 26]. Much of Harappa was destroyed in the 19th century; the lower deposits at Mohenjo Daro are waterlogged; and only the center of these two settlements has been excavated, leaving vast stretches

Map 4.

LOTHAL CITY PLAN

Lothal is the most extensively researched of the Indus coastal sites. A bead factory and Mesopotamian seal have been found there.

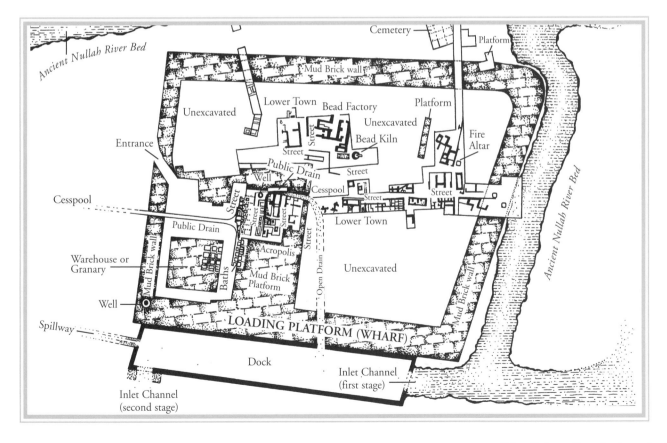

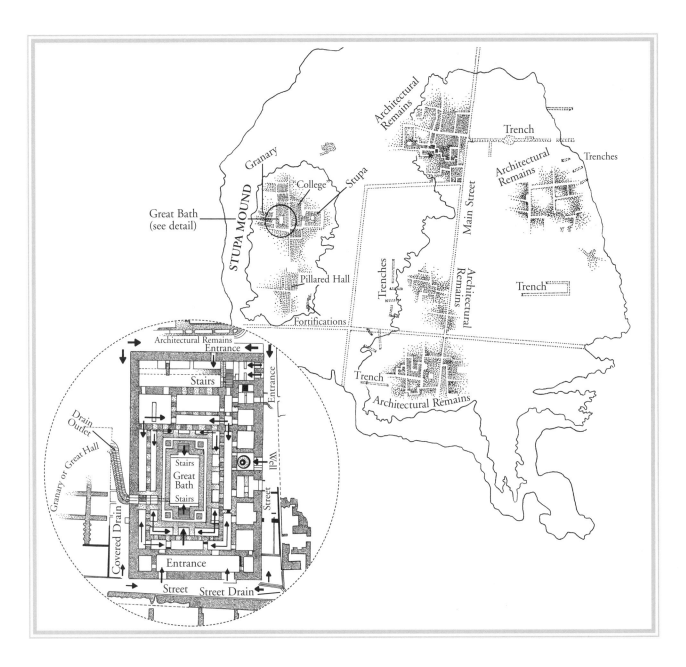

Granary

'College'

Stupa

Great Bath
(see detail)

STUPA MOUND

Pillared Hall

Fortifications

Architectural Remains

Trench

Trenches

Architectural Remains

Main Street

Trenches

Architectural Remains

Architectural Remains

Trench

Trench

Architectural Remains

Architectural Remains Entrance

Stairs

Entrance

Drain Outlet

Entrance

Well

Stairs
Great Bath
Stairs

Granary or Great Hall

Covered Drain

Street

Entrance

Street   Street Drain

Map 5.

MOHENJO DARO
CITY PLAN

*Mohenjo Daro is
the best known
Indus site. It is in
Sindh, Pakistan,
next to the Indus.*

unexplored and unknown [Maps 3 and 5]. Some of the smaller settlements like Lothal have been more comprehensively excavated [Map 4].

A great deal of the settlement evidence comes only from surface surveys. In suitable areas, these can provide a good indication of settlement distribution and density, such as the huge concentration of settlement along the Saraswati River and the paucity of settlement in Punjab. The types of material that have been collected from the surface of these sites—usually pieces of pottery but quite often also industrial debris such as copper slag or flint chips—give some clues to the variety of activities that took place at each. In some sites, the ruins of mounds survive and can be examined to reveal some clues to the architecture. But some areas are not suitable for such surveys—for example, the thick alluvial deposits in the Indus Valley itself mask the remains of former settlements unless, like those of Mohenjo Daro, they are substantial and rise above the alluvial plain. In some other regions settlement traces have been eroded away, so the picture obtained from surveys is not complete. And although sites are ranked by size, size alone is not necessarily an indicator of function, so we are to some extent guessing when we identify massive sites like Ganweriwala in the Saraswati Valley as cities.

Intensive surveys have been conducted in many regions, notably along much of the upper course of the former Saraswati River, in the Punjab and in Gujurat, as well as in the Indo-Iranian borderlands and along the Makran coast. These reveal that the settlement pattern differed in each region. The most densely settled area seems to have been in Bahawalpur, the central portion of the Saraswati Valley. Here many settlements of all sizes from less than 2 ha to more than 100 ha have been identified. The tentative conclusion to be drawn from this is that a dense network of farming settlements existed in this area, with many towns where a variety of industrial activities took place and at least one city, Ganweriwala. But this suggestion must remain just that—a suggestion—until some excavations are actually undertaken in selected sites to verify what has been proposed.

WHAT WERE THEY CALLED?

Excavations in the Indus region focused initially on the two massive and obvious settlements at Mohenjo Daro and Harappa. Like other Indus settlements—and the civilization itself for that matter—we have no idea what these cities were called by their inhabitants, because we cannot read their writing and we probably have no unbroken traditions carrying the ancient names forward into literate times. I say "probably" because Wheeler toyed with the possibility that Harappa could be identified with the place mentioned in the early Indo-Aryan oral text, the *Rigveda*, as "Hariyupiya," scene of an Aryan victory.

"In the aid of Abhyavartin Chayamana, Indra destroyed the seed of Varashikha.

At Hariyupiya he smote the vanguard of the Vrichivans, and the rear fled frightened."
(Possehl 1999 p. 45 quoting Rigveda book IV hymn 27 verses 4–5: Griffith 1896).

Nothing about this place in the text, however, can be pinned to a particular location, so it remains nothing but a charming possibility.

Mohenjo Daro is normally translated as the "Mound of the Dead," an appropriate name for a ruined city—but an interesting alternative is that the name means "Mound of the Mohanas" and derives from the Mohana, the people of the region who live today in houseboats on the Indus and earn their living by fishing. Neither name, however, brings us any closer to what the Indus people themselves called their great city.

Following the "lost Saraswati" farther east, the situation is not so dire. Surveys in the valleys of the Sutlej, Saraswati, and Drishadvati again show a considerable density of settlement, though less dense than in Bahawalpur, with sites of a range of sizes, and some of the larger sites (mostly 10–30 ha) have been excavated to some extent. These include Rupar in the Himalayan foothills, Mitathal and the massive site of Rakhigarhi (80 ha) in the east toward the present course of the Yamuna, Banawali in the center of this area, and Kalibangan at the confluence of the Drishadvati and the Saraswati.

In the Punjab the situation is very different. Very few sites have been located here, reflecting the overwhelming importance of pastoralism in this generally arid region where cultivation would have been confined to the banks of the rivers (the Chenab, Jhelum, Ravi, and Beas). The only major settlement in this region is the well-known and intensively excavated site of Harappa—but the very presence of such a huge site (estimated now to have been around 150 ha) here is surely a clue pointing to the Indus Civilization having been a unified state, since Harappa must have existed for the benefit of a much larger political unit than the sparsely populated region in which it lies.

Moving steadily westward, the next region is Baluchistan, highlands that had been occupied for millennia. Many settlements were located in this region over the course of the 20th century and quite a few of them were excavated. Their size and density reflect the opportunities available in the mountainous terrain. Dense settlement was supported by irrigated agriculture in the restricted fertile plateaus. Settlements were sparse elsewhere, except on the coast where there was access to marine resources and maritime trade routes. As well as supporting agriculture and pastoralism, the rivers cutting through the region offered routes through the mountains, encouraging trade. Settlements in this mountainous region were generally small, but with a few like Dabarkot, Kulli, and Mundigak rising to 15–25 ha. Nindowari may be an exception at a possible 50 ha. Pathani Damb is also said to be a vast site but no data are available on its actual size.

Encircled by these regions is the Indus Valley and the adjacent plains—a region that on ecological grounds should have been densely settled but where alluvial deposits are likely to have skewed the identification of ancient settlements toward the larger and therefore more visible and durable settlements. Nevertheless, a number of smaller sites have been located and excavated, including Allahdino, whose tiny 1.4-ha extent contrasts with its evident importance and organization. There are also a number of sites of intermediate size, including Chanhu Daro and Amri on the Indus and the more substantial (25 ha) Judeirjo Daro on the interface with the Kachi Plain, as well as the vast settlement of Mohenjo Daro, now reckoned at 250 ha.

Substantial settlements lay also in the delta of the Indus and Saraswati and along the interface between mainland India on the one hand, and the island of Kutch and the Saurashtra peninsula on the other. Of these Dholavira, at 100 ha, was the largest, but Rangpur was also a substantial settlement

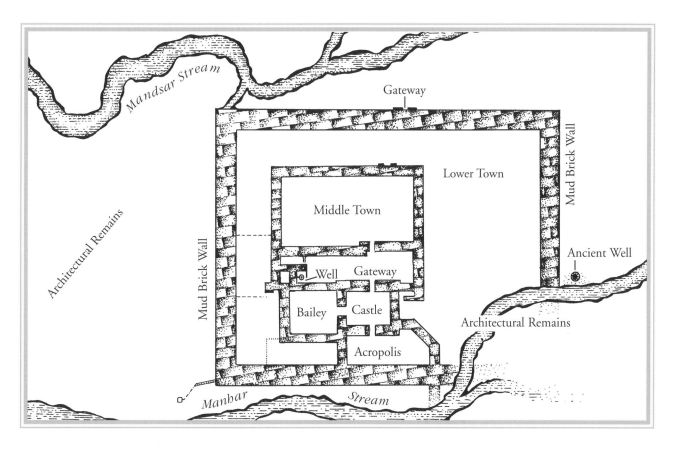

Map showing Dholavira City Plan with labels: Mandsar Stream, Gateway, Mud Brick Wall, Lower Town, Middle Town, Architectural Remains, Ancient Well, Well, Gateway, Bailey, Castle, Architectural Remains, Acropolis, Manhar Stream.

[Map 6]. Lothal, Desalpur, and Surkotada were smaller but excavation has shown them to have been internally complex. Within Kutch and Saurashtra themselves, the greater number of settlements were small. This is the only region where a number of excavations have actually been undertaken on smaller sites, such as Nesadi, Rojdi, and Kanewal that were thought to have been villages and pastoral camps—with encouraging results. A strong emphasis on farming and pastoralism here fits the local ecology, but the value of access to the sea routes and resources is underlined by the existence of settlements that seem designed to exploit them, such as the shell processing settlement at Nageshwar, and the recently discovered port (now underwater) at Dwarka.

The patterns of settlement density and size built up through field surveys have provided some preliminary clues to the nature of Indus settlement. Excavated sites, however, have shown that settlement size alone is not an adequate clue to settlement complexity, so it is now necessary to examine aspects of these excavated settlements in more detail.

Investigating the Indus settlements is not an easy task. Mohenjo Daro is largely buried beneath the deep alluvial deposits of later ages. Harappa, in contrast, was used in the 19th century as a brick quarry, destroying much of the original settlement. In addition, its citadel area has been built over by a Muslim cemetery and much of the ancient city lies under the modern town of Harappa. Both Mohenjo Daro and Harappa covered a vast area, and

Map 6.

DHOLAVIRA
CITY PLAN

Dholavira is located on Khadir Beit, an island in the Great Rann of Kutch in Gujarat State India. It has only been excavated since 1990. As large as Harappa and Mohenjo Daro, it has some of the best-preserved architecture. A tantalizing signboard with Indus script has also been discovered.

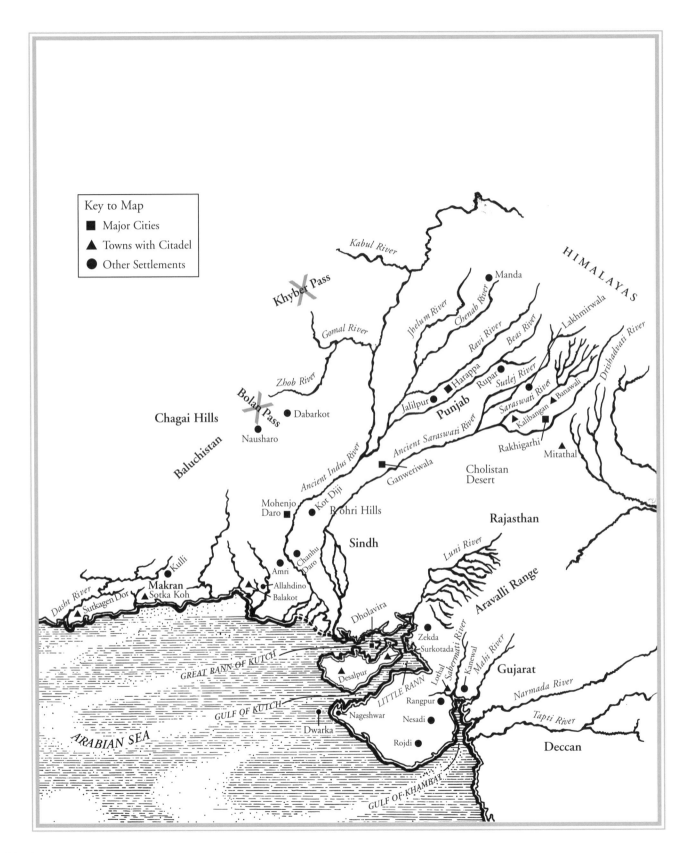

Key to Map
■ Major Cities
▲ Towns with Citadel
● Other Settlements

Kabul River

HIMALAYAS

Khyber Pass

Gomal River

● Manda

Jhelum River

Chenab River

Ravi River

Beas River

Lakhmirwala

Drishadvati River

Zhob River

Bolan Pass

Chagai Hills

● Dabarkot

Baluchistan

● Nausharo

Jalilpur ●

■ Harappa

Rupar ●

Sutlej River

Saraswati River

Banawali ▲

Punjab

▲ Kalibangan

■

Rakhigarhi ●

▲ Mitathal

Ancient Saraswati River

Cholistan
Desert

■
Ganweriwala

Rajasthan

Ancient Indus River

Mohenjo
Daro ■

● Kot Diji

Rohri Hills

Sindh

Luni River

Aravalli Range

Kulli ●

Dasht River

Makran

Sutkagen Dor ▲

▲ Sotka Koh

Amri ●

● Chanhu
   Daro

Allahdino
● Balakot

▲

Dholavira

Zekda ●
Surkotada ▲

Sabarmati River

Mahi River

Kanewal ●

Gujarat

Narmada River

GREAT RANN OF KUTCH

■

Desalpur ▲

LITTLE RANN

Lothal ▲

Rangpur ●

Tapti River

GULF OF KUTCH

Nageshwar ●

Nesadi ●

ARABIAN SEA

Dwarka ●

Rojdi ●

Deccan

GULF OF KHAMBAT

their excavations investigated only a portion of these sites. This is true also of many other settlements. So the picture we have of the Indus towns and cities is frustratingly incomplete [Map 7].

INDUS CITADELS

Cities of whatever place and time have two major components: public and residential. Often the public sector—administrative buildings, religious edifices, the place of residence of the rulers—lies at the heart of the city, providing a focus for dwellings that gradually grow up around it. The major Indus settlements, however, seem to have been deliberate creations rather than gradual developments—at Mohenjo Daro, Harappa, and smaller settlements like Lothal and Kalibangan there is evidence that massive mudbrick foundation platforms were constructed before the settlement was laid out above them, to raise it above the level of floodwaters. This deliberate planning is reflected in the formality of the striking division between the public and residential sectors of these settlements. In Mohenjo Daro and Harappa, the first two Indus cities excavated, there is a clear separation, with public buildings located on a higher walled mound to the west, to which the term *citadel* has generally been applied.

A number of other Indus settlements have a separate citadel mound like those at

Map 7.

MATURE
INDUS SITES
*Cities of the Indus
c.2600 B.C.*

IDENTIFIED CITADELS

NAME	ESTIMATED SIZE	REGION	GENERAL LOCATION
Balakot	2.8 ha	Central	coast west of Indus
Banawali	16 ha	Eastern	Saraswati River
Desalpur	1.3 ha	Southern	central Kutch
Dholavira	100 ha	Southern	island in Rann of Kutch
Ganweriwala	80 ha	Southern-Central	Saraswati River
Harappa	150 ha	Punjab	Ravi River
Kalibangan	11.5 ha	Eastern	Saraswati River
Lothal	4.8 ha	Southern	Bhogava River
Mitathal	7.2 ha	Eastern	south of Drishadvati River
Mohenjo Daro	250 ha	Central	Indus River
Rakhigarhi	80 ha	Eastern	Drishadvati River
Sotka Koh	16 ha	Western	Shadi Kaur River, Makran
Surkotada	1.4 ha	Southern	eastern Kutch
Sutkagen Dor	4.5 ha	Western	Dasht River, Makran

Mohenjo Daro and Harappa—at Kalibangan, for example, this is subdivided into two walled sectors. In some other settlements, however, the separation between public and private areas is achieved by walling off one part of the area within the city's walls. Surkotada in Gujurat, for instance, is a walled settlement that is divided into two, the western half, the citadel, being built over a massive platform, whereas the eastern half (regarded as the residential area though not actually excavated) has no such platform and is lower. At Dholavira, the massive settlement in the same region, the elevated southern sector is separated by walls from the rest of the city and is itself subdivided into two halves, the "Bailey" and the "Castle." The citadels at Lothal and Banawali are also a subdivision of the walled city.

Not all important Indus settlements had a citadel, however. In some settlements it may be that limited investigation has failed so far to identify a citadel that was actually present—but at Chanhu Daro, a 4.7-ha settlement with extensive workshops, the excavator, Ernest Mackay, explicitly states that there was no citadel mound.

The construction of citadels finds reflections more than 2,000 years later in the layout of the Indo-Greek cities of the northwest, such as Taxila, where a raised citadel or acropolis contained the royal palace and important public buildings. It is also a feature of cities in many other parts of the world at various times, such as ancient Greece and several American cultures. Often, this raised area was the heart of a city's defenses, the place of refuge for the citizens, and the location of their last stand when besieged. But perhaps more significantly, its elevation set it apart, investing the buildings on it with special importance and often restricting access

Figure 27.

DHOLAVIRA SIGNBOARD

This signboard was found at the impressive North Gate that led to the walled-in citadel at Dholavira. The inscription remains a mystery, like all Indus writing. It has been theorized to have sacred meaning, but perhaps we will never know.

DHOLAVIRA SIGNBOARD

In the 1989–1990 season at Dholavira, the excavators made a remarkable discovery. Lying on the floor of the chamber flanking the western side of the passage through the North Gate of the citadel were found nine or ten huge Indus "letters"—signs in the Indus script—made of a white crystalline material [Figure 27]. Each was about 37 cm high and their width ranged from 25 to 27 cm. It is to be supposed that these signs had once been set on a board, probably of wood, displayed over the gate. Perhaps it contained some sacred message, symbolically purifying those who passed under it. The signs included a circle divided by six radial lines, thought by many who have studied the script to be equivalent to the later dharmacakra—"the wheel of the law"—a symbol used in Buddhism to denote both the beginning of Buddha's preaching and the concept of dharma—righteousness and duty. The same symbol is associated with the cakravartin ("universal king")—the righteous monarch—and with the sun. The symbol appears several times in the inscription.

to them. Generally such structures would be public buildings of various types—temples (like those on the Athenian acropolis), administrative buildings, or royal palaces. It therefore seems probable that those Indus settlements that had a citadel were ones that had a special importance in the civilization. But the presence of a citadel was not necessarily correlated with size: the five massive sites all had citadels, but only some of the medium-sized sites and a number of the smaller ones. Thus, for example, in Gujurat, 1.4-ha Surkotada and 1.3-ha Desalpur each had a citadel, but the much larger settlement of Rangpur did not.

Artificial platforms were the foundation for these citadels in every case and were generally constructed at the time of the settlement's foundation or when it was rebuilt during the transformation into a Mature Indus settlement. The citadel at Mohenjo Daro was constructed as a vast brick platform, surrounded by a massive baked-brick retaining wall with bastions, giving protection against flooding. On this, rising 10 or 12 meters above the surrounding plains, were built a number of impressive public structures [*see* Figure 1].

At Dholavira, the "Castle" was the earliest substantial construction, built probably during the Early Indus Period, of mudbrick and stone rubble over the remains of an earlier small-scale occupation. Somewhat later a residential area sprang up to its north. The Mature Indus Period saw the addition of the "Bailey" on the west of the citadel, while the residential area was razed and transformed into a ceremonial open space. Farther north a new walled residential area was constructed. Reservoirs—vitally important in this arid area—were built beyond this and an outer wall was constructed around the whole settlement. Inside the wall the settlement expanded as time passed. The former residential area became the walled "Middle Town" and a great deal more housing was built in the eastern part of the settlement, within the outer walls. Massive and elaborate gateways belong to this period, controlling access to the citadel. Thus at Dholavira the settlement began with the citadel and grew into a major walled settlement covering around 100 ha with the citadel becoming a part of the settlement that was difficult of access and remote from everyday life.

PUBLIC BUILDINGS

Every town and city has a range of public buildings. Palaces and mansions, political and administrative buildings, temples, shrines, and churches, and arenas for public spectacles are to be found in cities the world over, their form and nature varying from place to place—Roman amphitheaters, Mesoamerican ball courts, Greek theatres, modern American football stadiums. Alongside these are buildings that are distinctive features of each individual culture—Roman bathhouses, modern European multi-story carparks. What public buildings do we find in the Indus Civilization and what do they tell us about the Indus people?

The citadel mounds of the Indus settlements seem predominantly to have been public in nature, although there were some workshops and houses. Access to the citadel was controlled and restricted by the way it was laid out. To arrive at the heart of the citadel at Kalibangan, for example, one had either to pass through the walled northern portion of the citadel, which may have been the residential area of the elite, and enter through a central gateway that divided the citadel in two, or approach through the southern gateway. The highest part of the citadel at Dholavira was reached only by passing through several lower walled compounds. The citadel was surrounded by a wall with an impressive gateway in each side. Above one gate was a signboard with an inscription [*see* Figure 27]. To gain access to the citadel at Mohenjo Daro, visitors had to enter via a gate on the western side and mount a substantial flight of stairs. At the top, they passed through another gate into a bathing place where, it is thought, visitors would have been required to wash to purify themselves before entering the sacred precinct. All citadel areas, whether on a separate mound or contained within the city, were massively walled with impressive gates, emphasizing their importance. Often the gate included one or several chambers. Several of the gates at Dholavira incorporated pillars of limestone blocks and beautifully carved stone bases that probably supported wooden pillars. Flights of steps or broad ramps led up to the gates from the town below.

Many of the buildings within the citadel were probably religious in nature. They are bewildering in their diversity, including structures as dissimilar as the Great Bath at Mohenjo Daro, and the row of "fire altars" (hearths interpreted as altars for the burning of sacred fires) at Kalibangan [*see* Color Plate 17]. Ceremonial activities may also have taken place in some of the large buildings that have been found on the citadels of several settlements. In the southern portion

Figure 28.

BATH AREA
IN HOUSE,
MOHENJO DARO

The bathroom was an important feature of almost every house at Mohenjo Daro. Water that was poured over the bather flowed across the bathroom's brick-paved floor to empty via a brick-built outlet into the efficient drainage network of the city.

Figure 29.

"GRANARY,"
HARAPPA

This large structure has the foundations of twelve rooms, arranged in two rows on either side of a central passage. The sleeper walls allowing the circulation of air led to its interpretation as a granary. Scholars now tend to see it as a public building for administrative or religious activities or even as a palace.

of the Mohenjo Daro citadel was a large hall with the brick bases for pillars. Wheeler likened this to the great assembly halls of the ancient Near East, and analogies closer to home could also be drawn, such as the Mauryan pillared hall at Pataliputra or the Buddhist halls of Sri Lanka, some 2,500 years later. Here it is likely that some kind of assembly would have taken place—perhaps administrative meetings of the elders of the city, or public audiences by the rulers to give laws and settle disputes. Adjacent to this hall was another smaller building that could have served an administrative function.

The citadels of all the settlements that have been excavated included some residential structures, in addition to the public buildings. We would have expected palaces to house the rulers of the civilization, but these have not been found. Instead evidence has emerged of structures not dissimilar from those of the lower town (the residential part of the settlement). Such structures were found in the northern part of the citadel at Kalibangan, in the area of the Mohenjo Daro citadel north of the Great Bath, in the citadel of Banawali, and in other settlements large and small. If these were the houses of those in authority as their location suggests, they give an interesting and unexpected picture of rulers who followed a modest and ascetic way of life.

Many early civilizations have large state storage facilities in which tribute, taxes, or

Color Plate 1.

DANCING GIRL, MOHENJO DARO

A rare and beautiful example of a bronze figurine that was cast using the complex cire perdue *or "lost wax" technique. The girl is wearing bangles on both arms; note the different sizes on her elbows and wrists. These bangles possibly signified her status in Indus society.*

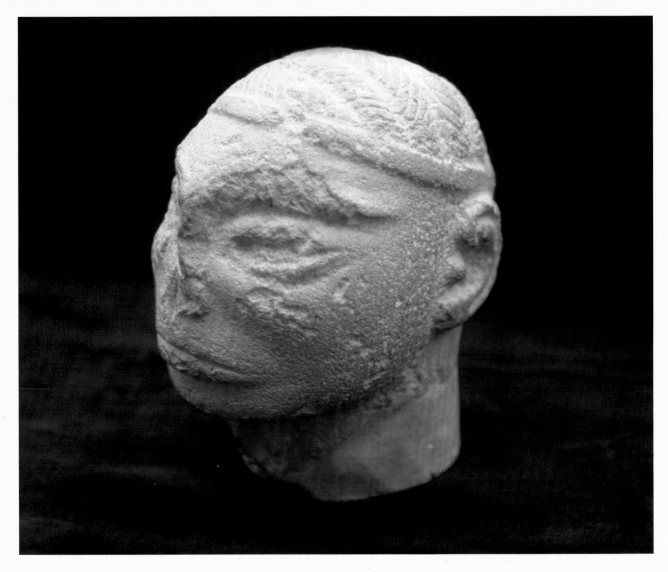

Color Plate 2. (above)

MALE HEAD, MOHENJO DARO

This fragment depicting a male head may have originally been part of a sculpture of a seated figure. The man's hair is shown neatly arranged in braids across the top, caught into a bun at the back and held in place by a band of ribbon, possibly of gold. A closely cropped moustache and beard cover his upper lip and chin.

Color Plate 3. (right)

"PRIEST KING," MOHENJO DARO

This famous sculpture, known as the "Priest King," is only 17.5 cm high. It has the typical characteristics of Indus sculptures of male figures, such as the neat hair bound in a ribbon and the closely cropped beard. In addition it has many unusual features, such as the circular object worn in the center of the headband and on the arm, and the elaborate garment draped over the left shoulder, leaving the right bare—which is still the proper way to indicate reverence both in India and throughout the Buddhist world when approaching a shrine or holy person. A pair of holes beneath the ears indicate that something was originally attached to this figure—perhaps a necklace or headdress of precious materials.

Color Plate 4.

MASK, MOHENJO DARO

This tiny mask of a bearded figure with horns may represent a deity. The mask was made in a mold and is perforated on either side. Therefore, it may have been produced to be worn as an amulet. Similar masks have been found at both Mohenjo Daro and Harappa.

Color Plate 5.

OX-DRAWN CART, HARAPPA

Terracotta models of carts pulled by a pair of bullocks have been found at many Indus settlements. These are strikingly similar to carts still in use in India and Pakistan.

Color Plate 6. (above)

HORNED TIGER SEAL, MOHENJO DARO

This seal depicting a composite beast can be seen in a religious context. The tiger is combined with the horns of a bull or water buffalo. Both the tiger stripes and the headdress appear on many Indus deities.

Color Plate 7. (right)

HEAD OF A FELINE FIGURINE, HARAPPA

The wild creatures of the Indus realms that seem most to have impressed their human neighbors included tigers. These probably played an important part in Indus religious beliefs. This small terracotta head may represent a tiger although the punctuated dots all over it may alternatively suggest a spotted leopard.

Color Plate 8. (above)

ELEPHANT SEAL

This is a typical Indus seal, showing an animal on the bottom and a brief inscription across the top. There are a numerous Indus artifacts that suggest the elephant might have been tamed. The elephant in this seal is covered with a cloth. This cloth could be simply for decoration, or possibly used as a type of saddle.

Color Plate 9. (left)

ELEPHANT HEAD FIGURINE, HARAPPA

Elephants provided the ivory much used by the Indus people. Clues from the few figurines and seals suggest that some of these powerful animals may have been domesticated—for instance, this model has traces of decoration like that today traditionally painted on the faces of domestic elephants on important occasions.

Color Plate 10. (above, left)

PROCESSION SEAL, MOHENJO DARO

This scene has been interpreted as depicting the goddess Durga within a pipal tree. Her current partner in sacred marriage, Rudra, kneels before her, perhaps offering the head of his predecessor, while his foster-mothers, the wives of the Seven Sages, form a procession in the foreground.

Color Plate 11. (above, right)

SEATED YOGI SEAL, MOHENJO DARO

Less well known than the famous seal depicting a deity ("proto-Shiva") surrounded by animals [see Figure 51], this seal shows a similar figure with three faces, seated in a yogic position, wearing many bangles, and crowned by a horned headdress with a central sprig of pipal leaves.

Color Plate 12. (top)

FLAT-BOTTOMED BOAT TABLET

One face of this three-sided tablet from Mohenjo Daro shows a boat that strikingly resembles the flat-bottomed houseboats still used on the Indus River. Important features include the central cabin or hut and the double steering oar that acted as a rudder.

Color Plate 13. (bottom)

DOCKYARD AT LOTHAL

There are archaeological finds that suggest the Indus people traded with both ancient Mesopotamia and Egypt. At Lothal we find a large brick basin constructed along the eastern side of the town. Its excavator believed it to be a dock into which boats would come from the nearby river to unload, although serious objections have been raised to this theory.

Color Plate 14. (above)

WELL

Massive brick wells supplied the inhabitants of Mohenjo Daro with water. As the successive demolition of buildings and reconstruction on their foundations gradually raised the level of the city's streets and houses, further courses of brick were added to the tops of the wells to maintain their level. Recent excavation of the soil and rubble around them has left many wells standing proud, like this example.

Color Plate 15. (above)

DRAIN

A sophisticated network of drains and sewers carried away waste-water from the houses of the Indus towns and cities. This corbelled drain, carrying water and sewage, was constructed in an abandoned gateway of the city of Harappa.

Color Plate 16. (right)

STREET

Brick-built houses line the small lanes that open off the main streets of Mohenjo Daro. Their high walls originally gleamed with white plaster and perhaps with colorful painted designs.

Color Plate 17. (below)

GREAT BATH

The impressive watertight basin of the Great Bath lies in the northern half of Mohenjo Daro's citadel, surrounded by small bathrooms. A colonnade flanked three sides of the basin, which must have been used for ritual bathing and purification.

Color Plate 18.

TERRA COTTA CONES

Some Indus artifacts—pots, jewelry, and metal fish-hooks, for instance—had uses that we can easily guess. Others are completely baffling—like these terracotta cones that have been found at both Harappa and Mohenjo Daro. Suggestions for their use include as plumb-bobs (but they do not have a convenient means of suspending them) or pens for writing (but there is no trace of ink on their worn tips). Might they have been spinning tops for Indus children to play with?

Color Plate 19. (above)

CUBICAL WEIGHTS, HARAPPA

Graduated weights made of various kinds of stone follow a standardized weight system that was adhered to throughout the Indus realms and which gave rise to a system of measuring weights used by later Indian cultures. The weights must have been employed in some official capacity, such as tax collection or the issuing of trade goods to authorized merchants.

Color Plate 20. (below)

LIBATION VESSELS, MOHENJO DARO

These crank conch shells (Turbinella pyrum) have been modified to form vessels and have been decorated with incised lines. By analogy with later use in India, these can probably be interpreted as vessels for pouring libations during religious ceremonies or for containing and dispensing holy water.

Color Plate 21. (left)

CEMETERY H DISH OR LID

Distinctive painted pottery with designs of animals, plants, and people were found in Cemetery H, a cemetery which was in use during the late period of occupation at Harappa, after 1900 B.C. Although some motifs were traditional to the Indus civilization, they were combined in novel ways with each other and with new motifs, creating a regional style that was found over the Punjab, Swat, and eastward into the northern part of the Ganges and Yamuna valleys. The dish is also decorated with trefoils, which so often show up in Indus art.

Color Plate 22. (below)

BURIAL, WOMAN AND INFANT, HARAPPA

This burial vividly illustrates the scant respect paid to the dead once they had been interred. Disturbed before the flesh had rotted, this woman's dead body was flipped over in her grave and some of her bangles removed from her left arm, which was broken in the process. The pots accompanying her burial were also moved about at this time. Between her legs can be seen the tiny body of an infant, buried within a small pit.

Color Plate 23. (left)

HAND-BUILT POT

This pot was built by hand and is therefore an uncommon shape and not completely symmetrical, like much of the Indus pottery. Like the dish in Color Plate 21, it is decorated with a traditional Indus motif: the net and the bird. This type of decoration was especially popular during the Ravi Phase (c. 3300 B.C.).

Color Plate 24. (below)

POLYCHROME POTTERY

These pottery fragments were excavated at Niai Buthi in the high plains of Baluchistan. They date from the 3rd millennium B.C.

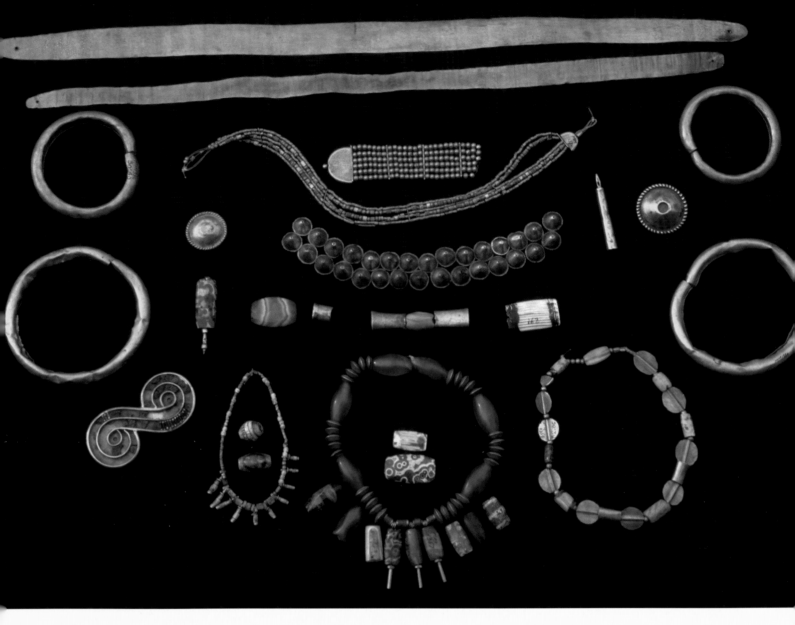

Color Plate 25.

JEWELRY

Several hoards of jewelry made of gold, carnelian, jasper, steatite, and agate have been found in houses at Mohenjo Daro and Harappa, as well as one in the tiny (1.4 ha) settlement of Allahdino. These included hollow gold bangles, chokers to wear round the neck, longer necklaces, earrings, and rings. The two gold bands were probably worn as a fillet around the hair, as depicted on many of the male statues—the ends of the bands are perforated to take a cord or other means of fastening. The elongated carnelian beads were a creation of exceptionally skilled craftsmanship.

religious offerings were stored—these were another set of public buildings that investigators have looked for. Near the Great Bath at Mohenjo Daro is a building that Wheeler thought to have been a granary. A close study of its features shows that it was more probably a pillared hall, because the brick podia that Wheeler thought had supported a raised granary floor are more likely to have been the bases of wooden columns. This building was constructed sometime before the Great Bath. When the latter was built, the hall was slightly modified. At Harappa, a rather different large structure was located to the north of the citadel mound, near the river [Figure 29]. Here a large mudbrick plinth supported a series of twelve rooms or divisions, arranged in two rows of six, provided with sleeper beams to allow air to circulate beneath. Circular working platforms, some with the remains of charred wheat and barley husks, were found nearby [Figure 30]. Wheeler used this as evidence to support the identification of the large structure as a granary. The building is somewhat reminiscent of the earlier compartmented storerooms from Mehrgarh. In the latter, however, there is actually evidence in the form of grain impressions and charred grain that these were indeed granaries.

In more recent times, grain has usually been stored in baskets or mud-plastered bins raised on a mud-plastered earthen or wooden plinth. The "granaries" at Mohenjo Daro and Harappa did not have such bins—if they had formerly contained baskets, inevitably some traces of spilt grain would have remained in them. The fact that grain is explicitly noted

to be absent in the suggested granaries at Harappa and Mohenjo Daro therefore makes this identification unlikely.

Recent excavations in the huge settlement at Rakhigarhi, however, claim to have exposed a granary with barley in one of its compartments—an extremely important discovery whose full publication is eagerly awaited. At Lothal the citadel also contained a large structure that the excavator, S. R. Rao, believed to have been a warehouse—constructed on a raised mudbrick podium, it contained sixty-four mudbrick blocks of which twelve have been uncovered, arranged in three rows of four separated by passages. Rao's claim is supported by the finds that came from the building, which included numerous seals and sealings from bales of goods that had been packed in reeds, woven cloth, and matting. So here at least there is evidence of a major storeroom, probably for manufactured goods intended for trade. The tiny (1.4 ha) settlement of Allahdino, which has been excavated in full, does not have a

Figure 30.

CIRCULAR PLAT-
FORM, HARAPPA

A series of circular platforms made of bricks set on edge were discovered near the so-called "granary" at Harappa and were initially interpreted as places where grain from the "granary" was ground. But many of these platforms had originally been contained within buildings whose bricks had, much later, been robbed, leaving only their foundations. These buildings were not contemporary with each other—so they did not represent a single large-scale operation.

separate citadel, but its buildings seem geared in part to the administration of the surrounding area. The center of the settlement here is dominated by a courtyard around which the buildings were arranged. The north wing of the largest building contained a number of pottery storage vessels, and a separate smaller structure contained others.

THE LOWER TOWN

Public religious and secular architecture is surprisingly elusive in the well-planned lower towns of the Indus settlements, in stark contrast to the prominent temples and palaces in the cities and towns of other primary civilizations. In some Indus settlements, domestic shrines have been identified, so these may have fulfilled the requirements of everyday worship. In the lower town at Mohenjo Daro, however, at least one possible major shrine was found.

Open areas within the settlements could have been places for people to meet or may have had some part in acts of worship. For example, the area immediately in front of the citadel at Dholavira was made into a large open space at the height of the settlement's prosperity and its location suggests it was connected with public activities. Other public rather than private structures include a large building at Mohenjo Daro with a staircase near its entrance leading to an upper floor that Ernest Mackay, who excavated it, believed to have had a number of rooms. He identified this building, situated near a probable gate giving access to the river, as a caravanserai—

a place where visiting merchants would have been accommodated.

Major Indus settlements were generally surrounded by walls with massive and imposing gateways. They must have conveyed a powerful message to a traveler approaching the settlement of solidity and strength in the face of nature. Towers and bastions may have occurred at intervals in the circuit of the wall, and there were generally a number of gateways. These were not designed primarily for defense, although strong wooden gates would have allowed them to be closed against any threat that arose. Guard rooms often flanked the gateway, probably accommodating a gatekeeper who could monitor the flow of people into and out of the city and, if need be, deny them access or egress.

At Harappa there were several separate walled areas. Here and at Mohenjo Daro there were also suburbs that were probably not walled. These have not been excavated, so we do not have datable material from them. We can surmise, however, that the suburbs developed gradually as the area within the city walls became too small to accommodate all who wished to live in the big city. Such extramural development is a familiar feature of towns and cities the world over. At Dholavira, the development of the settlement has been traced from its foundation in Early Indus times (earlier 3rd millennium B.C.) to its abandonment at some time in the 2nd millennium. Although initially only the area later occupied by the citadel was built up at this time, the settlement was surrounded from the beginning by a massive wall 11 meters wide at its base.

From what we know it seems that Mohenjo Daro's lower town, though larger than most, was typical of the general layout of Indus centers. Large main streets crossed the city north-south and east-west, dividing it into residential blocks. In some parts of the city, brick platforms stood outside the houses. These platforms, which were found also in the streets of Kalibangan, could have been places for people to sit and talk. Covered drains ran down the middle of the main streets, part of the impressive system of sanitation for which the civilization is justly famous. As in many modern Indian settlements, to avoid the dust of the main thoroughfares, the houses that lined these streets presented only blank walls—their entrances lay along lanes that ran off the main streets. The impression of the early excavators at Mohenjo Daro and Harappa was that the settlements were laid out in a checkerboard pattern. Although further investigations have shown the layout of the settlements to be less rigid and regular than this, they were nevertheless laid out using some precise criteria. Although the smaller streets do not follow a straight line but often take a crooked course, they are nevertheless composed of straight sections and do not curve or wander. And the plan of the settlements closely follows the cardinal directions, the streets diverging by no more than 2° from these in their orientation. Asko Parpola and a number of other scholars relate this to the astronomical knowledge of the Indus people and to the unknown religious beliefs that must lie behind this. They demonstrate that the cardinal orientation of the streets could have been achieved by aligning them with the set-ting point of particular stars and constellations, notably the bright stars Procyon in Canis Minor and Aldebaran in Arietis and the constellation of the Pleiades, which visibly set in the west in the Indus Period.

HOUSES

Unlike the principal thoroughfares, the lanes often followed a crooked course, accommodating the variation in the size of residential blocks and houses. Wheeler also suggests that the dog-leg arrangement of the lanes would break the force of the prevailing wind. Access to the houses was from these lanes [*see* Color Plate 16]. Although all that survive today are bare mudbrick walls and beaten earth streets, we may imagine settlements that were a blaze of colors—plastered walls decorated with painted designs akin to those on the Indus pottery, complemented by the colors of gorgeous cotton clothing. Doorsteps raised the householder above the level of the lane: it is not unlikely that these would have been decorated, as they often are today, with geometric patterns of red and white in auspicious designs. Neighbors must have stood here to converse, although they could also have looked out of the occasional window, provided with wood or stone lattice grills to allow air into the house and wooden shutters to enable them to be closed to the outside world. Numerous trees were probably planted along the streets—these would have provided shade, both for people engaged in casual conversations and formal meetings, and for men and women to sit and work.

Houses varied considerably in size and complexity. Some were small dwellings, the home of a single family, whereas others were substantial complexes that must have accommodated the large households of important people. Some of the larger houses were also surrounded by a number of smaller units, which suggests the quarters of families who depended upon the central household. Despite the differences in size, the housing in the major Indus settlements was generally of a high standard, suggesting that even the least important individuals led a comfortable existence. There were many features that were common to all or most of the houses. Often, especially in the larger houses, a small janitor's room faced directly on to the house doorway so that the visitor was first confronted and checked out by a doorkeeper. Once within the house, the visitor would turn immediately left or right into a passage that led into the courtyard, the center of the household, as it is in modern India. Here much of the day-to-day business of life would take place—preparing grain, fruit, and vegetables for storage or immediate eating; washing and drying clothes; spinning, weaving, and sewing, cooking, eating, playing, and sleeping. The windows and balconies of the house overlooked the courtyard, integrating the activities within the house with those outside.

A stair led from the courtyard to the upper part of the house—generally one and in some cases two upper stories. The stair probably continued upward to give access to the roof. Constructed of wooden beams covered by matting and plaster, the roof provided an additional place for the family to sit, talk,

and sleep, as they do today. As the upper-story rooms do not survive, we can only guess at what they were—storerooms, personal chambers, offices. At ground level, various rooms opened off the courtyard. These included a small kitchen with a hearth where food and water could be heated. Other rooms were for storage. In some settlements, namely Kalibangan, Banawali and Lothal, the houses also included a room set apart as a domestic shrine, a feature also common in modern Indian homes, although such shrines have not been found at Mohenjo Daro.

Houses of any size at Mohenjo Daro would also have a private well, sturdily constructed of wedge-shaped baked bricks—those without a well of their own, however, were well served by the public water supply [Color Plate 14]. Other cities were less generously provided with wells but also had an excellent drinking water supply in the form of reservoirs and cisterns. The area immediately inside the walls of the great settlement at Dholavira was taken up by enormous reservoirs that covered around a fifth of the enclosed area of the settlement. Water played an important—indeed a vital—part in the life of the Indus people, and their management and use of the domestic and urban water supply were way ahead of those of any other civilization of their time. Not for another 2,000-odd years were hydraulic engineers of this caliber to reemerge, with the Romans in the Old World and Chavin in the New.

One of the most impressive rooms of the Indus house was the bathroom [Figure 28]. Bathing would have followed the custom that still holds today, of pouring water over oneself with a small pot—but in some households there was the refinement of a "shower": a small stair along one side of the bathroom allowed another person to ascend and pour a steady stream of water over the bather. The bathroom floor, constructed of stone or sawn baked bricks, allowed the water to flow off into the efficient drainage system that served the city, via pottery drainpipes or drainage chutes [*see* Color Plate 15]. Wastewater was collected into small open drains in the lanes and from there flowed into the main drainage system. This ran along the main streets, hygienically covered by bricks or stone slabs. At intervals there were inspection covers so that the free flow of the drains could be checked and maintained.

Such drains are a feature of many of the major settlements, including Dholavira and Lothal, but not of all. Kalibangan, for example, had to make do with soakage jars to deal with the water from house drains. The quality of the urban water system may well be an important clue to the status of an Indus settlement: as well as lacking drains, Kalibangan has mainly mudbrick rather than baked brick buildings and a more rural style of houses, a series of features that may indicate that Kalibangan was a provincial town rather than a city, despite its considerable size (11.5 ha as compared to Lothal's 4.8).

The drains also carried off the effluent from the private latrines that were present in almost every house in Harappa and probably in Mohenjo Daro and elsewhere. A large jar set into the floor provided the latrine itself—often just a squatting hole, but some at Mohenjo Daro are furnished with seats for greater comfort. As in modern India, a small waterpot stood by the latrine for washing oneself afterward—occasionally a clumsy user would drop one of these pots into the latrine, where they naturally remained until retrieved by the archaeologists some 5,000 years later! Some of these jars were connected by a drain with the city drainage system and it seems they were periodically emptied, along with the drains and rubbish bins provided on the streets.

WORKSHOPS

The excavations at Mohenjo Daro and Harappa revealed substantial evidence of craft activity within the settlements. Some houses contained small workshops set into one side. Elsewhere there were whole streets of workshops. Here a great diversity of craft activities were carried out, notably bead and bangle-making, potting and figurine making, flint and metal toolmaking, and the manufacture of steatite seals. Large jars set into the floor of one structure may have been for dyeing, an indirect clue to the manufacture of cotton textiles. The early excavators, however, obtained only a general picture of craft activities within these two major settlements, and one of the principal concerns of recent work in both has been to find how craft production was organized and where manufacturing took place. At Mohenjo Daro, the Italian and German teams who are currently intensively investigating the site (from the Oriental Institute IsMEO and from Aachen Technical University, respectively) have carefully analyzed the records of Marshall and his assistants in an attempt to relate the recorded building levels to true stratigraphy so that the artifacts found can be assigned to their true context. And, using surface surveys, they have mapped the distribution of debris from various manufacturing processes—sherds of misfired pottery, fragments of stone and shell, pieces of copper slag—so as to identify areas where goods were produced.

At Harappa, where further excavation has been permitted, the American HARP (Harappa Archaeological Research Project) are investigating workshop areas in detail, using all the modern techniques available. This has shown, for example, that one area of the central mound (mound E) was devoted to the manufacture of pottery throughout the life of the long-lived settlement [*see* Figure 4]. Here there were several kilns, producing a variety of wares. Tools such as spatulas used in making the pottery, clay ready for use, and hematite for coloring the vessels lay scattered around them. The houses that opened off the nearby street were also craft workshops. Other such industrial quarters have been identified in Mohenjo Daro and Harappa and elsewhere. Wheeler excavated a large concentration of furnaces, probably for metalworking, and of circular working floors built of bricks, north of the citadel at Harappa. These were associated with small buildings that Wheeler claimed were barrack-like dwellings comparable to the "coolie-lines" where hired laborers dwelt in British India. We now think they are more likely to have been just workshops, used during the day by workers who returned after work to their homes within the city walls.

Mohenjo Daro and Harappa housed workers in the entire range of Indus crafts—and it is likely that Dholavira, Rakhigarhi, and Ganweriwala did the same. Smaller settlements, such as Chanhu Daro, concentrated on a more restricted range of crafts. For example, Balakot, on the coast near the mouth of the Indus, was a center for processing shells obtained from the coastal waters nearby. In many ways the minor settlements were smaller versions of the major centers. Their streets were aligned in cardinal directions and their houses arranged in blocks. Some local variation occurred. In Gujurat, for instance, stone was used in building instead of the baked brick that was so common in the Indus Valley itself. At Kalibangan, houses opened on to the main street, with entrances large enough to allow a bullock cart to drive into the courtyard. Not all towns had drains along their streets; instead they had sump jars that would have been regularly emptied.

THE CHANGING FACE OF INDUS SETTLEMENTS

Nearly 70 meters of deposits accumulated at Mohenjo Daro between its earliest settlement (probably in the late 4th millennium B.C., though Jansen has recently challenged the notion that there was an Early Indus settlement at this site) and its abandonment in the early centuries of the 2nd millennium B.C., and massive occupation deposits also accumulated at other Indus centers. As yet, however, we know little about the course of development at most of these settlements. It is hoped that the current investigations at Mohenjo Daro will yield some clues to this detailed settlement history. Work over the past decade at Harappa has already shed some light on the changes that occurred through time: details of the crucial transition period from early settlement to Mature Indus city have emerged, showing that this took place over at least a century rather than suddenly, and that the major changes, such as the construction of a massive peripheral wall, took place during the transition period itself rather than at the beginning of the Mature Indus Period. Several stages have also been uncovered in the period of decline. But as yet there is little evidence of major changes during the Mature Indus Period itself.

The situation at Dholavira is similar. In the transitional period, the massive outer wall was extended and reservoirs were constructed along its inner face on the south, west, and north. The walled citadel was extended by the construction beside it. To its north, the residential area immediately was cleared to create an open space that probably had a ceremonial function. A walled residential area was also found to its north. At the end of the transitional period, massive damage (possibly caused by an earthquake) was followed by more substantial reconstruction. A huge "lower town" was created in the eastern part of the enclosed area. This layout apparently remained unchanged until the period of urban decline in the Late Indus Period, when standards fell and parts of the settlement were abandoned.

The evidence is far too scanty to be able to say positively that no urban development took place during the Mature Indus Period. Nevertheless, there seems to be some indication that the planned transformation in the transitional phase fulfilled the requirements of Indus society so well that only minor changes were needed up until the Late Indus Period, when urban life declined.

CITIES AND TOWNS OF THE INDUS

Mohenjo Daro is the best-known and best-studied Indus settlement and is a prime candidate for consideration as a city. It lies in a central location within the Indus realms, halfway between the great northern settlement of Harappa and the sea, close to the great north-south highway provided by the Indus River. From here routes stretched up into the upland region of the Indo-Iranian borderlands, closely tied to the Indus lowlands; to its south lay the rich plains of the Indus and Saraswati. Its credentials as a city and its key importance are reflected in the great diversity of activities within it. Here we find the full range of the crafts practiced by the Indus people. Many inscribed objects including seals, copper tablets and stoneware bangles hint at a well-developed bureaucracy organized from this center. Large, impressive, and sometimes unique public buildings underline the settlement's importance and suggest its role in serving the entire Indus realms. Excavations over the past seventy-five years have exposed a city of massive size, but recent surveys over the surrounding alluvial plain have shown the settlement to have extended over a much larger area, more than 250 ha—and it may have housed as many as 100,000 people. All these lines of evidence suggest that Mohenjo Daro functioned as the principal city of the Indus Civilization.

Mohenjo Daro is the largest settlement, but there are several other settlements of impressive size. Like Mohenjo Daro, Harappa in the north is now known to have covered an area much larger than was previously suspected, probably around 150 ha, with a population of perhaps 60,000. It has been studied almost as intensively as Mohenjo Daro, and the evidence from it has revealed a similar range of industrial activity and similarly impressive public architecture. In addition, like Mohenjo Daro, Harappa has produced a great quantity and variety of inscribed objects, some unique to this settlement.

At the opposite extreme of the Indus realms, Dholavira in Kutch extends over 100 ha. Ganweriwala, centrally located on the fertile Saraswati River south of the Indus, covers 80 ha, as does Rakhigarhi in the east. Recent work at Dholavira has revealed some evidence of its importance, although it has yet to be published properly—at present we have only tantalizing brief summaries, such as those in *Indian Archaeology* where one brief notice of Rakhigarhi is also published. Far more needs to be known about the range of objects in use in Dholavira, the diversity of crafts that took place here, and the nature of its public architecture. Ganweriwala has yet to be excavated at all, although survey work has

shown that it is divided into citadel and lower town, like other major Indus settlements.

J. P. Joshi, a leading Indian archaeologist, claims to have located several other huge settlements within the Saraswati plain—Dhalewan, Gurni Kalan I, Hasanpur II, Lakhmirwala, and Baglian Da Theh, all said to be between 100 and 225 hectares in extent. These are situated in a small area along the Sirhind stream (a tributary of the modern Ghaggar) within 30 km of each other. Their closeness to each other throws doubt on their identification as contemporary cities and other explanations are possible. They could have been occupied not simultaneously but consecutively, for example. Or they could be smaller settlements whose remains have been scattered by the people who occupied the same sites in historical times. Or again, they might be smaller settlements that gradually shifted through the period of their occupation. We don't know—and we won't know unless they are excavated. These sites well illustrate the problems of depending on the surface collection of disturbed material to provide a picture of settlement patterns—it can only go so far.

Harappa, Ganweriwala, Dholavira, and Rakhigarhi may have enjoyed a similar status and role to Mohenjo Daro, acting as regional capitals controlling large areas. The location of these five settlements suggests to a number of scholars that the Indus Civilization can be divided into five domains, each controlled by one of these cities: Mohenjo Daro, the Central (Indus-Sindh) domain; Harappa, the Northern (Punjab) domain; Rakhigarhi, the Eastern domain; Dholavira, the Southern (Gujurat) domain; and Ganweriwala, the

Saraswati (Bahawalpur) domain. This excludes the highland areas to the west that were also part of the Indus domains. However, the mountainous topography, dissected by river valleys, divided this region into many separate zones, rather than uniting it into large regions. These five cities must have provided the economic, administrative, political, and religious focus for their respective regions, which in each case covered an area of more than 100,000 km².

Within these domains, there were other, much smaller centers similarly laid out with separate public and residential areas and cardinally oriented streets. These vary enormously in size, which seems to give little indication of their function—an important caveat when attempting to reconstruct settlement hierarchy on the basis of surveys. For example, Kalibangan, at 11.5 ha, has a substantial citadel mound, serving the administrative and ritual needs of its region, but the lower town has a somewhat rural air, with its unpaved streets, sump jars instead of drains, and houses with provision for parking carts. On the other hand, Lothal, which is only 4.8 ha in size, has not only a highly organized citadel mound with a substantial warehouse but also drains, paved streets, the huge water tank known as the "dock" (see Chapter 7), and a great variety of craft workshops. Tiny Allahdino, a mere 1.4 ha, seems largely composed of administrative buildings. Many of the undifferentiated rural settlements of peasant huts are many times larger than Allahdino—the 6-ha farming village of Kanewal, for example, or the 4-ha pastoral camp of Nesadi.

A considerable number of the excavated settlements cannot have been self-sufficient, but must have existed as pieces of a huge jigsaw, their specialized functions serving a large community and in some cases the whole civilization. At the top of the five-city settlement hierarchy sits Mohenjo Daro. Many scholars have drawn attention to the location of Harappa, not at the center of a settled region but on its periphery. Harappa served, therefore, not only as the administrative, industrial, and religious center for the agricultural area to its south and for the pastoral groups moving around in its hinterland, but also as the entry and control point for a range of materials imported from the areas to its north. This argues that its role was as part of a larger polity, the integrated state.

Among the other types of settlement that can be identified are regional towns such as Kalibangan, providing administrative and other services for their region; towns like Lothal combining these roles with craft production on a huge scale, for internal consumption or external trade; specialized industrial settlements like Nageshwar, processing local raw materials; tiny centers like Allahdino providing limited administrative and other services for a small area, and presumably answerable to the authorities in a larger town; and farming villages and pastoral camps, like Kanewal and Nesadi. As excavations continue, the variety of Indus settlements multiplies—but despite their differences, they are united by their shared culture, including many architectural features, and by their contribution to the unified state from which they all benefited.

CHAPTER SIX

INDUS RELIGION

THE ENIGMA OF THE INDUS RELIGION

Many of the finest creations of early societies have been designed for the gods and put economic, political, and social power in the hands of their representatives. In many civilizations the supreme authority was invested in religious leaders. In those states where kings ruled, the priesthood also enjoyed very great power, giving or withholding divine sanction (in medieval Europe, for example). Alternatively, the king was often the representative of the gods (as in a number of Central and South American civilizations).

Knowledge of the nature of Indus religion and the role it played in Indus life, therefore, is crucial to understanding how the Indus Civilization worked. From the study of Indus citadel mounds and their buildings, it seems that religion was of great importance to the Indus people. Many who have studied the civilization have suggested that it was a theocracy. But remarkably little tangible evidence survives of the religious practices and beliefs of the Indus people. A number of objects, buildings, and images seem highly likely to have been connected with the Indus religion, but we do not know anything about the religious beliefs and practices behind them.

There are some clues to be found in the religious practices, iconography ,and beliefs of cultures contemporary with the Indus Civilization, such as Mesopotamia, and those of later Indian cultures. Helpful though this may be in some ways, we must be cautious in assuming shared beliefs and practices between the Indus Civilization and its contemporaries and successors.

THE DIVERSITY OF INDUS RELIGIOUS STRUCTURES

Buildings in or on which to worship and glorify the gods are an important feature of civilized societies the world over. Investigations of the early cities of Mesopotamia have revealed long sequences of temples, tracing back from the magnificent complexes of the late 3rd mil-

Figure 31.

"PRIEST-KING" SCULPTURE, MOHENJO DARO— REAR VIEW

Unlike most sculptures and other representations of men, this figure does not wear his hair in a double bun, which would normally be held in place by the fillet around the head. Instead the back is flat and the hair is not shown, indicating that originally this area was covered— probably by an elaborate headdress. Perhaps a buffalo-horned headdress, like those crowning the "proto-Shiva" deity on many seals, could have been placed on this sculpture on ceremonial occasions such as religious festivals.

TREFOILS

The garment of the Priest-King sculpture found at Mohenjo Daro is decorated with trefoils that had once held a red pigment [Figure 31]. Asko Parpola has made a particular study of the multilayered symbolism of these trefoils and the garment itself. He notes parallels with Mesopotamian and Central Asian art where these signs decorated figurines of bulls, a creature with sacred connections. In Mesopotamia such trefoils symbolized stars, and cloaks decorated with them were known as "sky-garments" and were worn by both gods and priest-kings. A similar robe, studded with stars or celestial raindrops, is worn by the water god Varuna in the later Indian Vedic texts and here they also represent the thousand eyes by which the god views all that passes in the world. This robe was also mentioned in the *Vedas* as being worn by kings during their consecration. Parpola also argues that the trefoil could represent the three-lobed hearth, used not only in the home but also in Vedic sacrifices, and the vulva or womb— the *yoni,* symbol of the goddess Durga and counterpart to the *lingam,* symbol of Shiva. In this context, trefoils decorate a finely polished red stone stand from Mohenjo Daro that had probably originally supported a lingam.

lennium B.C., with their ziggurat towers, to the humble shrines of 3,000 years before. Every civilization has its own distinctive form of shrine or temple, but in general it is possible to recognize them and to distinguish them from domestic architecture. So where are those of the Indus Civilization? We do not know.

Since the days of Marshall's first investigations of the Indus cities, people have been searching for the religious monuments of the Indus Civilization. What they have found has been very puzzling. There have been few buildings that suggest a religious function— the Great Bath at Mohenjo Daro has always seemed a good candidate and a few other buildings also seem possibilities. Also, there is little consistency, the structures identified as possibly religious in one city or town being different from those of others—a striking contrast to the cultural uniformity indicated by many other aspects of the Indus Civilization, but one that finds echoes in the diversity of later Indian beliefs and practices.

In the lower town at Mohenjo Daro, one building stands out from others. It has been suggested that this was a temple. A double doorway leads into a passage, between two blocks of rooms, the left-hand one of which had no access into the passage or the rest of the complex but which may nevertheless be related. At the end of the passage is a courtyard in which there is a circular brick surround. It is likely that this once contained a tree, probably one with sacred significance. From this courtyard two staircases facing each other lead up to a second, raised courtyard, off which open a number of rooms, some leading into others.

This building is unusual in a number of ways, in addition to its unique layout. Nowhere within it is there a well, a real rarity in this city and one that emphasizes a nondomestic role. The objects that were found within it were not the usual range of domestic utensils, which would generally include a wide selection of different pots and stone and metal tools. This building, in contrast, contained several pieces of stone sculpture depicting seated men—extremely rare in Mohenjo Daro and almost unknown in other cities—as well as a large number of seals, all bearing the same unicorn motif, many small pottery vessels, terracotta figurines, and jewelry. These are all types of object that might easily have been offerings.

Other buildings in Mohenjo Daro have less convincingly been identified as religious structures, although there is certainly a possibility that they were shrines. And in other cities and towns, similar difficulties have been encountered in the search for Indus temples. The citadels, however, seem likely to have held sacred architecture. We can surmise, for instance, that the large halls in the citadels at Mohenjo Daro, Harappa, and elsewhere were public buildings in which ceremonies or meetings took place that could have been religious or secular.

WATER

Ascending the grand staircase into the citadel at Mohenjo Daro, visitors entered the complex. The visitors were probably required to purify themselves in the bathroom at the top of the stair. From here a zigzag route led into the heart of the complex: along a street, turning to enter one of the two doors of the building on one's left, and passing through an antechamber into the pillared courtyard within which lay the Great Bath [Color Plate 17]. This is a large rectangular basin, carefully constructed so as to be watertight. An outer baked brick shell held an inner wall, with mudbrick packing between them. Within this a thick layer of bitumen (natural tar) provided a seal within which the bath was constructed of closely fitted bricks placed on edge, the gaps between them filled with gypsum plaster. Steps led down from the courtyard to a ledge running across each end of the bath and thence down into the water.

Scholars seem by and large united in considering that this was a religious structure, connected with ritual bathing. Ritual purification has played a key role in religion in the Indian subcontinent over the last 2,500 years and must presumably have done so 2,000 years earlier. Clockwise circumambulation (pradakshina) has been an important form of worship in the subcontinent for several millennia and it is possible that the colonnade was used to perform this act of worship around the Great Bath. A large well lay in a room to the east of the colonnade while around the east and northern sides were a series of bathrooms, where perhaps the worshipper might ritually wash before entering the bath itself.

Although the Great Bath is unique (and probably uniquely holy to the Indus people), the citadels of many towns and cities, such as Lothal and Kalibangan, also had a series of bathrooms. As I showed in the previous chapter, fine bathrooms that connected to an excellent and efficient drainage system were a feature of many Indus houses, in striking contrast to the sanitary arrangements of other societies of the time. It therefore seems reasonable to see here a concern with cleanliness that went beyond the needs of hygiene—an indication that the notion of ritual purity, so important an element of Indian religion, was already a feature of the Indus belief system. As Dumont argued in *Homo Hierarchicus,* his famous study of the caste system, contact with organic life in its many forms introduces ritual pollution, and bathing can remove this in many cases. Given its vital role in sustaining life and supporting agriculture in both the Indus-Saraswati plains and the mountains to their northwest, water might be expected to have played an important role in Indus religion, even without its ritually purifying properties.

FIRE

Fire is an element of almost equal importance to water, both in everyday life and as an agent of ritual purification in Indian religion. Fire was a key element in the religion of the Indo-Aryans who entered the subcontinent during the 2nd millennium B.C. The embodiment of the god Agni, fire represented the sun, light, and heat and played a central role in sacrifices. Fire might therefore have been an addition to Indian religion in the 2nd millennium—but the evidence suggests that it also previously had a religious role in Indus life. At Kalibangan, Lothal, Banawali, and Rakhigarhi, and probably in other towns and cities, bathing facilities on the citadels were associated with what are taken to be sacred hearths (fire altars). At Kalibangan these consisted of a row of seven (a significant number in later Indian religion) clay-lined pits in which charcoal and ash were found, along with clay stele perhaps representing the lingam (sacred phallus) and examples of the enigmatic terracotta "cakes"—small triangular objects of baked brick whose function is still unknown. On another platform at Kalibangan, a single fire altar was found alongside a rectangular pit containing antlers and the bones of cattle, presumably from animal sacrifices. In the lower town here, many of the houses also had a room containing a fire altar and therefore presumably set aside as a domestic shrine. Many Indian houses today also have their own shrine, where incense is burned and grain, fruit, and flowers are offered to the gods.

SACRED IMAGES

Household shrines today may contain an image of one of the gods, whereas temples are the house of massive statues of the deity. Hindu religion, however, does not regard these images as embodiments of the gods themselves so much as a focus for devotions and as a housing within which the god may choose to manifest him- or herself. Is it possible to identify any comparable images of deities among the artistic creations of the Indus people?

The three-dimensional artwork of the Indus Civilization falls into two main groups. There are numerous terracotta figurines of people and animals and there are a very few pieces of sculpture, in stone or bronze. Of course there were also very probably figures in wood that have perished. The rarity of stone statuary should perhaps not surprise us because the use of stone for sculpture was also rare or absent in later art up until the reign of Ashoka in the 3rd century B.C.

Sculptures have been found in only a few of the cities, notably Mohenjo Daro. The usual subject of the stone sculptures was a seated or half-kneeling male figure wearing a robe that left the right shoulder exposed, similar to the style of dress of later Buddhist monks. Where the head survives, the figure is generally bearded and wears a headband, probably made of gold because thin gold bands with holes for a thread to tie them have been found at Mohenjo Daro and elsewhere [Color Plate 2]. The figure's hair is generally neatly arranged and may be braided. It is often tied in a double bun—an arrangement of long hair in a large bun divided in two by a ribbon or fillet worn round the head [*see* Figure 43]. This style is also common on representations of men on seals and is quite widespread outside the subcontinent, being clearly depicted, for example, on the superb mid–3rd millennium B.C. gold helmet of Meskalamdug from the Royal Graves at Ur in Mesopotamia. The finest example of these Indus sculptures is the torso known as the "Priest-King," a calm, austere figure, wearing a robe covered with trefoils that originally held a red paste [Color Plate 3]. The garment on which this is modeled was probably sewn with appliqués in some fine material. Asko Parpola believes these trefoils to have had

COMPOSITE BEASTS

One of the rare Indus stone sculptures depicts a curious hybrid animal—a bull with an elephant's trunk and the horns of a ram. Other composite creatures are shown on several seals and in terracotta figurines from Nausharo. Some of these combine the heads and bodies of three creatures that are com-monly found elsewhere in Indus and later Indian religious iconography—the water buffalo, the tiger, and the elephant [*see* Color Plate 6]. Other examples incorporate features of Markhor goats and antelopes [*see* Figure 32]. One example has a cobra instead of a tail—another creature steeped in religious significance in India.

several layers of religious significance, and the design crops up again on stone stands that may once have held sacred stone phalli. Although some people have suggested that these sculptures are cult images, a greater proportion of scholars now consider them to be portraits of rulers or important individuals. On the other hand, it is possible, as in other cultures, that both meanings are intended, the figure showing the ruler in the guise of the deity.

Two small sculptures from Harappa, in contrast, depict a naked male, carved in a very naturalistic style—very different in feel to other Indus art and thought by some scholars to be intrusive pieces of considerably later date. One is clearly dancing, while the other, which is broken, also appears to be moving. They can, perhaps, be considered alongside the famous bronze figure of a dancing girl from Mohenjo Daro, and could equally be

Figure 32.

SEAL,
MOHENJO DARO

*One of the rare
representations of
composite beasts,
this seal portrays an
animal with three
heads, those of a goat,
an antelope, and a
bull, all animals that
feature repeatedly in
scenes and images
that probably have a
religious context.*

depictions of individuals engaged in a dance that could well be ritual in nature, or of gods, perhaps a parallel to the later images of Shiva Nataraja (Lord of the Dance), dancing the destruction of the universe.

Finally there are a few examples of animals sculpted in stone or cast in bronze, including several rams and a strange composite beast [Figure 32]. Given the rarity of Indus sculptures and the exceptional quality of most of them, it is clear that they were of some considerable significance, but whether this significance was religious or not is unknown.

We are probably on firmer ground with the remaining examples of Indus artwork: the figurines and seals. Figurines are ubiquitous and it has often been suggested that they were toys [Figure 35]. Some at least, however, are likely to have served originally as votive offerings, their role in ritual being confined to the ceremony for which they were made or obtained, after which they may have been discarded, to be picked up and played with by children. Almost every creature that the Indus people were familiar with is to be seen here as figurines or images on seals—from fishes and hares to elephants and rhinos [Figure 33]. Other creatures are also represented that have no counterpart in the real world. Among these are "unicorns," a creature frequently depicted on the seals, which occasionally turn up in the form of a figurine. These unicorns, and occasionally other animals, were shown on the seals facing a curious object consisting of a stick bearing a hemispherical bowl surmounted by a ridged cylinder [*see* Figure 45]. No one knows what this is but there has been plenty of speculation—an incense burner, an offering stand, a sacred brazier? One intriguing suggestion is that it was a filter for preparing the sacred drink, soma, that is mentioned in the religious texts of the later Indo-Aryans—but no one knows what that was either and whether it was made from a plant native to the sub-

continent, so the suggestion does not get us much further forward. Whatever the object was—and it also is found carved in the round in ivory—it is usually interpreted as a ritual object.

BULL FIGURINES

Massive bulls are a popular subject for figurines, perhaps marking the beginning of the tradition of sacred cattle in the subcontinent [Figure 34]. On the other hand, the presence of cattle bones in the fire altars, implying their sacrifice, indicates that the sacredness of cattle had not yet developed to the stage where cattle were protected. Similarly the sacrifice of cattle shows that the notion of massive pollution coming from contact with

Figure 33.

RHINOCEROS FIGURINE, HARAPPA

Powerful beasts such as the rhino, but also including the tiger, elephant, and bull, played an important role in the imagery of the Indus people. Oftentimes, these animals are depicted in what appears to be sacred contexts. But it is also possible this little figurine was a toy or the Indus version of a knickknack.

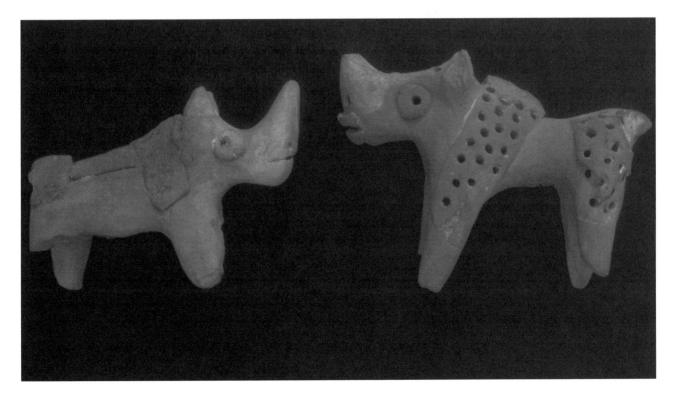

Figure 34.

BULL FIGURINE,
HARAPPA

*Many of the Indus
figurines depict
animals, giving a
lively picture of the
domestic and wild
fauna that inhabited
the world of the Indus
people. Although
many of the Indus
cattle were zebus,
descendants of the
indigenous Indian
Bos namadicus,
others were humpless
species like this
splendid bull.*

dead cattle (making leather-workers among the most ritually polluted members of society) had also not developed.

FEMALE FIGURINES

Female figurines had been made in the Indo-Iranian borderlands for thousands of years and continued to be popular in later millennia when they represented mother goddesses who played an important part in folk religion [*see* Figure 12]. In more recent times, such figurines have been used in rituals connected with fertility—to bring about conception, to protect in childbirth, to guard the health of children—and the Indus figurines similarly reflect such preoccupations, with their emphasis on generous breasts and

wide hips, and an occasional suckling baby. The less common male figures also link with fertility because they emphasize the phallus, as do the male animals that are represented.

DEITIES

Modern Indian religion is the result of many transformations and is manifest in many different ways in different areas or among different groups. Stark contrasts exist—between extremes of asceticism and tantric indulgence, between animal sacrifice and concern to protect the lives of even the smallest creature, between devotion to a single deity and worship of a multiplicity of gods, between the benign and malignant aspects of individual deities. Nevertheless, beneath this surface flows a common stream: the many gods are but aspects of a single supreme power, encompassing everything within the universe, good and bad. Nature plays an important part in mediating between the human and the divine, so many plants and animals are venerated. Among these are cobras and trees, particularly pipal, banyan, acacia, and neem. Looking at the seals made by the Indus people we can see that these trees were already attracting such veneration. Many seals depict these trees, particularly pipal and banyan, containing figures that can be identified as gods and goddesses [*see* Color plate 10]. Pipal leaves had been a familiar decoration on pottery of the Indus region and the Indo-Iranian borderlands since much earlier times, often combined with the horns of bulls or water buffaloes, and together they

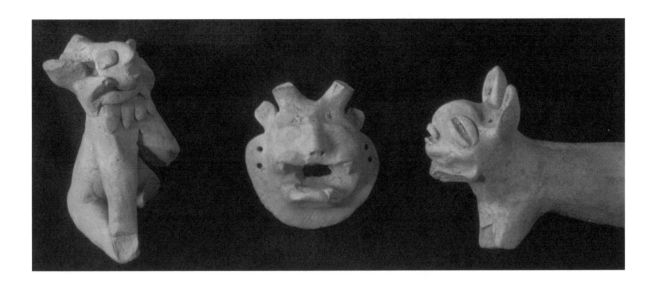

form headdresses worn by many of these deities [Figure 37 and see below]. Sometimes the trees are shown standing in a pot or railing, as sacred trees were protected in later times—and here we may recall the brick ring in the supposed shrine at Mohenjo Daro, which could well have protected such a tree.

Other seals show scenes in which a figure sits in a tree while a tiger prowls below. Some of the terracotta figurines depict tigers or other felines [Figure 36]. Tiger stripes are shown on some of the deities and there are also composite beasts of which the tiger forms a principal element [Color Plate 6]. Tigers also appear in scenes of combat between man and beast, as do water buffaloes, and they are also matched against each other. It would seem that these two wild and magnificent creatures played a major and balancing role in the iconography of the Indus Civilization, both individually and in combination. Both appear in later Indian religion, as vehicles for deities, as manifestations of gods in their more terrible forms, and as their opponents—for instance, the goddess Chamundi riding a tiger and slaying the buffalo demon, Mahisasura.

The Indus seals depict a number of scenes showing figures that are remarkably similar to later deities. Principal among these is one interpreted as the great god Shiva, depicted in various roles, as Lord of the Wild Beasts or as Nataraja, the Lord of the Dance. Shiva is generally shown wearing buffalo horns, which sometimes form a trident headdress. Many representations show this figure seated in a yogic position. Unlike later representations of Shiva and of other important religious figures such as the Buddha, who generally sit in the lotus position adopted for meditation, these Indus figures are seated in a much more difficult position with the legs folded beneath the body and the feet pointing downward—the mulabandasana position [Color Plate 11]. Shiva is later regarded as the lord of Yoga, among his many roles. By the 1st millennium B.C. Shiva was established as one of the major gods, but no trace of his worship is to be found in the earliest texts of the Indo-Aryans who invaded the northwest in

Figure 35.

FIGURINES,

HARAPPA

These three terracotta figurines combine human and animal features and were probably representations of religious or mythological figures familiar to their Indus audience. The feline figurine with a woman's face and headdress, on the left, had a hole in its base to allow it to be held on a stick. Such figurines may have been used as puppets to retell legendary stories in the context of religious ceremonies, or just for entertainment.

the 2nd millennium B.C. and who established military dominance over the indigenous groups they encountered. This adds weight to the suggestion that Shiva originated in the horned deity of the Indus folk. His worship is intimately connected with fertility, and he is often represented by a lingam. Objects that could be interpreted as lingams have been found in Indus cities, including stone stele in the fire altars of Kalibangan, and in some cases they were mounted on a stone pedestal, thought to represent the yoni (vulva or womb), sometimes decorated with the same trefoil pattern that adorned the robe of the Priest King [*see* Figure 31].

In his attempts to decipher the Indus script via plausible interpretations of some individual signs (see Chapter 8), Asko Parpola has studied the iconography of the Indus seals in great detail. He has uncovered a strong interest by the Indus people in the stars, planets, and other heavenly bodies and their movements, which seem to have had considerable significance in Indus religion. Astral deities and mythology are a feature of the later religion of the subcontinent. Comparison with the known movements of the stars and planets show that the star calendar used in Vedic times since at least 1000 B.C. was compiled around 2300 B.C. The calendar was not introduced into India by the Indo-Aryans, which indicates that it was already in use in the Indian subcontinent and was therefore that of the Indus people. Among the principal heavenly bodies that Parpola considered important to the Indus people were Saturn, Venus, the North Star, the Great Bear, and the Pleiades.

A famous seal from Mohenjo Daro allows Parpola to develop his theme in some detail [Color Plate 10]. Here we have a goddess, her divinity indicated by her headdress, standing within a pipal tree. Before her kneels a male worshipper with before him an offering (identified by a number of scholars as a severed head, although this is not entirely clear) and a large ram behind. In the foreground, seven figures (probably female) walk hand in hand in procession. Parpola identifies the goddess as Durga (present in the heavens as Venus or Aldebaran), to whom human sacrifices were made until quite recently, and the kneeling figure is identified as the youthful god known variously as Skanda, Rudra, or Kumara, who is bound to the goddess in a sacred marriage that will culminate in his sacrifice. Rudra was nursed in his youth by the wives of the Seven Sages (who appear in the heavens as the stars of the Great Bear) and these may be the seven ladies in procession along the front of the scene—they appear among the stars as the Pleiades. Such reconstructions might be stretching the evidence too far, but they provide an important first step in attempting to reconstruct something of the religious beliefs of the Indus people. Half a world and 3,000 years away, similar detailed consideration of the known position of constellations and the later belief systems of the local people have been instrumental in gaining an insight into the religion and cosmology of the Maya Civilization, underlining the value of such exercises.

EXTERNAL CLUES

Although many features of modern Hindu belief and practice can plausibly be traced back to what we see in the Indus evidence, suggesting continuities, other insights come from comparisons with the sacred imagery of contemporary cultures in Western Asia, especially Sumer and its neighbor Elam. A frequent scene in the artwork and iconography of this area is a struggle between a hero or god and two ferocious wild animals. The hero wrestles with a pair of bulls or lions, or the animals themselves wrestle, an upright bull against a pair of lions, or a lion against two bulls. While the Indus versions are faithful to the form of these contest scenes, the bulls are replaced by water buffaloes and the lions by tigers, showing how the people of the Indus Valley had reinterpreted and adapted aspects of the

Figure 37.

MOLDED TABLET, HARAPPA

This scene on one face of a molded tablet presumably depicts a religious story whose subject matter would be well known to its Indus audience. On the left, a figure spears a ferocious buffalo, watched by a buffalo-horned deity, generally interpreted as "proto-Shiva" seated in a yogic posture.

mythology and religious beliefs common to the whole vast Western Asiatic region [*see* Figure 37]. This conflict scene has been interpreted by Western Asiatic scholars as a representation of the eternal opposition between natural forces—between day and night, sun and moon, summer and winter, heat and cold, fire and water, life and death. In the Indian context, given the association of tigers with goddesses, buffaloes with gods, one might add the antithesis of male and female principles to this list of binary cosmic oppositions. Again within the same geographical area the iconography includes a variety of imaginary beasts. The Indian examples differ from those farther to the west in incorporating Indian creatures such as elephants among the elements that compose such creatures.

FUNERARY RITES

Archaeologists often use burials as an important source of inferences about religion. But the paucity of Indus religious structures and artwork is matched by the rarity of burials found at Indus sites. In part this is due to accidents of discovery, because flat graves buried beneath accumulations of alluvium are harder to locate than the ruins of substantial brick buildings. It seems particularly surprising, however, that to date there have been no burials or cemeteries discovered that stand out by the lavishness of their funerary structures or the wealth of their grave goods and which could be thought to represent the rulers of Indus society.

Wheeler excavated a cemetery (R-37) at Harappa and recent excavations have continued to investigate the graves here. Cemeteries were also excavated at Kalibangan, Lothal, and Dholavira. Bodies were generally placed in an oval or rectangular pit. Sometimes this had a lining of mudbricks or contained a wooden coffin. Although usually the wood preserved only as a stain, Wheeler was able to identify one as being made of rosewood with a deodar (cedar) lid. The body was laid in the grave fully extended, with the head to the north, feet to the south, the direction associated in later Indian religion with Yama, the god of death. At Kalibangan a layer of clay was placed on the floor of the grave before the body was buried. Sometimes the deceased was wrapped in a cloth or reed shroud and generally still had the ornaments that had been worn in life—women with shell bangles on both arms or just their left, anklets of steatite beads, and a stone amulet around their neck, men and women with a few beads tied on a thread at wrist or waist. A number of pots were buried with them, sometimes arranged beneath the body [Figure 38]. Although no trace now survives, we may reasonably assume that these contained food and drink. In some cases, the deceased wore more elaborate and abundant jewelry—long bead necklaces, sometimes including gold beads, worn around the neck or used to tie up the hair—and some of the women were buried with a copper mirror.

In some cases the graves were marked by a low mound of earth or, in one instance, mud bricks. At Kalibangan, the graves were neatly arranged in groups of six to eight and

each was associated with a "cenotaph," a rectangular or oval pit that was left open and in which a number of pots were placed. This may perhaps be interpreted as an offering place belonging to an individual family. A similar situation may have existed at Dholavira, where one conventional burial was uncovered along with four circular pits marked by cairns and two stone-lined rectangular pits. These contained pottery but no bodies. The arrangement of burials in the cemeteries at Harappa and Lothal was much more haphazard than at Kalibangan, later burials often cutting and disturbing those already buried, something that seems to have been rare at Kalibangan. Scant respect was accorded to the dead when their graves were disturbed—

jewelry was sometimes taken from them, and broken pottery, old bones, and half-decomposed corpses were removed and thrown into pits nearby [Color Plate 25]. In the northern part of the Kalibangan cemetery there were circular pits containing pottery and collected disarticulated bones, either from disturbed graves or representing a separate rite of disposal.

All the cemeteries that have been located lie outside the walled areas of the towns and cities. In contrast, toward the end of the Indus Civilization, when civic standards were breaking down, burials of a very different nature were made actually in the heart of Mohenjo Daro. Instead of carefully placing the body in a grave with its possessions, corpses were disposed of higgledy-piggledy in

Figure 38.

UNDECORATED POTTERY, HARAPPA

Toward the end of the Indus Period, the citizens of Harappa buried their dead with undecorated pottery, like the vessels shown here. On occasion, they covered painted pots with a plain red slip, hiding the decoration.

abandoned streets or empty houses. These are Wheeler's famous "massacre" victims—not, we now know, killed by invaders, but perhaps the casualties of disease [*see* Figure 56]. Where the bones bear witness to violence in one or two cases, these were blows that the victims had survived. Malaria, however, seems to have been endemic, not surprising in a society that made so much use of water, the breeding ground for malarial mosquitoes.

The Indus burial practices have provided some tantalizing clues about their religious beliefs. Burials were made in separate cemeteries outside the city, in which individuals were carefully placed wearing the clothing and ornaments that distinguished their place in society (see Chapter 7). Sometimes they were placed on a layer of pots or of clay soil that separated them from the ground, a practice that was still in use in some of the South Indian megaliths 2,000 years later. They were accompanied by offerings probably of food and drink, in pottery vessels [*see* Figure 38]. Where disease or civic breakdown disrupted life, the rites were not performed and individuals were disposed of in a perfunctory manner—but the decline of the civilization did not generally affect burial practices, as we see the continuation of the traditional extended burials at Harappa in the lower level of cemetery H, dating from the final period of the city.

Except in unusual circumstances, therefore, it was clearly important that the Indus individual was laid to rest in the appropriate manner. Once this had been done, however, it did not seem to matter what happened to the body and its accompanying offerings after-

ward, given the way bones, pots, personal ornaments, and even incompletely decayed bodies were treated when they were encountered in digging a new grave. Perhaps the Indus people believed that the transition to the afterlife required a rite of passage that involved burial, but that after this was performed, the soul had departed and had no further use for its bodily remains. This presents a marked contrast to the beliefs of the Egyptians of the same period who were evolving elaborate techniques to mummify and preserve the bodies of their dead—but may find some echo in contemporary Mesopotamia, where it was a regular practice to dig into graves and remove and "recycle" the valuable offerings placed in them. Indus burial rites contrast with the classic Hindu rite of cremation—but although this became widespread during the 1st millennium B.C., it is by no means the only way of disposing of the dead practiced in India, where a great diversity of rites are still in use.

EVOLUTION OF INDUS RELIGION

Diversity characterizes Indian religion in general, where the worship of Shiva and Vishnu, rebirth, and the quest for nirvana underlie a bewildering diversity of local cults and practices associated with different castes or groups. In part this has been built up through the ages, with new ideas being introduced by many groups of historically attested outsiders who have invaded the Indian subcontinent and have been absorbed, starting with the Indo-Aryans during the 2nd millennium B.C. Other developments such as Buddhism and Jainism are of indigenous inspiration. Practices and beliefs and devotion to the worship of particular deities are strongly linked to group identity, and changes in religious adherence and practice have often been associated with the attempt by a particular group to advance their position in the caste hierarchy.

Going back into the Indus Period, we should expect considerable diversity already to be present, for the people of the Indus Civ-ilization not only included the descendants of the hunter-gatherer peoples of the plains and the pastoralists and farmers of the hills, but had also been linked for millennia with the inhabitants of the great sweep of the Iranian plateau and its neighbors in Mesopotamia and Central Asia. To these, 3rd-millennium B.C., sea trade added the peoples of the Persian Gulf.

As with so many other aspects of Indus life, what we can confidently say about Indus religion is extremely limited and everything else is speculation based on tenuous clues. Burial practices that are consistent throughout the Indus realms suggest an underlying and generally held belief with regard to death and the afterlife—though we cannot say what this belief may have been. Mother goddess figurines and venerated trees and animals show the strength of the folk cults that thrived throughout Indian history. The god and goddess that repeatedly appear on seals suggest the cult of Shiva or at least a god with many of his attributes, along with his female counter-

part, the prototype of Durga—so we can focus on looking for clues from our knowledge of these deities in later times to build some picture of Indus beliefs and practices.

An unexpected feature of Indus worship has been the discovery, doubted at first but repeated now at many sites including the recent excavations at Rakhigarhi, of the sacrificial hearths known as fire altars. Fire altars are a central feature of the religion of the Indo-Aryans, and their apparent discovery in the Indus Civilization has fueled the cause of those who are convinced—wrongly, as I and many other scholars believe—that the Indus people were also Indo-Aryans, while it has proved an embarrassment to those who don't support this view. But are the Indus hearths really fire altars in the Vedic sense? The similarities have been overemphasized and the shared elements of fire and animal sacrifice are too common, being found in many religions, to be a culturally diagnostic link.

More significant are the presence within the Indus hearths of clay stelae and their association with bathing platforms. The multiplicity of bathing facilities, from the Great Bath at Mohenjo Daro, through the bathrooms on every citadel mound to the private bathrooms in the houses, with their excellent drains carrying off the used water, seem a keynote of the Indus Civilization. Water is associated in Indian religion with purification, not physical cleansing but the removal of ritual pollution. Its importance here may be giving us a vital clue not only to Indus religion but also to understanding the nature of Indus society—and I shall follow up this clue in the next chapter.

CHAPTER SEVEN

INDUS SOCIETY

THE MEANING OF SOCIETY

Humans do not exist in isolation—they live in societies in which everyone has to cope with other people, finding ways to manage interactions. As societies grow larger, so the complexity of the organization they require also grows. Leaders become rulers—kings or archpriests—supported by a hierarchy of lesser leaders or bureaucrats with responsibility for organizing parts of the society; tax collectors, census takers, magistrates, overseers, local lords and administrators, parish priests, and the like. Societies that fail to evolve the means to organize themselves collapse into anarchy and fall victim to internal conflicts or external aggressors.

The very existence of a civilization—at the most basic level, a very large number of people densely packed within a substantial region—implies that that society has successfully devised ways of organizing its members. So we do not need to ask whether the Indus Civilization was organized—this is a sine qua non—but how it was organized. In a very real sense, the nature of its organization reveals the nature of the society.

A HYPOTHETICAL PICTURE

The Indus Civilization seems clearly to have been a united, single society, rather than a federation of similar communities—an empire rather than a collection of city-states, although not all scholars agree with this view. At the apex of Indus society was a ruler sanctioned by the gods—perhaps the Priest-King of the famous sculpture. On current evidence the centrally located city of Mohenjo Daro, with its elaborate ritual bath, could well have been the seat of government and place of residence of the ruler and his immediate circle. But if in the future excavations are conducted at Ganweriwala, centrally located in the densely settled Saraswati

Figure 39.

RUINS AT
MOHENJO DARO
*It is easy to imagine
that Mohenjo Daro,
the largest known
Indus city, was the
capital of a highly
structured civiliza-
tion. The fact is that
evidence for whether
this city, or any other
major site, was the
seat of government
or the center of
religious activity is
almost exclusively
circumstantial.*

plain, it is possible that this could turn out to have been the administrative heart of the civilization. If that proves to be the case, Mohenjo Daro's role was as center of greatest holiness and place of pilgrimage. Within each of the cities lesser priests and perhaps merchants probably formed a hierarchy and bureaucracy through whom a high proportion of the products of every craft worker would be gathered in as tax and other goods and necessities issued. Each city and town would have a major priest as local ruler, to whom the products of the city would be conveyed for local distribution as appropriate. The local priests would also have acted as local tax collectors, ensuring the supply of local specialist goods and raw materials needed to keep the system operating. Rather than being seen overtly as taxes, these goods and materials were probably collected as compulsory offerings, owed to the gods at appropriate times and seasons, and perhaps surrendered in the context of festivals.

THE UNIFORMITY OF INDUS CULTURE

Indus religious structures and practices are diverse. This probably reflects the heterogeneity of the people who lived in the Indus realms and their beliefs. Heterogeneity of beliefs and practices is a familiar feature of many societies across the globe, so it would not be surprising if each sector of the Indus community had its own deities and ways of worship.

This reflection of the heterogeneous makeup of Indus society contrasts strongly with the evidence of the essential unity of its organization, a unity that can be seen in the uniformity of material culture throughout the Indus realms. In the periods before and after the Indus Civilization, tools were generally made from local raw materials, but the Indus people had only the best. High-quality goods were produced in large quantities from such materials and were widely distributed, being found in every urban center, from huge cities like Mohenjo Daro to tiny towns like Balakot and even in the houses of farmers in the few villages that have been excavated. The same styles are found throughout the Indus realms. Many everyday objects were made locally in every town, following remarkably standardized designs. More specialized products, made from raw materials that were not readily available or whose manufacture required more highly developed skills of craftsmanship, such as fine painted pottery or carved steatite seals, were made only in the major centers but were widely distributed. Individual towns might also be involved in the initial processing of local raw materials, but again, the finished products ended up in households over a wide area.

THE ORGANIZATION OF INDUS SOCIETY

Uniformity in household objects and their efficient distribution argues for a well-organized bureaucracy under some type of central or federal control. Another clue lies in the standardized system of weights and measures, used throughout the civilization. The weights were made of stone, and were generally cubical in shape [*see* Color Plate 19]. However, fine jasper or agate weights in the form of truncated spheres also occur. The system of weights was not only uniform throughout the Indus Civilization, but also endured after its decline, giving rise to the weight system used in historical times, one that is still used in the subcontinent today.

The most common Indus weight was equivalent to about 13.7 grams. Taking this as the basic unit the Indus people used smaller weights that were $\frac{1}{16}$, $\frac{1}{8}$, $\frac{1}{4}$, and $\frac{1}{2}$ of this basic unit and larger ones that were multiples of 2, 4, 10, 12.5, 20, 40, 100, 200, 400, 500, and 800 times the basic unit.

The basis for the whole weight system was probably the ratti, around 0.109 gram, the weight of a seed of the gunja creeper (*Abrus precatorius*), equivalent to $\frac{1}{128}$ part of the Indus basic unit. The ratti is still used in India as a jeweler's weight and was the basis, among other things, for the weight standards of the first Indian coins that were first issued in the 7th century B.C. A number of the early states issued coins of 1 or 2 karshapanas, a karshapana being 32 rattis, so these coins were equivalent to the Indus weights of $\frac{1}{4}$ and $\frac{1}{2}$ the basic unit.

What is the significance of the Indus weights? The fact that a way of measuring quantities of materials was standardized throughout the length and breadth of the Indus realms amply demonstrates the existence of a statewide system of organization that could dictate, monitor, and guarantee such a uniform system. But what was the purpose of these weights?

In contemporary Mesopotamia, weights (on a different standard than those of the Indus) were used mainly in administrative contexts. In the 21st century B.C., the Sumerian king, Shulgi, standardized the Sumerian weights and measures. The copious Sumerian administrative documents that survive refer to weights of goods received or issued, in taxation or payment of dues, in payment for services, and in official trading. They also include property documents such as records of land sales, with payment to those witnessing the transaction. The Sumerians used weights of silver, and to a lesser extent barley, tin, and copper, as a standard by which to calculate the value of other goods, as a medium of exchange between different commodities, and as a means of paying directly, all functions that were fulfilled by coinage at a much later date. Many of the documents refer to foreign trading expeditions: merchants setting out on official expeditions were issued with weighed commodities for exchange, and on their return the weight and value of the goods they delivered was recorded. That the Indus weight system was also involved in such trading transactions is amply demonstrated by the occasional discovery of Indus weights in places outside the Indus region with which the Indus people traded: Mesopotamia, Susa (the capital of Elam, Mesopotamia's highland neighbor), Dilmun (Bahrain), and Magan (Oman).

It is highly probable that the Indus weights, like those of Mesopotamia, were used in regulating the issue and receipt of trade goods by the authorities and the official measuring of goods received in taxation or issued in official payment. Groups of weights are often found near Indus city gateways, suggesting that they were used by officials who were regulating the flow of goods into and out of the cities. Whatever their precise use, the very existence of a system of weights standardized throughout the Indus region implies official control and regulation of the movement of commodities.

WHO RAN THE INDUS STATE?

Behind the issue and monitoring of a system of uniform weights, and their use throughout the Indus realms, must lie a well-organized bureaucratic system capable of enforcing standardization over this enormous area and with official reasons for doing so, whether for regulating taxes, levying customs' dues, organizing official trade, issuing payments to state employees, or handing out benefits to those in need. State sponsorship, regulation, and supervision can also be seen in the layout of the towns and cities, which were conceived and built to a regular plan, with variations as locally required.

Although we see the hand of authority in these features, the rulers themselves are elusive, and even the elite are hard to pin down. One could argue that, given the small numbers of cemeteries that have been found, the royal graves lie yet undiscovered. This is certainly a possibility, although it becomes increasingly unlikely as the volume of evidence of the civilization grows. Burial in the Indus Civilization was a relatively low-key affair. Individuals were buried with a few pottery vessels and personal ornaments. Some were better endowed than others—we could suggest, for example, that those interred in a wooden coffin and wrapped in a shroud were people of a higher social standing than those simply laid in a grave pit. Similarly, a small number of burials contain a far larger amount of jewelry than usual and may therefore have been of important individuals. None of the burial sites are lavishly endowed, nor are there any more elaborate forms of burial such as mausoleums to indicate that special efforts were made in laying to rest the leaders of society. And whereas in most stratified societies the elite show signs of being better nourished than the ordinary folk, no such differences can be seen in the bones of the Indus people that have been studied—on the contrary, these show that everyone had access to an adequate and balanced food supply.

They also were comfortably provided for in other ways. No one seems to have wanted for any essential objects, and the same high-quality goods were present in households in villages and in cities. However, there is an indication that some individuals had copper or bronze tools whereas others had similar objects made of flint: this may give a clue to the existence of some social differentiation. There are few overt signs of an elite that enjoyed exceptional wealth, but some substantial house complexes at Mohenjo Daro and other principal cities have yielded caches of gold and silver objects and rich jewelry [*see* Color Plate 25].

All the houses in the Indus towns and cities provided a comfortable existence with good facilities. The different sizes and internal complexity of these houses, however, may also be a clue to differing social status—some would have accommodated a single nuclear family while others had space not only for a large extended family but also for a substantial number of dependents or servants. Those houses whose entrance was guarded or monitored by a janitor seated in a cubicle facing the door may well have been the homes of important individuals in the Indus hierarchy.

One would have expected the Indus rulers themselves to reside on the citadel mounds of the cities, but no obvious palaces exist there or in other parts of the city, as they do in other early civilizations. Like religious structures, palaces take many different forms in different cultures, but they generally have a number of common elements. One, naturally, would be a set of private rooms, probably luxuriously or expensively furnished. The rooms would be set apart, and made relatively inaccessible so as to maintain their privacy and, in some societies, to guard the sanctity of the ruler. Another element would be the public rooms, where the ruler would conduct public business, giving audience to domestic petitioners and foreign dignitaries. A third sector would house the administrative offices—official records, the offices of bureaucrats—and there would probably be a large service sector, with workshops, kitchens, storerooms, and so on. But if the Indus Civilization had such buildings, they have yet to be recognized.

THE BEGINNINGS OF THE CASTE SYSTEM?

Why are the Indus rulers so difficult to find? The answer must lie in the nature of their authority and the way of life and ideology associated with it. It has plausibly been suggested that the Indus rulers exercised power through religious authority. There is little evidence with which to test this theory, but some support may come from a consideration of the later caste system. This unique way of organizing society has its basis in tenets of the Hindu religion.

In Hinduism individuals belong by birth to one of a great variety of hierarchically ordered occupational groups. But unlike the classes of most societies, here there is no scope for movement out of the social position into which one is born, which is determined on the basis of one's performance in a former life. The hierarchical ordering of these castes is determined by their degree of ritual purity. Contact with many elements of organic life causes ritual pollution.

By the mid–1st millennium B.C., the caste system was well established. Many guilds of hereditary craftsmen existed in towns, their membership often coinciding with that of a subcaste. Some distinctions between different occupational groups are mentioned in the Vedic texts of the 2nd-millennium B.C. Indo-

PEOPLES OF THE INDUS

Identifying the peoples of the past is never an easy matter. Even where quite definite historical information exists of the movement—through colonization, immigration, or conquest—of a group of people from area A to area B, it is rarely easy to pin them down using archaeological evidence. And it is very unusual for the situation to be clear-cut. A band of raiders may call themselves "Saxons," for instance, but it is highly likely that this group name conceals a motley collection of Jutes, Angles, Frisians and other adventurers along with a Saxon princeling and his warband. In the Indus and adjacent regions we have three sets of information about the people who may have been there in the 3rd and 2nd millennia B.C., and they don't necessarily all paint the same picture.

For a start we have a certain amount of rather confusing literary evidence. We know that the Sumerians referred to the Indus Civilization as the people of "Meluhha"—but we don't know if this is a name that the Indus people used themselves. The earliest Indian literature, the *Vedas*, oral texts passed down faithfully for many centuries before they were finally committed to writing, are the hymns of a people who called themselves the Aryas, nomadic pastoralists, horse riders and warriors. Their literature shows that they moved gradually from an area to the north, on the Iranian plateau, into the Punjab, and thence farther into the subcontinent, and later texts have them firmly established in the Ganges Valley. They contrasted themselves with dark-skinned enemies, battles against whom feature prominently in their hymns. These enemies went by many names, some obviously those of individual communities, but the most commonly used was "Dasa," along with "Dasyu" and "Pani." It is generally considered that these enemies dwelt within the northern areas of the Indian subcontinent—but Asko Parpola has argued most convincingly that they lived further north, in Bactria, at the time when the Aryas were fighting them.

Next there is the linguistic evidence, which I discuss at some length in the next chapter. This seems to show that speakers of the Indo-Aryan (also known as plain "Aryan") languages, a branch of the Indo-European language family that covered Europe, Iran and northern India by the late 1st millennium B.C., entered the Indus region during the 2nd millennium B.C. where they encountered large numbers of people speaking languages belonging to the Dravidian family that is now largely confined to South India. And finally there were probably still some groups speaking a variety of other, indigenous, languages such as Munda, languages that survive today in a few small pockets, mostly in Central India.

Archaeological evidence presents the third strand of information, allowing us to identify indigenous hunter-gatherer groups who had lived in the region since time immemorial; the Indus Civilization whose people had colonized the region from the adjacent highlands where their ancestors had lived for many millennia, giving way (when the civilization collapsed in the early 2nd millennium) to regional farming communities; and a small number of quite diverse groups with weapons, horses, and new burial practices, scattered through the region and beyond (in Swat, for instance) from the 2nd millennium onward.

What "story" can we make from these three strands of information? Some bits fall neatly into place—an indigenous substratum of hunter-gatherers in the Indus region speaking a variety of tribal languages overlain by the arrival in the late 4th millennium of Dravidian speakers bringing farming, who flourished for some centuries as the Indus Civilization and subsequently declined into smaller farming communities. But the Aryan bit is much more hazy. Because the Indo-Aryan language eventually became dominant, many people are tempted to see the Aryas/Indo-Aryan speakers as a huge flood of incomers rather than a trickle—or even to see them as the people of the Indus Civilization, though there is no support for this view. Were the Aryas of the Vedic hymns the first Indo-Aryan speakers to enter the subcontinent or were there earlier waves? Can we identify later waves as well? Who were the Dasas and what language did they speak? These are matters that are fiercely debated and for which there is still not nearly enough evidence to build a coherent story.

Aryans invaders, but these were not hereditary. The caste system known in the 1st millennium B.C. is far more elaborate and incorporates the concept of ritual purity that is absent in the earlier texts. Although undoubtedly the full-fledged caste system owed much to the mingling of Indo-Aryan and indigenous groups, we may well seek its origins in the social organization of the Indus Civilization. The great degree of craft specialization observed here may point this way. Although we do not have enough evidence at present to consider in any detail the theory that the caste system underlay the Indus social order, we may at least search for relevant clues.

As different activities convey different degrees of pollution, a whole hierarchy is created by the activities that individual groups can perform, and by other related practices—for instance, vegetarianism is more pure than meat-eating and various types of meat, such as game, are less polluting than others. Those at the apex of the hierarchy, the Brahmins, must guard themselves from any danger of pollution. This is achieved by assigning polluting activities, such as dealing with the dead and with waste materials, to segregated groups at the bottom of the hierarchy—the untouchables, or Harijans as they are now called.

The concern with bathing and the separation of pure from impure materials, such as wastewater, suggests a concern with ritual purity as well as practical hygiene. Those whose job it was to maintain the efficiency of the drainage system and to empty and clean the rubbish containers and drains would have been tainted with ritual impurity,

making them untouchable. A similar status would have been accorded to those who handled corpses and buried the dead. The scant respect paid to the remains of the dead would support the idea that corpses were ritually polluting and that the people who dug the graves were not the relatives of the deceased. Untouchability was well established before the mid 1st millennium B.C., when religious reformers like the Buddha objected strongly to it. It would therefore not seem too far-fetched to suggest that the concept of ritual purity was one that was already present in India when the Indo-Aryans entered the subcontinent and that it was from the descendants of the Indus people that the concept found its way into the religion and social organization of the 1st millennium B.C.

Looking back many centuries to the time when the Aryans first entered the subcontinent and left a record of their lives in the religious poems of the *Rigveda*, the role of the priests was very different from that of later Brahmins. A social transformation took place during the later 2nd and early 1st millennia B.C. as the invading Aryans and their warrior kings and indigenous peoples became integrated. Because the elevated status of the Brahmins in the 1st millennium B.C. does not match the far humbler status of the earlier Aryan priests, it seems likely that the Brahmins represented the descendants of the former native ruling class, surviving as the leaders of the farming communities who succeeded the civilization and now assimilated into the military-based hierarchy of the invaders. If this is so, it is a powerful argu-

Figure 40.

BANGLES,
HARAPPA AND
MOHENJO DARO

Bangles made from
metal were quite
uncommon and
presumably belonged
to important
individuals. These
two from Harappa
and Mohenjo Daro,
respectively, were
made from rods of
copper or bronze bent
round in a circle.
The bangles could
be slipped over the
hand, prying the ends
apart if necessary.

ment in support of the idea that the rulers of the Indus Civilization were the priesthood.

IDENTIFYING RANK

If we accept the suggestion that the Indus rulers were the forerunners of the Brahmins, we need to alter the nature of our search for them. Temporal rulers may well be distinguished by the richness of their burials and the grandeur of their residences. This may equally be true of societies where temporal and spiritual powers are tightly interwoven (as for example in the hierarchy of the Catholic Church in medieval Europe). But a society whose rulers are distinguished by the high degree of their ritual purity will leave completely different clues. It is within this context that we should look again at the abundant bathrooms on the citadels at Mohenjo Daro and other Indus cities.

The ritual purity of the Brahmins is maintained in part by segregation, so we should expect the quarters of ritually pure religious leaders to be particularly inaccessi-

ble, within a maze of outer rooms. And in the Indian context, holiness is often expressed in terms of detachment from the pleasures and pains of the world. Extreme austerity rather than lavish wealth might well be the setting of the Indus rulers—so we should be looking not for rich burials and finely furnished apartments but for much more subtle clues. For example, some of the Indus burials were interred within a wooden coffin or wrapped in a shroud of reeds or cloth. Others were laid upon a bed of clay or a layer of pots. Are these burials perhaps "purer"—ritually separated from the earth? And we need to look again at the objects that are associated with different individuals or structures. Rather than apply criteria of wealth (bronze more precious than stone and gold or silver most precious of all, for instance), we perhaps need to look at materials and objects in terms of their purity—for example, in traditional Indian society, gold is purer than silver, silver purer than bronze, and bronze purer than copper. This could be a profitable line of enquiry—although it may well be impossible to identify such intangible evidence.

Can we use items of dress to distinguish the status of individuals in Indus society? Bangles are an important element in traditional Indian dress [Figure 40]. Different types are worn by different communities within society, like the massive bone bangles of the Lambadi pastoralists in the south. Bangles are worn in large numbers by women, different types showing whether they are engaged or married, while the bangles of a widow are broken on her husband's death. Men may also wear bangles, the best-known example being the *kara* worn by all Sikhs as a sign of loyalty to their guru. The Indus figurines and statues and the depictions of gods or people on seals show that the Indus people also wore bangles as an important part of their dress [*see* Color Plates I and II]. Finds from burials bear this out. Women usually wore a number of bangles either on both arms or just on their left arm, narrow ones around the wrist and wider ones above the elbow. Most bangles were made of terracotta, generally handmade and therefore somewhat irregular; these may have been for everyday wear like the ubiquitous glass bangles worn today. Many also were made of shell—those worn by women buried at Harappa were all of shell. There were two main varieties. One was made by cutting a wide section from a conch shell, producing a large sturdy bangle that could have been worn even by women engaged in heavy manual work. The other, far more fragile variety was made from thin rings sawn from a conch shell, giving a characteristic shape, circular with a slightly thickened portion at one side protruding into the center, making the inside kidney- or heart-shaped. This shape was imi-

tated in fine bangles made of faience, either white or blue-green in color. Other bangles were made of a copper rod bent round into a circle, while a few were manufactured from hammered gold sheet. As faience, copper, and gold bangles were far less common than those of terracotta or shell, they may indicate that their wearers were members of the elite.

The elite may also have worn other pieces of special jewelry. A few finger or toe

Figure 41.

FEMALE FIGURINE, HARAPPA

This terracotta figurine from Harappa represents a lavishly adorned lady, wearing a fan-shaped headdress, two chokers around her neck and throat.

also by the craftsmanship involved. Microscopic beads of steatite, only a millimeter wide, show extraordinary skill and patience in their manufacture, whether they were drilled and ground by hand or made from an extruded steatite paste [Figure 42]. Necklaces and other ornaments, like the hair ornament found on a man buried at Harappa, were made of thousands of these beads, representing an amazing amount of labor.

Hairstyles were probably another way of showing the social standing of individuals. Female figurines often wear their hair folded up over a pannier or fan-shaped frame, or piled over the top of their heads. Others have a simpler bun or wear a turban. It seems likely that the more elaborate and time-consuming the coiffure, the more leisure and servants the lady in question was likely to have had—and this is borne out by the heavy quantities of jewelry worn by such individuals. A few of the women buried at Harappa had mirrors, which would have been useful for creating and checking such hairdos. Many individuals on the seals, including figures that were probably gods and goddesses, wear their hair in a long plait. The gender of these individuals is much disputed and it seems probable that both males and females actually wore their hair like this, but that it had some important significance—either denoting some kind of permanent ritual status or being adopted for festivals or other religious ceremonies. Male statues and figurines generally wore their hair in a bun divided horizontally by a headband or combed straight, though they might also wear a turban, and the majority are bearded [Figure 43].

rings of silver wire have been found and these may have been indicators of high status, while other individuals had rings of copper. The figurines show that women generally wore ear ornaments, necklaces, and pendants. A cylindrical or truncated conical stone amulet was worn by the women buried at Harappa, suspended round the neck, and these amulets are common at other sites. Given their numbers they may well have been an ornament that indicated that their wearers were married, like a number of the pieces of jewelry worn by Indian women today.

Many figurines wear neck chokers with pendant beads and single and multiple stranded bead necklaces of graduated lengths, virtually covering their chests [Figure 41]. Others wear few or none, like the recently excavated models from Nausharo of women grinding grain and kneading dough. By analogy with other societies, the quantity of jewelry worn seems likely to have been an indicator of status. The types of material used would also have probably related to social position. Value was likely to have been measured not only by the rarity and desirability of the raw material but

Figure 44.

The fillet (probably representing one of gold) worn by the famous "Priest-King" sculpture has in its center a disc or ring. Sometimes this is interpreted as an eye bead, perhaps of precious metal inlaid with semiprecious stone. Alternatively this could represent a stoneware bangle, one of the small, superbly crafted stoneware rings made with such care and skill at Mohenjo Daro, rings whose purpose is unknown but which seem likely to have been badges of office.

As well as jewelry, the Indus people wore clothes of cotton and probably wool. Here the artwork is less helpful than usual, because often the figurines are depicted naked. The stone statue of the Priest-King wears an elaborately decorated robe, draped to expose his chest and right shoulder, in the manner of later Buddhist monks, and other more complete stone statues show this robe was worn over a garment like the modern dhoti, which was wound around the waist and frequently drawn up between the legs to tuck in at the back. The latter may have been common male dress, particularly as other representations on seals of possible males sometimes wear what looks like a skirt but that could well be the dhoti in the untucked state. The robe, however, may have been confined to the priests or rulers. Women appear to have worn a short skirt that covered the thighs and was covered in some cases by a substantial belt made of strings of beads.

At present the evidence of how people dressed seems to offer a promising line of inquiry for reconstructing Indus social organization. There is a strong suggestion that people's jewelry, clothing, and hairstyles reflected both their place in the social hierarchy and other aspects of their status—their married or unmarried state, for example.

STONEWARE BANGLES—
A TECHNOLOGICAL PUZZLE AND MORE

Among the finds made in the 1930s excavations at Mohenjo Daro was a strange vitrified mass of pottery, clay, and bangles, which Mackay listed in his report as "Muffles and Crucibles." This material and the debris still in situ in its find spot were reexamined in detail fifty years later by M. A. Halim of the Pakistan Department of Archaeology and Massimo Vidale of IsMEO to see if they could understand what had taken place to produce this overfired material. They also conducted chemical and physical analyses of it. They succeeded in solving the technological puzzle—but revealed another mystery.

The debris resulted from the disastrous misfiring of a highly sophisticated arrangement for firing stoneware bangles. Wheelthrown, using carefully prepared clay, these bangles were made to an exact small size and were incised with an inscription. They were placed in pairs in small lidded bowls stacked in a column of five that was coated in clay. This was placed within a large jar and again coated with chaff-tempered clay, including a massive outer cap, very effectively sealing the bangles from the air during firing. The sealed vessel was arranged on heaped-up piles of terracotta bangles within a kiln that was fired at a high temperature. The finished bangles are a mottled grayish black, resembling fine-grained metamorphic stone.

Clearly these were a very sophisticated and complex product. Their great importance to the Indus people is emphasized by the fact that an Indus sign was inscribed on the inner clay layer, while a seal was impressed on the outer clay cover. For what purpose were these bangles used?

WRITTEN AUTHORITY

In the 1980s a puzzling piece of industrial debris was made to yield its technological secrets. It revealed that the people of Mohenjo Daro had expended a considerable amount of time and expertise in the production of small, very fine stoneware bangles. These were incised with signs in the Indus script. The various layers of clay used in constructing the containers in which they were fired were also incised with Indus signs and finished with the impression of a seal on the outside. Writing in early civilizations, where literacy was confined to an often very restricted group, was used as a means of wielding spiritual or temporal control and power. The use of the Indus signs here therefore implies either official control of the production of these bangles or an attempt to give them spiritual protection during the firing process, or both. We do not actually know the purpose of these stoneware bangles but they were clearly important. They may have been made at Harappa as well as Mohenjo Daro, and their use was also almost exclusively confined to these two cities. These two are the best known of the five principal settlements of the civilization, regional centers of power and administration where we would expect to find badges or symbols that identify the holders of high office. Can these stoneware bangles be such symbols?

Figure 45.

UNICORN SEAL, HARAPPA

The "unicorn" is the emblem most commonly depicted on Indus seals and there is considerable debate about its identity. Some scholars have taken this to be a depiction of a long-horned bull or antelope, one horn being hidden by the other. However, other two-horned animals depicted on the seals have both horns shown—and some figurines from Chanhu Daro are of a creature with one massive central horn, suggesting that this is also intended genuinely to represent a single-horned animal. We can only guess at its iconographic significance and the stories that must have surrounded it.

Their uniform narrow diameter, 5.5-6 cm, makes it unlikely that the bangles were worn on the wrist or ankle. More probably they would have been sewn on to clothing or worn in some other way, for example, as a pendant or on a belt. It may be significant that the Priest-King statue wears a circle in the center of his headband, and another on a band on his upper arm—these would match the stoneware bangles in size if the statue were life-sized [Figure 44]. It therefore seems a distinct possibility that the stoneware bangles were worn as badges of office by leading members of the hierarchy.

Other objects that bear writing in the Indus script are also likely to have had some official significance. One of the most characteristic finds from Indus towns are the square seals. Made of steatite (soapstone), each seal bears an inscription, usually short, and a picture, generally of a single animal, although scenes also occur. At some sites, such as Lothal, clay impressions of the seals have been found. The patterns left on their reverse show that they were attached to cords or sacking used to package bales of goods. We can plausibly see these sealings as part of an official system for controlling and recording goods and their distribution, and sanctioning their issue. The seals had a semicircular boss on the back so that they could be suspended, presumably on a cord round the neck or on a belt or wrist strap. These and other inscribed objects, such as small faience or steatite tablets and button seals, may have been issued as badges of authority to merchants traveling on official business and to other individuals who needed to show their authority or prove their credentials. In historical times, tokens with an official seal were used as passes within a system controlling road traffic.

What clues do these inscribed objects hold for us? Their distribution must be able to tell us something about the civilization's political geography and organization. So must a study of the spatial patterning of both repeated elements of the inscriptions and common images (such as the "unicorn"). The great majority of inscribed materials have been found at Mohenjo Daro and Harappa. Only these two of the five great cities have been adequately explored, but it is likely that a similar repertoire of inscribed materials was also in use in Ganweriwala, Dholavira, and Rakhigarhi. Before excavations began at the latter site in 1997, many seals were looted from its ruins. The evidence available shows that seals were in use in all towns and cities, including far-off Shortugai, and seal impressions from them have been found in a number, including Mohenjo Daro, Harappa, and Lothal. Some have also been found abroad, in Sumerian cities, Susa, and the Gulf. Their link with traders and the management of traded commodities therefore seems probable. A number of pottery vessels, such as large

jars or small drinking cups, have a few signs that were impressed on them before they were fired—perhaps an indication of their contents or ownership. Graffiti, perhaps a less formal use of writing, were scratched on some vessels at some time after the vessel was fired—the personal mark of the owner or a check mark by an official, perhaps.

Other inscribed materials are less widespread, and again the majority have been found in Mohenjo Daro and Harappa. From Harappa come a number of small inscribed objects: rods of steatite from the lower levels and small steatite, terracotta, or faience tablets from the upper. These bear a short inscription on one side and what may be a number on the other. The incised steatite examples often repeated the same inscription, while multiple copies of the same design in terracotta were produced in molds. Kenoyer suggests they may have been accounting tokens, whereas others see them more as offerings or amulets. While these may have all been produced at Harappa, they are found in small numbers in other cities, including Mohenjo Daro.

At Mohenjo Daro alone, more than a hundred inscribed copper tablets have been found. These bear an inscription on the face and a design on the other. Very often a particular design is paired with a particular inscription, and the repertoire of inscriptions and pictures is quite restricted. The designs include composite animals and a wild man with the hindquarters of a bull, armed with a bow and wearing a horned headdress—perhaps a form of the "proto-Shiva" deity familiar from the seals. The pictures on these tablets may well have had a common religious theme. Their restricted distribution and unusual designs as well as their rarely used material put them in a class of their own, and it is tempting to see them as some kind of symbol of authority related to the ruling priesthood. Eight copper tablets of a rather different sort were also found at Harappa. Inscribed ivory and bone rods may also have had some ritual significance.

Finally, there are a number of tools and pieces of jewelry that bore writing: bronze axes and chisels, gold jewelry from Mohenjo Daro, bone hairpins, and painted terracotta bangles. While in some cases these inscriptions may denote ownership, they are more likely generally to have been protective signs with some religious significance—to ward off the powers of evil, for instance, or to ensure the safe use of the tool. Or, in the case of some of the tools, those that seem from their quality more likely to have had a votive than a functional purpose, they may name the person or group that was dedicating the object.

CLANS, CITIES, OR PROFESSIONS?

The diversity of contexts in which writing is found reflects the diversity of its probable functions—to indicate ownership, to give divine protection, to identify goods and individuals. The seals seem most likely to provide an understanding of the political and bureaucratic organization of the Indus society. Most seals, in addition to their written inscription, carry a picture—generally of an animal—although some show scenes that are likely to reflect religious themes. The most common animal is the "unicorn" [Figure 45].

Many scholars see the animals depicted as representations of particular groups. Some think of them as clan totems and argue that the most commonly represented creature, the unicorn, is the sign of the ruling house, which rose to prominence at the beginning of the civilization, with other, politically defeated clans occupying positions of lesser status in the hierarchy. Other scholars argue that the animals are totems associated with individual cities, the unicorn representing the powerful city of Mohenjo Daro. Still others associate the different animals with different social or occupational groups within the society. Thus the rare seals depicting a zebu may be associated with the rulers themselves, while the unicorn seals may represent the elite, whoever they were, and other animals or designs stood for lesser groups. To my mind, this third suggestion seems the most plausible. Undoubtedly elements of all three could be involved—one might argue, for instance, that the ruling house came from Mohenjo Daro and belonged to the dominant clan. I am uneasy with the notion of clans, however, because the impression one gains is of a society organized into social groups that each have their separate occupation, rather than into geographically defined groups that encompass people practicing a number of different occupations.

If the pictures on the seals represent groups, there are two possible ways in which they may do so. One is as an identification of the individual—giving his or her occupation,

Figure 46.

BULL SEAL,

HARAPPA

This magnificent portrait of a zebu bull is one of only a few depicted on Indus seals, almost all of which were found at either Mohenjo Daro or Harappa. It has been suggested that the zebu motif may have represented the highest authority in the Indus realms.

group affiliation, or place of residence. The other is as a symbol of an issuing authority, showing who the individual was working for or was countenanced by. Undoubtedly they could have functioned in both ways on different seals and in different contexts—for example, the zebu seals being the personal seals of the highest authority, the high priest as we think, while the unicorn seals could have been issued to people representing the priesthood in general, such as merchants on official trade missions [Figure 46].

And what of the writing itself? If the pictures show the issuing authority, recognizable by literate and illiterate people alike, the writing may contain more personal information that was of relevance only to the handful of people who were able to read. Obviously we would like to be able to read it too—but many have tried and so far all have failed.

A

B

F

C

D

G

CHAPTER EIGHT

THE ENIGMATIC INDUS SCRIPT

WRITING

Writing was developed for different purposes in different cultures. That of the Sumerians and their neighbors in Elam was initially used largely for accounting—recording things issued or received by the authorities. The Chinese developed writing so that they could consult their gods on the possibility of a successful outcome in future events such as royal childbirth and hunting expeditions. The partial writing systems that emerged in Mesoamerica were concerned with the calendar and the repeating cycles of time, particularly as they affected major events. Of the Mesoamerican cultures, only the Maya went on to develop a true and complete writing system able to record everything, and they still used this mainly to inscribe records of time and events, such as dynastic history and accounts of their military successes and of the sacrifice of captured rival kings.

Like the inhabitants of almost all early civilizations around the globe, the Indus people developed a writing system. If we could decipher it, it should give us further vital insights into the Indus way of life.

As we have seen, the Indus people wrote on a number of different media. In addition to the steatite seals and clay sealings on which the script is mainly found, there are also a limited number of copper tablets and inscribed personal possessions, quite a few inscribed pottery vessels, small stamped or molded tablets, and a few triangular bar seals. It is extremely likely that other documents once existed, written, as in later times, on wood, cloth, bark, palm leaves, or other perishable materials; but these, alas, have long since decayed away. The script on the surviving pieces is sophisticated and clearly not in its earliest stage of development when it is first seen in use around 2600 B.C. The search for its antecedents takes us back into the 4th millennium B.C. when we find a few simple graffiti scratched on pots, probably the personal marks of the potters who made them.

These markings are similar to graffiti used in the same way in later times, after the end of the Indus Civilization, and to signs in the Indus script itself—but before we start claiming

Figure 47.

SEALS AND TABLETS

Although the seals are the most common inscribed objects, the Indus script was used on a variety of other objects as well. Seals A, B, E, and H, and Tablet G are from Mohenjo Daro. Seals C and F, and Tablet D, are from a single house at Harappa, possibly the home of a merchant.

Figure 48.

Button Seal

*A seal from the
Early Indus Period
(2800-2600 B.C.),
this "button" or
stamp seal was an
indication of the
development in the
organization of
society. It probably
reflected the need of
people in power to
mark their control
over the movement
of commodities.*

Map 8. (opposite)

Indus Script
Find Sites

*About 3700 inscribed
objects are known.*

continuity, it should be pointed out that they bear a strong resemblance to all sorts of other graffiti and incomplete scripts, such as signs used in early prehistoric Europe or on Easter Island a few hundred years ago, and probably to the doodles we have all done on our telephone pads while hanging on the phone line. Simple geometric signs, like triangles, arrows, wavy lines, and circles, are common to all cultures and recur without the people using them ever coming into contact with one another.

Far more significant in this search are signs that began to be inscribed on pottery at Harappa and several other early sites during the Early Indus Period [Map 8]. A number of these inscriptions resemble more distinctive Indus signs, such as the **U** or **V** shape with short lines added to the top of the arms [Figure 47-H]. Some of these begin to be used in sequences familiar from the Mature Indus script. Well and good—the Indus script

evolved in the Indus region and was not imported from somewhere else. This means that the use to which writing was put elsewhere at that time—in Mesopotamia and parts of the Iranian plateau—is unlikely to provide any clue to the purpose of the Indus script. Far from it, indeed—it is quite clear from the nature of Indus inscribed objects and the contexts in which they were found that the Indus script was not being used for the kind of economic record-keeping for which the Sumerians and Elamites devised their script. Or at least, the surviving inscribed objects were not generally being used in this way, although we don't know what other written materials that have vanished may have been used for.

CRACKING
ANCIENT CODES

What survives of Indus script are extremely brief inscriptions on the seals and tablets and other media. Breaking the code of ancient scripts requires some clues. Egyptian hieroglyphs were successfully deciphered when the Rosetta stone, a parallel text, was discovered in the late 18th century. The Rosetta stone bore the same long inscription in Egyptian and Greek scripts, with the personal names of the rulers conveniently placed in cartouches in the hieroglyphic text. From this starting point it was possible for the decipherer, Jean-François Champollion, to build up a knowledge of the phonetic value of many of the symbols, which were used to write a known

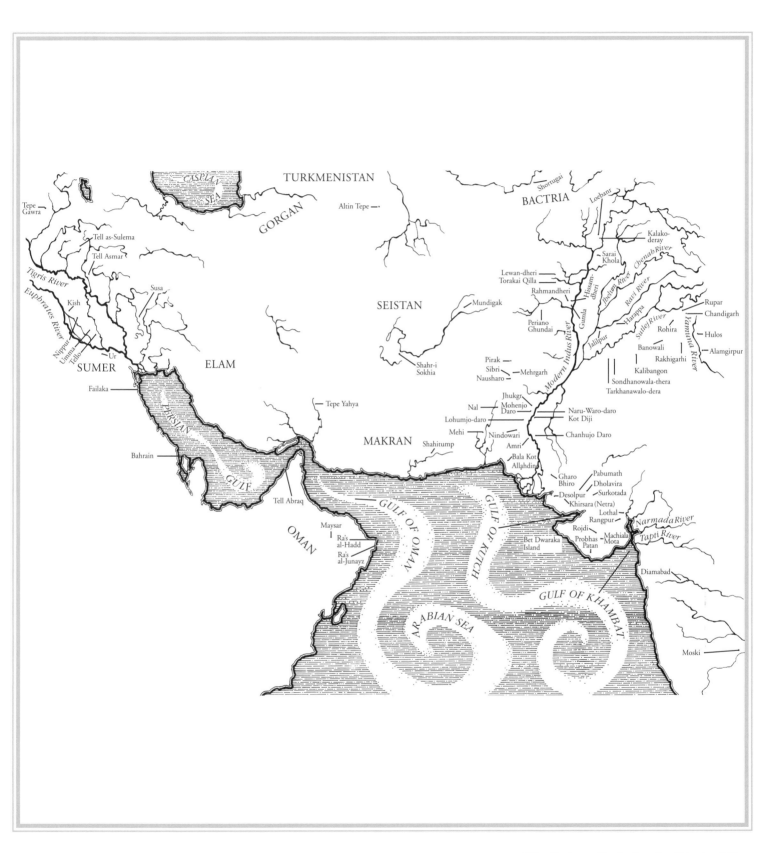

Map 9. (opposite)

Present Day
Distribution
of Dravidian
Languages

Today the majority of Dravidian languages are clustered in southern India. Telugu is the main language of the South-Central group; Kannada and Tamil, which is also spoken in Sri Lanka, are the two main languages of the South Dravidian group. The only Dravidian language spoken in the area of the Indus Civilization is Brahui, one of the North Dravidian group. Making up the Central Dravidian group are seven minor languages, all of which are probably doomed to extinction.

language, an early version of the Coptic language spoken in Egypt in historical times. The Egyptian hieroglyphs are a mixed system, but some of the signs were used alphabetically and this proved extremely helpful.

The script of the Mycenaeans, Linear B, for a long time eluded decipherment. Painstaking analysis of its structure revealed that it was an inflected language (like Latin and Greek) and that the signs were probably syllabic, each one consisting of a vowel combined with a consonant or standing alone. The breakthrough came when the architect Michael Ventris recognized that some repeated sign sequences were probably the names of the places where they were found. He matched the syllables of their names with the Linear B signs and applied the resultant sound values to his tables of words and endings. To Ventris' amazement, he discovered that the script had been used to write an early form of the Greek language, the details of which he was able to work out in conjunction with the distinguished classicist John Chadwick. The Linear B script and the associated pictographic signs give many clues to reading the similar Linear A script used by the Minoans in previous centuries. Unfortunately, the Linear A script was used to write a language completely different from Greek and unlike any others we know, and remains undeciphered to this day.

It proved possible to decipher Sumerian using the lexical texts of later Mesopotamian cultures, which exhaustively listed Sumerian words and their later equivalents. It was basically using a dictionary to learn a new language and script—a daunting but possible task. Maya glyphs, whose "code" has now been "cracked" but which are still incompletely deciphered, have proved the hardest decipherment problem to date. A complex series of clues have been found, including texts in a later version of the script, complete with translation or commentary in Spanish; knowledge of the family of languages to which that of the Maya belongs; and plentiful information on Maya culture, giving clues to the content of the texts. Even so, the complexity of Maya glyphs means that they are still being deciphered one by one—there is no universal key that will unlock them all at one fell swoop, as there was to a large extent with Egyptian hieroglyphs or Linear B symbols. The same Maya words may be written down using syllabic signs, pictographic signs, or a combination of both; single signs may have a number of completely different meanings; and a number of different signs often exist for the same syllable—so there is plenty of scope for confusion.

WHAT LANGUAGE DID THE INDUS PEOPLE SPEAK?

From this survey, it is obvious that before a script can be deciphered, it is necessary to know the language it has been used to write. Alternatively, a bilingual text is needed that will act as a dictionary for deciphering an unknown language (as was the case with Sumerian). So the first thing to find out is

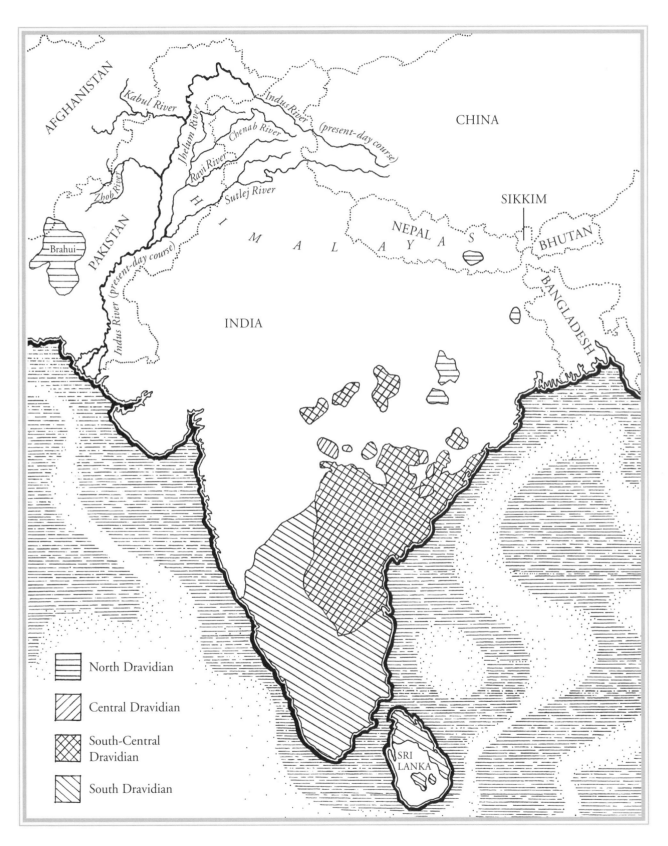

North Dravidian

Central Dravidian

South-Central
Dravidian

South Dravidian

what language the Indus people (or at least the literate Indus people) spoke.

The origin of the Indus language is a hotly debated question that is often seen as having ethnic implications. A number of languages are spoken in the subcontinent today. Some that are in common use were introduced in recent times and are obviously of no relevance to this debate—English being the prime example. The Sino-Tibetan languages, such as Naga, spoken in Burma and Tibet, lie too far east to concern us in our quest, because the Indus people penetrated no farther east than the western banks of the Ganges. A few communities in India speak languages belonging to the Austro-Asiatic language family, to which many of the languages of South-East Asia also belong. These languages, which include Munda, Mundari, and Santali, are spoken by tribal groups in parts of northeast and central India. Another central Indian tribal language, Nahali, may also belong to the Austro-Asiatic family or may be an isolate related to no other surviving language. Burushaski, spoken by a tribe in Kashmir, is also unrelated to any known surviving language. Although so restricted today, the ancestors of these languages were probably much more widely spoken in Indus times. Many of the indigenous peoples of the subcontinent would have spoken early forms of these languages, whereas others may have spoken languages, that have since died out completely.

The majority of Indians today speak languages that belong to two main families: Dravidian and the Indo-Aryan branch of Indo-European. These are largely divided between an Indo-Aryan-speaking north and a Dravidian-speaking south, although there are pockets of Dravidian speakers also in the northwest and in central and eastern India. The identification of the Indus people with one or other of these major language families is perceived by some individuals or groups in a political light, in that the modern speakers of its languages could be seen as having historical ownership of the subcontinent.

Dravidian and the Indo-Aryan branch of Indo-European are the main candidates for the Indus language, but other suggestions have been made that muddy the waters of debate still further. Often their proponents have a theoretical axe to grind—for instance, attempts to identify the Indus language with Sumerian may go hand in hand with theories that attempt to derive the Indus Civilization from that of ancient Mesopotamia. Nothing useful has come out of such attempts.

Several teams, notably those working in Finland, of whom Asko Parpola is the leading light, and those working in Russia, led by the great linguist Yuri Knorozov, have used sophisticated computer techniques to analyze the structure of the Indus script. These studies have revealed that the underlying language is agglutinative and uses suffixes. In other words, it builds up meaning by adding bits to the word root—sometimes creating whole sentences in a single word—and these bits are added on to the end rather than the beginning of the word. By contrast the Indo-Aryan languages, and the other languages of the huge Indo-European language family to which they belong, are inflected—they change a part of the word, particularly its ending, to show differences in tense or person. For example, in Italian we have "penso" (I think) but "pensa" (he thinks) and "pensero" (I shall think). The Indo-Aryan languages do not seem a likely candidate if the computer analyses are correct—which they seem to be.

The Dravidian languages, on the other hand, are agglutinative and use suffixes—a close match. On structural grounds, however, this would equally fit the family of Altaic languages spoken in Central Asia. These might perhaps have been more widespread in antiquity—but to support their candidature it would be necessary to find archaeological evidence of this, and currently the connection between Central Asia and the Indus region in the 7th to 3rd millennia B.C. seems confined to trade links. In addition, there is plentiful evidence that the Dravidian languages were being spoken in India by at least the 2nd millennium B.C., and none for the presence of Altaic languages. The same is true, but more so, of the Uralic languages, spoken now in the northern Urals, Siberia, Finland, and Hungary—structurally they are possible candidates, but historically they are not.

The history and present distribution of the Dravidian and Indo-European languages makes it most likely that the Indus people spoke an early form of Dravidian [Map 9]. The migrations of Indo-Aryan speakers can be traced in their early literature, the *Vedas*. The geographical information that they contain shows that the Indo-Aryans (who it is thought came originally from the area north of the Black and Caspian Seas) entered the northwest during the 2nd millennium B.C.

and thence moved eastward into the Ganges Valley by the early centuries of the 1st millennium. Although we cannot discount the possibility of some Indo-Aryan speakers being present on the fringes of the Indus and Baluchistan at a somewhat earlier date, there is nothing to suggest that their numbers were large. At the time of the *Rigveda*, the earliest text, the Indo-Aryans were a warlike pastoral people, riding horses and pursuing a nomadic lifestyle similar to that of many of their relatives in Iran and Central Asia. As they settled in the subcontinent, they gradually took up farming as well. The language even of their earliest texts includes a number of borrowings from Dravidian languages, which were clearly being spoken by people with whom the Indo-Aryans came into contact when they first arrived, and these borrowings become more marked as time goes on. They were of all sorts, affecting grammar, pronunciation, and vocabulary. Among the words adopted by the Indo-Aryan speakers were ones for "plough" and "threshing floor," new concepts, as well as "pungent-tasting," referring to indigenous spices.

Similarly, a few words from Austro-Asiatic or other indigenous languages were borrowed into the Dravidian languages at an early stage in their development: these include a number of plants and animals native to the subcontinent. This fits the scenario I have put forward, that the Indus people and their ancestors entered the subcontinent from the northwest and came into contact with indigenous peoples, from whom they would have learned the names of the new flora and fauna they were now observing. Although the majority of Dravidian speakers now live in the south—Karnataka, Kerala, Tamilnadu, and Andhra Pradesh, as well as northern Sri Lanka—there are also small groups farther north. Koraga, spoken on the west coast, is possibly related to Kurux and Malto, languages now spoken by groups in central India who, according to their own traditions, moved along the Narmada River in historical times. Far to the north, in the Brahui Hills on the edge of the Iranian plateau, another Dravidian language, Brahui, is spoken.

An intriguing additional piece of information is that a linguistic link has been demonstrated between the Dravidian languages and the Elamite language of early western Iran. Brahui, in fact, is thought to be closer to the original shared proto-Elamo-Dravidian language than to the Dravidian languages of the subcontinent. The link with Elamite may tie in with the suggested evidence for the spread of farming from the Near East into the Indo-Iranian borderlands in the 8th millennium B.C. If this involved the movement of people as well as of crops and animals, we would expect the language of the immigrants to be related to that of the region from which they had originated—in other words that they should all speak "proto-proto-Elamo-Dravidian." This is certainly a possibility. Alternatively, studies of the bones and teeth of the early inhabitants of Mehrgarh show that they were physically related to other early peoples of India rather than those of Western Asia and that immigration is therefore unlikely at this stage.

Alternatively, the link between Elamite and Dravidian may have been at a more recent date. In the 5th and 4th millennia B.C., when international trade across the Iranian plateau developed, changes appear in the teeth of people living in the Indo-Iranian borderlands that relate them more closely to Western Asians. It could, therefore, be at this period that the proto-Dravidian language reached the subcontinent, spoken by new settlers in the region. Thereafter, there appears to be a very plausible pattern of the simultaneous spread of farming and Dravidian languages in the subcontinent. The pattern of development of the Dravidian languages (its family tree) closely fits a spread into the south via western India, identical to the archaeological picture of the spread of farming communities. Many words reconstructed as forming part of the proto-Dravidian language from which the later Dravidian languages spring relate to farming, showing that its speakers were farmers.

We may therefore suggest as a reasonable hypothesis that the first farmers in the northwest were Dravidian speakers and that the Indus Civilization that developed from the culture of the first farmers was also Dravidian-speaking. This does not, of course, mean that there were no other languages spoken in the area. Groups like the fishing community at Jalilpur before the time of the Indus Civilization and contemporaries of the Indus people such as the inhabitants of Ganeshwar or Langnaj probably spoke other languages, perhaps members of the Austro-Asiatic family or of other language families that have died out.

Although the evidence the Indus people spoke a Dravidian language is not conclusive, there are many other small pointers in the same direction. Many place names in the Indus region as well as in south India are Dravidian in etymology. Taken as a whole, there seems no reasonable doubt that the Dravidian languages were once much more widely spoken than now. In the 2nd millennium B.C., incoming Indo-Aryans mingled with the successors of the Indus Civilization, giving rise to a hybrid culture in which there was considerable bilingualism. By the 1st millennium, the language of the warlike Indo-Aryans had become dominant, due to their military superiority, but it had changed in the mouths of the local Dravidian speakers so that a significant proportion of its structure and pronunciation had become Dravidian and its vocabulary a mixture of both Indo-Aryan and Dravidian.

DRAVIDIAN WORDS

If the language that the Indus script was used to write was Dravidian, this takes us a certain way toward decipherment. The range of decipherments can be narrowed considerably to those that make sense using the vocabulary, word order, and other grammatical features of the Dravidian languages. This shows a structural pattern in which to fit our attempts at decipherment. It also means that we can suggest sound values for any pictographic signs that can unambiguously be identified.

This, unfortunately, is not that easy. The Indus script as we know it is a fully formed

and sophisticated script, not in its early stages of development. Few of the signs are clearly pictographic—they have evolved into more abstract forms in most cases. A few retain a more obviously pictographic form, but even these are not entirely unambiguous. Take the inscriptions shown in Figure 47, for instance. One sign, which occurs in both texts in C and E, strikes most investigators as a representation of a fish—but it has also been identified as a hank of rope. Another, on the extreme left in B, is usually taken to be a jar—but it could equally represent a fig tree or a cow's head. What may be a crab to some scholars (on the right-hand text of Figure 47-E) looks like a pair of tongs to others. Cultural and archaeological considerations are important—for example, the symbol above the animal's horns on the broken seal in Figure 47-D looks unambiguously like a spoked wheel to our eyes but it must represent something else, because at the time of the Indus Civilization, spoked wheels had not been invented anywhere in the world and only solid wheels were in use. An interpretation of this sign as a sun disk seems a logical suggestion.

If we can identify and put sounds to some of our signs, we are already making considerable progress. We can even go a little further. One of the features of most early scripts is the use of the rebus principle. This is the use of puns to get round the difficulty of representing unpictorial or abstract things. A sign representing a concept that is easy to draw can be used also to represent other words that sound the same or almost the same but which are difficult to show visually.

An example that is often quoted is the English word "belief," which can be written pictographically using a bee and a leaf. Using puns like this greatly extends the range of ideas that can be represented using a pictographic script.

It is likely that the Indus people employed the rebus principle. For example, the proto-Dravidian word for "fish" is "min" but this also means "star" or "god." The fish, a common creature in Indus art as well as a written sign, is thought by many scholars to be depicted swimming, as do the stars, in the waters of the heavens. Perhaps the fish sign, therefore, can also be taken to represent the word "god." Asko Parpola, who has studied these in great detail, proposes interpreting these as stars and constellations that are known to have been associated with gods and other heavenly beings in later times. For example, he identifies the fish sign combined with the number six as the Pleiades, called Arumin (six stars) and known in mythology as six of the wives of the Seven Sages. The Seven Sages themselves are represented in the heavens by the constellation of the Great Bear (along with their one faithful wife, Arundhati, the star Alcor) and this may be the meaning of the Indus fish sign combined with the number seven. Parpola also offers other star and constellation names for other combined fish signs, such as the fish with a ^ above it (Figure 47-F in the right hand text) and explanations for some of the other signs. This is a promising line to take, although it is not going to get us very far, given the small number of truly pictographic signs in the Indus script.

ANALYZING THE SCRIPT

Early attempts to decipher the Indus script relied heavily on intuition and on the decipherer's preconceptions. Consequently, little progress was made for a long time. Over the past thirty years, however, a number of teams or individuals, particularly the Finns and Russians and the Indian scholar Iravathan Mahadevan, have worked systematically on the inscriptions. They established basic information about the script without which no attempt at decipherment can possibly succeed.

There are a number of different ways in which spoken sounds can be recorded as writing. The one with which we are most familiar, the alphabet, was the most recent type to develop. Alphabetic scripts in principle have a single sign for each vowel and consonant used in the language, making it possible to write down any word so that its pronunciation is unambiguous. As alphabets are borrowed from the language they were devised for and used to write other languages, modifications can be made to render new sounds—accents, diacritical marks, and changes to the form of the letter, like é, ü, ø, or combinations of letters, like "th" or "oi." The fit between sound and letter, however, is rather variable. In Italian, for example, the match is excellent—but it is very easy to think of examples in English where this is not so, such as the great range of pronunciations of "-ough" or downright oddities like Cholmondesley (Chumley). The immediate precursor of the true alphabet, which was first used by the Greeks, was the alphabet without vowels. This was developed in the Levant in the mid to late centuries of the 2nd millennium B.C. A consonantal alphabet suits a certain kind of language where the context makes the appropriate vowel sound obvious and it is still used—Arabic script is of this type. Alphabetic scripts can be recognized by the small number of different signs that they require, generally somewhere between twenty and thirty-five, and the number of signs that are needed to make a word—ranging in English from one to more than thirty.

Syllabic scripts require a considerably larger number of different signs—probably no less than fifty and ranging up to several hundred. Linear B has about ninety. Each sign represents a vowel on its own or in combination with one or two consonants. Sometimes, as in many Indian scripts, there is a basic consonant form that changes in a regular way in combination with the different vowels. In other scripts, however, such as Linear B, there is no obvious similarity between the different combinations of the same vowel or consonant.

The first scripts that developed, more than 5,000 years ago in Mesopotamia and Egypt and later in China and elsewhere, were originally logographic and pictographic—in other words, each sign represented a full word (Greek *logos* = word) and was often written as a picture of the object in question. Soon the rebus principle came into use and signs were

Figure 49.

INSCRIBED SHERD

This inscribed sherd dates to 2300 B.C. It is obvious that the writing had evolved from simple singular signs and symbols. This particular sherd from Harappa was inscribed as a sherd, and seems less detailed than many of the other seals and materials with writing. There is speculation that it is in fact an ancient form of "scrap paper."

used to represent words of different meaning that sounded the same. The Sumerian script often included a determinative alongside these—an additional symbol that allowed one to identify the appropriate meaning of the main sign by showing what class of word it belonged to, such as a place name or the name of a god. Although Egyptian hieroglyphs always retained their pictorial quality, it was not long before the Sumerian pictograms began to be simplified to make writing them easier and they became progressively less recognizable. At the same time, the message conveyed by the writing became more complicated, moving over a few hundred years from simple lists of numbers and commodities to full and grammatically complete sentences. This was made possible by frequently using the signs as phonemes—as syllables and other parts of words. By 2500 B.C. the Sumerian script was a complete writing system that could record anything, such as myths and legends.

The early scripts are a mixture of logographs and phonetic signs that convey sounds.

The Chinese script has retained a high proportion of logographs, though it does also use phonetic signs. The number of signs in use depends to a considerable extent upon the relative proportions of these two sign types and whether the phonetic signs are polysyllabic, syllabic, or alphabetic (in other words, whether they represent several syllables, a single syllable, or a letter). The Chinese script uses thousands of signs; although there were as many as 6,000 Egyptian hieroglyphs, only about 700–1,000 were in use at any one time and far fewer were needed for most purposes. Sumerian cuneiform, which had a large number of syllabic signs by the mid–3rd millennium, used about 600 signs.

Counting the number of signs used in the Indus script should give us some indication of what kind of script we are dealing with. A rough count gives us somewhere in the region of 400 signs. Clearly this is far too many for an alphabetic script (which is historically implausible anyway, given that the alphabet was invented around 1500 B.C.) and too few for a purely logographic script. Some of its signs must have been logographic, however, because there are quite a few Indus inscriptions that consist of a single sign that must convey a complete word or idea. It is therefore probable that the Indus script used a combination of logographs and phonetic signs, of which many are likely to have been syllabic.

A good starting point for deciphering the script is to identify those signs that stand alone. These signs are probably acting as logographs—although this does not mean that they cannot also have been used in other places as phonemes. We can also look for regular combinations of signs and for signs that always follow a particular order or appear regularly in a certain position. Looking closely at the script, however, we are up against another problem. How many signs are there actually? Parpola's count identifies 398 separate signs. But there are many signs that look like each other—Parpola finds no less than 1,839 variants. Some of these are likely to be due to different "handwriting"—the different way in which people wrote the same sign. These different versions of the same sign are called "allographs." Others, however, must be completely different signs, with different sounds and meanings. How can we tell which are which? To take an example, compare the symbols shaped a bit like a letter "Y" with added lines at the top, which occurs at the right-hand end of the texts in Figure 47-A and G. They look almost the same, but not quite. Are they two versions of the same sign or two different signs? For comparison, we might consider the very different ways different individuals write the letter "s" in our own script and its similarity to the number "5."

Added to this problem of allographs is a related one—ligatures. Ligatures are separate signs written in combination, often in such a way that part of each of the signs is removed. A good example is the sign at the right-hand end of the Figure 47-B. Here we have a human figure (a common sign) combined with a yoke with an oval suspended on each side and, instead of a head, a headdress made of the jar sign (which can be seen as a separate sign at the right-hand end of the same row, on the right-hand seal). Can we recognize which signs are ligatures and which signs go to make them up? Which, on the contrary, are completely separate signs? All this makes the study of the script very complicated [Figure 50]. Some progress has been made, although it is very slow and very partial. One set of signs about which there is fairly general agreement is the series of short lines, often arranged in two rows, one above the other [for example, Figure 47-A]. These were probably numerals.

RIGHT TO LEFT OR LEFT TO RIGHT?

One important piece of information has been satisfactorily demonstrated—the direction in which the Indus script is written. It is assumed that the seals showed the mirror image of what they should so that they would read the right way around when stamped on sealings. So before looking at the seal texts, they are turned the other way around.

Figure 51.

BROKEN SEAL,
YOGI CHARACTER

*The decipherment of
the text on this seal
has been a point of
contention amongst
scholars for years.
But its imagery also
provides viewers
with much to ponder.
The central figure
seated in the yogic
position—legs folded
beneath the body—
wears the horns of a
bull or water buffalo.
The seal also bears
images of four*

(continued opposite)

Several pieces of evidence now suggest that the script was written from right to left. For a start, inscriptions that do not fill the whole upper line of a seal always begin on the right. Ones that run over on to another line either start again on the right side or occasionally run around on to the next line going left to right (backward but continuous). Sometimes the writer started on the right using normal-sized signs but ran out of space toward the end and cramped the last few signs on the left. All this seems fairly convincing evidence that the writing ran from right to left.

Proof that this is so was demonstrated by Mahadevan and comes from the internal evidence of the sign sequences. His studies showed that certain signs often appear in the same place in the inscriptions. In particular, the "jar" sign is frequently at the left-hand end of the text. Certain other signs, such as the "sun wheel," frequently appear at the right-hand end and there are several regular combinations, of signs to the right of the jar sign, to the left of the sun wheel, and together elsewhere. By looking at the signs that ended up on the second line when text was broken into two lines, it was possible to demonstrate that the jar sign comes at the end of texts, and the sun wheel and others from the right side at the beginning. So the writing was definitely from right to left.

This is very important because it provides clues to the sign combinations and syntax of the Indus script, leading on to results like the demonstration that the script was agglutinative and used suffixes. This, as we have seen, is an important clue in our attempt to identify the Indus language, as it fits very well with the theory that the language is an early form of Dravidian, and does not support the identification of the language as early Indo-Aryan.

DECIPHERMENT?

These studies have made some progress toward unraveling the mysteries of the Indus script. But the decipherment can only go so far because of the extreme brevity of the texts. The vast majority are short inscriptions on seals comprising a few signs only; and no text so far discovered is longer than two lines. Comparison with the early use of writing in other civilizations suggests that the texts on the seals probably gave either names or titles, and this fits in with the idea that the seals combined personal identification with official authorization. The task at present, therefore, seems akin to attempting decipherment from a telephone directory! Longer texts are needed.

A number of scholars, however, have not been daunted by the apparent hopelessness of the task. Some have offered complete decipherments, but the sense of the resulting "translated" texts has not been convincing.

For instance, the following are "readings" of the text of the famous "proto-Shiva" seal from Mohenjo Daro [Figure 51], quoted by Possehl in his 1996 volume on the Indus script:

- Bedrich Hrozny 1939: "Here is the tribute offered to the god Kueya."

- Swami Sankarananda 1943: "The (aquatic) birds have covered all the waterways."

- Finnish team: "Man of the Star (Shiva), the lord of . . . ."

- Prof. B. M. Barua 1946: "ajala-upasa" equivalent to Sanskrit acal-upasya meaning "The mountain-worshipped one."

- Prof. Bankabehari Chakravorty 1975: "Satta Kosika" (a name—Kosika present in Dictionary of Pali Proper Names).

- M.V.N. Krishna Rao 1982: "Makhanasan" (variant of makhahan, an epithet of Indra in Vedic literature).

- B. Priyanka 1988: "Trama mahisa-ha (great three-faced buffalo deity)." (This one sounds very plausible but has been arrived at by very dubious means, by comparison with Brahmi and using Indo-European as the underlying language. The syllabic values he has allocated to the signs have in many cases been arrived at by trial and error, accepting values that give words that make sense rather than because there is a logical reason for them—a circular approach.)

- W. A. Fairservis 1992: "An-il the Ruler, he (who) gathers the assembled clans."

- Parpola, whose approach is more cautious and systematic, reads the last three signs of the inscription—three common signs: jar, fish, man—as "min-a al" meaning "man [or servant] of the god."

Others are more reserved in their claims, but seem likely to be making more solid progress: for example, some argue that names or titles would probably have included the names and attributes of gods or have been paralleled in later names and titles, and have offered some plausible suggestions for these. Others have begun studying individual groups of objects whose inscriptions may be of a limited nature that may allow them to be identified. Looking at inscribed artifacts, like bronze axes, has allowed Parpola, for instance, to identify a sign that he believes may symbolize the concept of "king" or "ruler." It may one day be possible to gain some insight into the social, economic, and political organization of the Indus Civilization from its written clues.

important animals in Indus iconography: the bull, the rhino, the elephant, and the tiger. Of these, the bull and the elephant continued to play an important role in Indian iconography, while the tiger was later replaced by the lion. The fourth "noble beast" in later times was the horse, not introduced into the Indus region until the 2nd millennium B.C. Together these four creatures represented the cardinal directions. All these elements combined create an image pregnant with meaning.

CHAPTER NINE

TRADE AND LOCAL AND INTERNATIONAL RELATIONS

THE IMPORTANCE OF TRADE

Trade has generally been viewed as a vital aspect of civilizations and in many cases as the "prime mover" that catalyzed the emergence of civilization in particular regions. This is because raw materials are not evenly spread over Earth's surface. Hunter-gatherer societies generally move around to obtain many of these resources, and pastoralists also frequently move, sometimes over enormous distances like the steppe peoples of Central Asia.

Settled communities are tied to one place and therefore have to organize ways of obtaining the things they need. One way is by maintaining links with their neighbors and with their kin in other communities, creating a long chain of connections by which the products of distant lands eventually reach them. For example, the early farming communities of the Near East traded obsidian (volcanic glass, highly prized for making exceptionally sharp tools) over distances up to 800 km, in a series of hundreds of short moves. Central Asian turquoise and Persian Gulf coast shell must have reached the 7th millennium B.C. farming settlement of Mehrgarh in the same way.

An alternative way of obtaining raw materials is to trade directly with the people of the areas in which these materials are found or to establish colonies in these areas to get the goods themselves, by mining, quarrying, and other appropriate means. Traders and prospectors may engage in these activities as part of a wider economic strategy—in parts of South Asia and elsewhere, for example, pastoralists have for millennia carried trade goods as they moved between seasonal pastures.

As societies became more complex, their needs also grew. The luxuries of one generation become the vital needs of their descendants. In addition to the basic needs, now magnified

Figure 52.

MESOPOTAMIAN CYLINDER SEAL

This 21st century B.C cylinder seal from the Mesopotamian port city of Lagash is one of several that suggests Indus merchants living in the city were involved in trading along coast of the Arabian Sea.

GILGAMESH

The world's first written story is the Epic of Gilgamesh, king of Uruk. Although a historical character recorded in the Mesopotamian king lists, Gilgamesh became the focus for a host of legendary stories that gradually accreted to his name. In his youth, Gilgamesh acted the tyrant. The gods therefore created the wild man Enkidu to be his match. Enkidu came to Uruk, and met Gilgamesh in single combat. Wrestling together, they came to appreciate their superhuman similarities and became bosom companions. Together Gilgamesh and Enkidu traveled to the Amanus Mountains in the west where they slew the demon Humbaba, guardian of the cedar forest, and together they defied the power of Uruk's patron goddess Inanna—but these impieties cost Enkidu his life. The wild man was carried off by a divinely inflicted fever, and Gilgamesh was powerless to save his friend. He descended into madness in which he wandered far and wide in search of immortality, to preserve himself from such an end. Coming to Dilmun, he encountered the immortal Ziusudra, survivor of the Great Flood, and obtained the Plant of Life, which could bestow immortality. But on his return journey, the plant was eaten by a snake and Gilgamesh was forced to come to terms with human mortality. Returning to Uruk, he was consoled by the knowledge of the strength of his city and of its walls that he had rebuilt. Henceforth he became a mature and wise ruler, feted by his subjects.

(metal ores for tools instead of the more commonly available stone, for instance), societies required prestige goods to emphasize the growing status differences between individuals and groups—like gold for the trappings of kings—and materials to offer to the gods. Civilizations often developed in areas where immense agricultural potential was matched by a scarcity of important raw materials, encouraging the creation of an infrastructure to support foreign trade—to organize and finance expeditions and supply goods for trading.

Mesopotamia fits this picture very closely, and it has been convincingly argued that the need to conduct trade with neighboring regions was one of the main catalysts to the emergence of civilization here. Many people studying the Indus Civilization have suggested that trade played the same role in its emergence.

THE LAND OF MELUHHA

Although the Indus script still defies decipherment, we are actually not entirely without written information about the Indus Civilization. Several thousand miles away, the Sumerians of southern Mesopotamia had invented and begun to use writing around 3200 B.C., and by the mid–3rd millennium they were using a well-developed script not only to keep economic records but also to write legal

Figure 53. (opposite)

SUMERIAN TABLET

In the poem inscribed on this Sumerian clay tablet the god Enki describes Meluhha, thought to be a name for the Indus Civilization. The tablet, dating to about 1500 B.C, was discovered in 1898 by University of Pennsylvania archaeologists Herman Hilprecht and John Peters at the Iraqi site of Nippur.

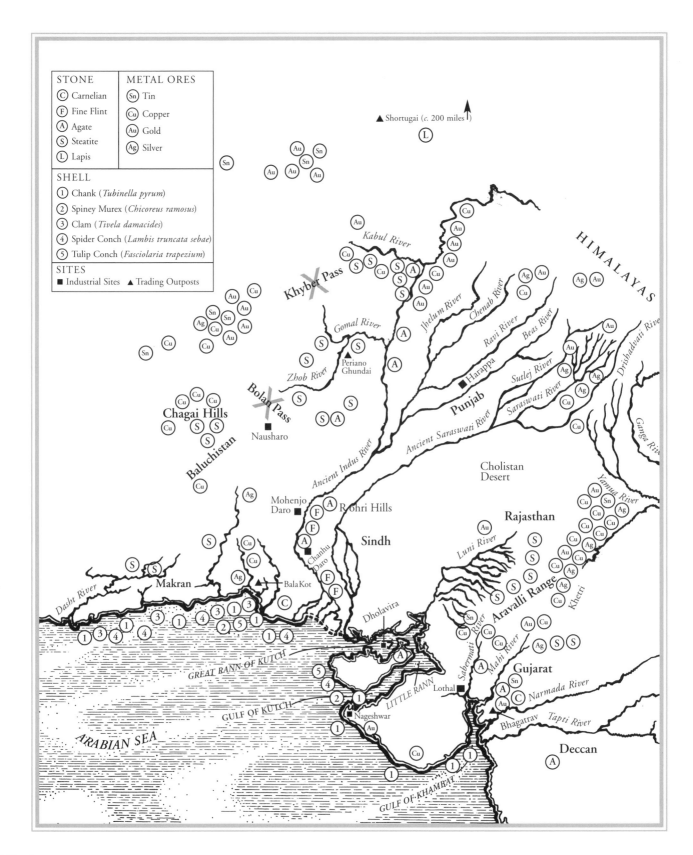

THE RISE OF MESOPOTAMIAN STATES

Civilization first emerged in Sumer and Akkad, the lands of southern Mesopotamia. Here in the late 4th millennium B.C. cities began to appear, their priestly rulers controlling the neighboring agricultural lands. Among the first was Uruk and it was here that writing was developed and first used, as a means of recording goods coming into and being issued from the temple. The city-states expanded rapidly and by 2800 B.C. were coming into conflict with one another. Now military prowess counted for as much as organizational ability and warrior kings began to emerge, usurping the traditional power of the priesthood. The legendary king Gilgamesh of Uruk was one such ruler. Individual cities grew increasingly powerful, trading widely and sometimes succeeding in controlling their neighbors. The wealth of the Royal Graves at Ur gives a glimpse of the splendors of this age. In 2334 B.C., Sargon, king of the city of Akkad in the central Euphrates Valley, succeeded in conquering the other cities of Mesopotamia and for the first time unified the region in the Akkadian Empire. He and his successors extended the power of Mesopotamia as far west as the Mediterranean and as far east as the Zagros Mountains. But by 2193 B.C. the empire had dwindled away and individual cities like Lagash were jockeying for power. In 2112 B.C. Ur-Nammu of Ur succeeded in reuniting Mesopotamia under the rule of the Third Dynasty of Ur, whose power endured until 2004 B.C. Again other cities rose to fill the power vacuum, notably Isin and Larsa, but it was not until 1792 B.C. that Mesopotamia was again united by the great Babylonian king, Hammurabi.

documents, literature, and even school exercises [Figure 53]. They were very active traders by land and sea, in contact with lands from the Mediterranean to the Indus, and they wrote of what they observed or heard. From their texts we can piece together some picture of the 3rd-millennium world in which they moved and of changing international relations. Many 3rd-millennium texts survive only as later copies and translations, and so inevitably some errors in copying and anachronisms have been introduced—but used with care, these texts are an invaluable reflection of this period.

Voyaging by sea from Sumer around 2300 B.C., the traveler would come first to the land of Dilmun, "the place where the sun rises"—the island of Bahrain and the adjacent Eastern Province of Saudi Arabia. Dilmun was blessed with "sweet water" from its artesian springs. Landfall would come next in Magan, land of copper mines, now identified as Oman (probably along with the Makran coast on the opposite side of the southern end of the Persian Gulf), and finally the voyager would sweep round into the Indian Ocean and sail on to Meluhha—the Indus Civilization. Studies of the information contained in the texts and archaeological work in the lands around the Persian Gulf have allowed these three foreign trading partners of Mesopotamia to be confi-

Map 10. (opposite)

INDUS RESOURCES

The list of natural resources to which the Indus people had local access seems to leave little to be looked for overseas, unless the volume required was so huge that local supplies could not keep pace with demand.

THE ROYAL CEMETERY AT UR

In 1919, Sir Leonard Woolley began excavations in the great Sumerian city of Ur, and in 1927 struck the magnificently furnished grave of a king—Meskalamdug, who ruled around 2800 B.C. Among the objects placed in his grave was a helmet of beaten gold in the shape of a wig, in which every strand and curl of hair was lovingly rendered. In the following year, Woolley came upon the first of sixteen royal tombs, each built of stone or mudbrick and set in a large pit. This grave, belonging to queen Puabi, demonstrated the wealth of the city and the astounding lavishness of royal burials of the period between 2600 and 2400 B.C. The queen was laid to rest on a bier within the burial chamber, clad in her finery, which included a lavish gold and lapis lazuli floral headdress and enormous gold earrings, surrounded by gold and silver vessels and other rich objects and accompanied by two maidservants similarly finely attired. In the pit outside the chamber were many of the queen's treasures and the sacrificed bodies of many servants and guards, who had apparently willingly entered the grave with their queen. The other Royal Tombs contained equally outstanding grave goods—including many strings of carnelian beads made by Indus craftsmen. One of the finest offerings was a sculpture of a pair of goats standing on their hind legs to eat a plant beautifully constructed of gold stems and flowers. The goats themselves had fleeces of gold and silver with lapis lazuli covering their shoulders and horns.

dently identified. Archaeological evidence, however, has also highlighted some discrepancies that are themselves extremely valuable in helping us to reconstruct trade relations at this time.

Archaeologists working in the Gulf have found evidence that the geographical areas to which the Mesopotamians attached these names changed through time. In the early 3rd millennium B.C., "Dilmun" may have been applied more loosely to include Oman, while "Magan" at this time probably referred just to the Iranian Makran. Later in the millennium Dilmun was used more specifically as the name for the islands of Bahrain and Tarut and the adjacent Arabian coast, while by the early 2nd millennium it also included the island of Failaka, much closer to Mesopotamia.

Meanwhile, Magan had shifted to become the Mesopotamian name for Oman. "Meluhha" was certainly the Indus region in the 3rd and early 2nd millennia, but by the 15th century B.C. there had been a remarkable change and the name was given to Ethiopia, from which Mesopotamia now imported many of the same commodities as it had received from the Indus, such as timber and ivory.

The pattern of trade was not static either. The Mesopotamians recorded the lands from which they obtained particular commodities but of course these need not have been their original source. Dilmun acted as an entrepot for much of the Gulf trade during certain periods, trading their own imports on as exports to Mesopotamia—and the goods that the Indus people traded included many that they themselves had obtained from distant lands [Map 10].

EARLY SUMER AND ITS NEIGHBORS

Mesopotamia was a rich and fertile land, producing abundant crops and feeding many animals. By the 4th millennium B.C. its farmers were supporting a substantial number of other people who dwelt in the emerging towns—craftsmen making pottery from local clays and textiles from the wool of their sheep; priests and traders; and warrior kings by the early centuries of the 3rd millennium. But Kalam, "the Land," as its people called it, lacked many commodities that were necessary or desirable for everyday life and for the glorification of its gods and rulers—things like hard stone for grinding grain, timber for building houses and ships and for making furniture, copper for making tools, gold and silver and gemstones to adorn the temples and their finest artifacts. These materials they had to obtain from neighboring lands, trading their surplus grain and other agricultural produce, and various manufactured goods such as textiles, perfumes, oil, and pottery.

Sumer and Akkad, the lands of Mesopotamia, enjoyed trading relations at various times with Anatolia and other lands to its west and north, but it is those to the south and east that are of relevance to the Indus Civilization. Immediately east of Mesopotamia rise the mountains of the Zagros range, which define the western edge

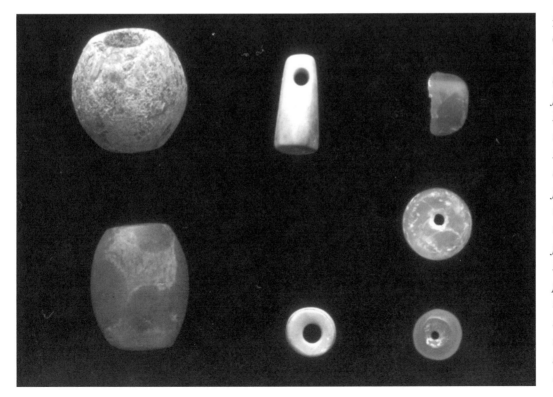

Figure 54.

CARNELIAN BEADS
Carnelian was a quintessential export for the Indus people. It is frequently mentioned in the Mesopotamian texts, often as an import from Dilmun, though in some inscriptions it was clearly identified as coming from Meluhha. The Indus people did ship the unworked carnelian to Sumerian craftsmen, as identical beads are found at Sumerian sites.

of the Iranian plateau. This region was inhabited by the Elamites, with whom the cultures of Mesopotamia were in constant interaction throughout their history, often trading with them but equally frequently at war. Indeed, some of the finest pieces of Mesopotamian art were found at Susa, the Elamite capital, where they had been taken as the spoils of war. Like Mesopotamia, Elam was in the throes of urbanization during the 4th and early 3rd millennia. Beyond Elam and to its north lay lesser communities that also developed thriving towns, supported by the international trade network that was coming into being. One Sumerian text, "Enmerkar and the Lord of Aratta," vividly recounts the story of attempts by a legendary early-3rd-millennium king of Uruk, Enmerkar, to obtain a supply of exotic goods—gold, silver, and lapis lazuli—from his counterpart in the distant land of Aratta, "beyond the seven mountains of Anshan." After issuing a series of unsuccessful threats, he sent a caravan of donkeys heavily laden with barley and obtained the desired commodities as a return gift or trading exchange.

Excavations in a number of these trading towns on the Iranian plateau have revealed the reality behind such trading expeditions, often uncovering the remains of major industrial activity related to this trade. At Tepe Yahya, for example, fine stone vessels were produced from chlorite (or steatite), a soft stone that was locally available. Chlorite vessels were traded from here to Mesopotamia, settlements in the Gulf, and elsewhere. The towns of the Indo-Iranian borderlands, and beyond them the early settlements in the

Indus Valley at the eastern end of the Iranian plateau, were integrated into this trading network.

The Sumerians particularly valued lapis lazuli. This was mined in the hills around Badakhshan in Afghanistan and traded by the local people. It reached Shahr-i Sokhta in Seistan in the form of raw nodules, and here it was worked to reduce its bulk. Skilled workers removed the cortex (outer "rind") and impurities and prepared the lapis for export either as pure clean nodules or as finished items such as beads. Lapis lazuli was traded to centers throughout the network, turning up in small amounts in Baluchistan, Elam, and the Gulf, but the greater part went to Mesopotamia. Here it was used as one of the main prestige materials to decorate many valuable objects, such as the lyres and gaming boards included as grave offerings in the Royal Cemetery at Ur, dated around 2600–2400 B.C. Other offerings included carnelian beads imported from the Indus Civilization.

Not content with this overland trade, Mesopotamians had also been exploring the Gulf by sea in search of raw materials. They had known the Bahrain region from as early as the 5th millennium B.C., and in the early 3rd millennium they were trading pottery with Tarut and with Oman, obtaining some of the copper ores in which the Oman peninsula abounds. By the middle of the millennium, Bahrain was growing in importance as an entrepot in the trade. With its precious springs of "sweet water" and fine natural harbors, it was a natural port of call of any vessel sailing through the Gulf. It was already established in Sumerian mythology as the Paradise land, home to Ziusudra, the immortal survivor of the legendary Mesopotamian Flood, which he, like Noah, had weathered in an ark, along with animals both wild and domestic. The waters around Bahrain yielded "fish-eyes" (pearls) and it was probably a pearl that the hero-king, Gilgamesh of Uruk, obtained here as the "Plant of Life," with which he hoped to secure immortality. His aspirations were frustrated by a snake that ate the pearl while he slept. Pearls and mother-of-pearl were exported from Dilmun to Mesopotamia along with the fine dates that were cultivated on Bahrain.

INTERNATIONAL VISITORS TO UR

In the 24th century B.C., the Indus Civilization, whose goods had been reaching Mesopotamia for many years, finally appears on the Mesopotamian literary stage. In 2334 B.C. southern Mesopotamia was united for the first time into a single kingdom by Sargon of Akkad, who founded the Akkadian dynasty. Referring to himself in the third person, he boasted in one of his inscriptions that during his reign, "Ships from Meluhha, ships from Magan, ships from Dilmun he made lie at anchor at the harbor of Akkad," his capital city, which lay far up the Euphrates River. Massive foreign seaborne trade was now at its height, dominated, in their view, by the Mesopotamian powers. Sargon's grandson, Naram-Sin, whose thirty-seven-year reign

began in 2254 B.C., called himself "King of the Four Regions of the World" and "King of the Universe" (as well as "God of Agade") and implied that he controlled the Indus. Writing of a massive uprising that he put down, he includes "...ibra, man of Meluhha" (the name of the man of Meluhha is incomplete in the inscription), among the rebellious rulers—but reading between the lines, Meluhha was well beyond the reach of his army. He may have attacked as far south as Magan, for he says he "marched against Magan and personally caught Mandannu, its king"—but it is obvious that the Mesopotamian kings were prone to exaggerate the extent of their conquests from a remark in an inscription of Naram-Sin's father, Manishtushu (who came to the throne in 2269 B.C.). After boasting of conquering Anshan and Sherihum (east of Elam), he adds, "These are no lies. It is absolutely true!"

After the fall of the Akkadian dynasty in 2193 B.C. there was a period of political disintegration, during which various Mesopotamian city-states reasserted their independence. One of the foremost was Lagash, under their great ruler Gudea (2141–2122 B.C.), who made use of the established trade network to acquire exotic materials for a great temple he was building in his capital city, Girsu. The land was again united in the 21st century B.C. under Ur-Nammu, who founded the Third Dynasty of Ur (Ur III), the second Mesopotamian empire. Many documents were discovered at Ur in the merchant quarter: these refer still to boats from Magan (Oman), but do not now speak of those from Meluhha, even though Meluhhan merchants were certainly still in Mesopotamia. We know little of the seafarers of Magan themselves, but their relatives on the northern coast of the Oman peninsula traded their copper and received Mesopotamian goods in return throughout the second half of the 3rd millennium. The people of the interior and the southern shores of Oman, unlike their northern counterparts, were trading with Indus rather than Mesopotamian merchants. The settlement of Ras al Junayz, on the south coast, was one of those directly engaged in trade with the Indus—Indus weights and seals with Indus script on them were being used within the settlement. A warehouse or magazine here contained a number of slabs of bitumen probably standing ready for export to the Indus (where, for instance, bitumen had been used to make the Great Bath watertight). Magan seems also to have supplied the Indus with some copper, although the Indus people had several other copper sources. Incense and other produce from farther west in Arabia would also have passed in this way through southern Magan and across the sea to the Indus.

From the Akkadian Period onward, the bulk of Mesopotamia's trade was conducted by sea, and long-distance overland trade routes withered away, although overland trade continued over shorter distances. The Indus Civilization was instrumental in bringing about this major change. Sea trade, though not without its risks, such as storms and pirates, was a far more efficient means than overland transport of carrying goods in bulk over long distances. It also gave much more control over the management of trade, bringing the Indus people into direct com-

mercial relations with the Mesopotamians themselves rather than depending on middlemen. By the time of Sargon, therefore, if not before, the Indus people were plying the sea lanes and anchoring in Sumerian ports.

Although the later texts, of the Ur III Period, no longer mention the arrival of ships from Meluhha, there are numerous clues that attest the actual presence of merchants from the Indus region in Mesopotamia at this time, presumably keeping an eye on Indus business interests. The city of Lagash was home to an enclave of Meluhhan merchants who must have managed the Sumerian end of the trade network. Instead of the square Indus seals whose impression could be stamped directly, they used the local type of seal, an inscribed cylinder that was rolled across clay to make an impression of the design [Figure 52]. On these they inscribed designs based around Indus animals. Looking at the arrangement of signs on these seals, scholars have been able to work out that they are placed in unusual sequences—this means that the inscriptions probably gave non-Indus names or titles, which hints that Indus merchants were involved in the local organization of trade.

CHANGES IN THE GULF

Although Dilmun is rarely mentioned in Ur III texts and the Sumerians at this time seem to have been obtaining their copper directly from Magan, the island of Bahrain and the other areas that made up Dilmun continued to grow in prosperity during this period, importing considerable quantities of Mesopotamian goods and trading with the Meluhhans. A number of their characteristic round seals bear writing in the Indus script—as in Sumer, these signs are arranged in an unusual way, suggesting that the words written here are in a non-Indus language. The pattern of trade altered again when in 2004 B.C. the Elamites sacked and looted Ur and carried off the king, bringing to an end the Ur III dynasty. The political unity that Mesopotamia had known for most of three centuries was destroyed and individual cities fended for themselves. Previously overseas trading expeditions had been officially financed by the temple or the palace; now merchants were largely self-financed and they had neither the resources to make long-distance expeditions nor the backup resources needed to insure against disasters on a large scale. Mesopotamian trading expeditions and the vessels in which they were undertaken were therefore scaled down, and the texts now make it clear that they traveled only as far as Dilmun, three days' sailing from Ur.

As a result, Dilmun now gained new importance as the middleman in the international trade network, providing Mesopotamia with goods and raw materials from the Gulf and Meluhha and growing rich on the proceeds. The town of Qala'at al Bahrain had substantial warehouses in its center and many of its houses contained seals and weights, a sign that many of the inhabitants derived their prosperity from direct involvement in the trade. The weights followed two systems, that of Mesopotamia and that of the Indus,

so that the Dilmunites could measure and convert quantities to the satisfaction of both sets of customers. In Mesopotamian texts the Indus weight system is now referred to as the "standard of Dilmun," emphasizing Sumer's loss of contact with the Indus region. The texts also note, however, that the Meluhhans were trading with Dilmun. This must have been a two-way process because a seal of Dilmun type has been found in the Indus trading town of Lothal and another in the recently discovered Indus port at Dwarka. Curiously, there is little evidence of the presence of Dilmunites in Oman, although this must be the source of the copper that Dilmun was trading to Mesopotamia. Probably by now the Omanis themselves were actively involved in the trade.

Magan and Meluhha were also involved in another trade route by this time (early 2nd millennium B.C.), one that followed the southern coast of Arabia and reached into Africa. Incense was probably the main commodity that traveled east along this route, but new crops were also introduced that were to have an enormous impact on the Indian subcontinent: sorghum, finger millet *(Eleusine),* and bulrush millet *(Pennisetum).* These were under cultivation in Arabia by the 4th millennium B.C. but seem not to have been introduced to Gujurat, the region of the Indus realms where their cultivation took off, until the late 3rd millennium B.C. This was to have far-reaching repercussions.

The 18th century B.C. saw the virtual collapse of the Gulf trading network, due to major political changes in the two great civilizations involved. In Mesopotamia, Hammurabi, the great Babylonian king, reunited its lands and peoples by 1750 B.C., creating a huge empire. But unlike earlier Mesopotamian states, this was centered on Babylon, whose focus of interest lay to the north. Mesopotamian trade was now largely with Anatolia and the Levant, and the cities of the south declined in importance, along with their seaborne trade. Salination of the land, the result of millennia of irrigation, was also undermining the prosperity of southern Mesopotamian agriculture. The Indus Civilization declined around the same time and unlike southern Mesopotamia did not revive in later centuries. Did the loss of its overseas market cause or contribute to the Indus collapse? To answer this it is necessary to look more closely at Indus involvement in the Gulf trade network.

MELUHHA—SOURCE OF MANY OF SUMER'S IMPORTS

Meluhha is described in a Sumerian poem that recounts the creation of the world, "Enki and the World Order" [*see* Figure 52]. Here the god Enki is dictating the form that Meluhha was to take:

"Black land, your trees will be large trees, they will be mesu-groves of the highland,

Your reeds will be large reeds, they will be reeds of the highland,

Heroes work them as weapons in the battlefields,

Your bulls will be large bulls, they will be the bulls of the highland,

Their roar will be the roar of the bulls of the highland,

The great laws of the gods will be perfected for you.

All fowls of the highland wear carnelian beards,

Your birds will be haia birds,

Their cries will fill the royal palaces,

Your silver will be gold,

Your copper will be bronze-tin,

Land, everything you have will increase."

Meluhha's attributes listed in the Creation text are ones that are likely to have struck a Mesopotamian visiting India. Cattle were the Indus domestic animal par excellence, and the majority were the humped zebu cattle of the subcontinent, very different from the cattle of West Asia and therefore noteworthy to the Mesopotamians as a feature of the land of Meluhha. The haia bird that is mentioned is probably a peacock—this would certainly fit the description of its noisiness. In the 1st millennium, Indian merchants brought a peacock trained to sing and dance to Babylonia. In other texts, Meluhha is said to be the home also of the dar bird, identified by scholars as the black francolin *(Francolinus)*. Francolin bones have been found in at least one Indus town.

From the many texts we can get some idea of the range of materials that the Mesopotamians imported from Meluhha— various types of timber, stone and metal, ivory, and animals as well as exotic birds like those already discussed. Often there is archaeological evidence of these imports to back up the textual references. Some of these materials are very clearly of Indus origin; others cannot so easily be identified but may match products of the Indian subcontinent. Others again are obviously not products of the Indus region itself but were materials that the Indus people were importing for their own use and which they must also have traded on to Mesopotamia.

Lapis lazuli, from Badakhshan in Afghanistan or the Chagai Hills in Baluchistan, falls into the latter category. The greater part of the lapis that Indus people obtained was most likely traded to Mesopotamia, where it was extremely highly valued. Carnelian ("red stone") was frequently mentioned in the Mesopotamian texts, often as an import from Dilmun, though in Gudea's inscriptions it was clearly identified as coming from Meluhha [Figure 54]. Mines at Rajpipla and elsewhere in the Deccan and Gujurat produced large quantities of carnelian, agate, and other hard stone that the Indus people worked into fine beads. Identical carnelian beads have been found at many Sumerian sites and these must have been imports from the Indus Civilization, along with the unworked carnelian that was used by Sumerian craftsmen.

Ivory from Indian elephants was used in great quantities by the Indus people—at Mohenjo Daro, objects made of ivory were more common than those of bone, and were in everyday use as combs, pins, sticks for applying kohl (eye makeup), dice, and many other small items. Mesopotamian texts refer to Meluhha as the source of ivory birds.

Other ivory objects and unworked pieces are said to come from Dilmun, but this may be because they fall in the Late Period when Dilmun was acting as the middleman in trade between the Gulf and Mesopotamia. The Dilmunites probably made a considerable profit on this exchange as ivory was highly prized and rare in Mesopotamia.

Timbers of various sorts were important imports since Mesopotamia lacked substantial trees for building houses and other buildings, boats, and furniture. The highland mesu wood mentioned in the Enki text was probably sissoo (*Dalbergia sissoo*), which grew in the Punjab and was used at Mohenjo Daro in house building. From it the Sumerians made boats, chariots, and furniture. Another wood, used for furniture and building construction, was called kusabku—"sea-wood." This might have been mangrove, which was found as an import at Saar on Bahrain (although it could equally have come here from the Emirates or the Makran, where it also grows). The identification of sea-wood as mangrove is problematic, since mangrove is not suitable for fine purposes, such as its use in a throne inlaid with lapis lazuli that is mentioned in one Sumerian text. Alternatively, teak, native to the Deccan and the coastal region south of Bombay, and found at Lothal, is as much used for boat building as it is water-resistant. So teak could well be the sea-wood referred to in the Sumerian texts—it is a very fine timber highly suitable for decorative furniture.

Many other kinds of Meluhhan timber are mentioned. One is called *sullum meluhhi*, "black wood of Meluhha," and may perhaps have been ebony, native to south India. We do not know for certain if the Indus people had trade relations with south India that would have enabled them to obtain ebony, although it seems possible. No trace of ebony has yet been found at Indus sites themselves. The lack of wood at these sites is not conclusive evidence that the Indus people did not use it, because wood does not generally survive and the few extant pieces cannot be fully representative of all the types of timber used by the Indus people. The Mesopotamians also claimed to import "Meluhha date-palm" as timber. Why? The Indus people did indeed grow these trees, but the date palm was the one tree that flourished in southern Mesopotamia itself. Perhaps the name refers to a different type of tree that bore some resemblance to the date palm.

Finally "Enki and the World Order" refers to reeds, another puzzle to understand. There are several possible explanations. Reeds are said to have been imported by the Sumerians from Magan as well and were used for containers and arrowshafts as well as furniture: the Magan reed was probably bamboo. The Indus people themselves imported bamboo from the Makran region and used it in their buildings and for oars and masts, and as a packing material at Lothal. So possibly the "highland reeds" were bamboo. Alternatively, it is possible that this could refer to sugarcane, which grew wild in the Punjab. A type of reed, *Saccharum arundinaceum*, is known from Harappa. The other timbers used by the Indus people themselves, including deodar, rosewood, tamarisk, pine, elm, and acacia, seem not to have been imported by the Sumerians.

Meluhha is listed by the Mesopotamians as a source of copper and gold dust, both of which they also imported from Magan. The trade in copper was probably quite a complicated one. The Indus people obtained much of their copper from the inhabitants of the Aravalli Hills to their south and had done so since Early Indus times. They also probably obtained copper from the Las Bela region of Baluchistan. There were other sources farther north, in the Chagai Hills and at several places on their trade routes into Iran and Afghanistan. Across the Gulf lay Oman, ancient Magan, which was by the mid–3rd millennium a major exporter of copper, in which the region abounds. Weights and other Indus artifacts show that merchants from the Indus lands were trading here and copper is likely to have been one of their main objectives. Mesopotamia also had access to copper from a number of sources: Anatolia, Cyprus, and Palestine as well as the regions to its south. The Sumerians seem to have obtained some copper directly from Oman throughout the 3rd millennium, but, as we have seen, during the latter part Meluhha and Dilmun also acted as intermediaries and Sumer had no direct contact with Oman after about 2000 B.C.

Tin was a rare commodity in the ancient world, but one to which Sumer and Meluhha both had access—both civilizations alloyed it with copper to make bronze. Its source is uncertain. One reference, in an inscription of Gudea, suggests some of Sumer's tin came from Meluhha, although the greater part seems likely to have come from Afghanistan. The Indus people themselves could perhaps have extracted alluvial tin from their rivers, though this is by no means certain. A source of tin was recently discovered in the Tusham area of the Aravalli Hills, in the region inhabited by the Ganeshwar culture, which also supplied the Indus people with copper, and it is possible that this source was known and worked in Indus times. The people of the Indus may also have obtained tin from the region around their outpost at Shortugai in Afghanistan, where tin and gold and lapis lazuli were available. Gold dust was probably panned by the Indus people on the upper reaches of the Indus River, as it is still today. Karnataka in south India was another possible source of Indus gold. The export of gold dust to Mesopotamia would suggest that quite substantial quantities were available to the Indus people one way or another. This is borne out by the large number of pieces of gold jewelry that have been found in their towns and cities [see Color Plate 25].

WHAT WAS EXPORTED TO MELUHHA?

What evidence is there of the goods and materials that were traveling in the opposite direction? Mesopotamian texts give some indication of the range of commodities that they exported to the lands with which they traded. There was the surplus of local agricultural produce, such as barley, wheat, dates, leather and wool, and dried fish, along with goods manufactured from local materials such as fine woolen textiles, perfumed ointments, and oil. Then there were goods and materials imported from other regions, such as silver from Anatolia or Elam—such materials were imported in larger quantities than the Mesopotamians required and were traded on. Finally goods manufactured in Mesopotamia from imported materials were also traded.

Archaeological evidence allows us to trace exports that were not perishable—pottery, for example. Some pottery was exported for its own sake, other pottery vessels as containers for foodstuffs, cosmetics, and aromatics. Modern scientific techniques of investigation can sometimes detect and identify residues of substances that were once carried in the pottery, such as oil. Despite this, many of Mesopotamia's exports are "invisible"— they have long since been consumed completely or have perished. (This is of course also true of many of Mesopotamia's imports but we have the surviving textual evidence here to complete the picture.) So although we know what goods and materials Mesopotamia was sending out, we have no idea if the Meluhhans were among the customers for these particular commodities.

What did the Indus people actually want from the west? When we look at the list of commodities that Mesopotamia and the Gulf had to offer, there seems little that the Indus people could not obtain closer to home or produce themselves in abundance. Very few Mesopotamian objects have been found in Indus sites—some pottery of the type known as "reserved slip ware," occasional cylinder seals, a handful of small stone objects that may be Mesopotamian—a few curios, not the serious basis of a major trade network. The Indus people had no need of Mesopotamian grain or other foodstuffs as their own fields produced abundant supplies. Sesame, used by the Sumerians to make the oil they exported, is thought to have been introduced to Mesopotamia originally from India, and was certainly cultivated by the Indus people. The Indus people had their own sheep and goats to produce hair and wool for making textiles and in addition they had cotton. Nevertheless, it is possible that the foreign patterns of Mesopotamian textiles were considered desirable by the Indus people, that Mesopotamian or Dilmun dates were preferred to local dates, just as in the modern world the apple-growing and dairy-farming inhabitants of Britain import French "Golden Delicious" apples and New Zealand butter.

The list of raw materials to which the Indus people had local access also seems to leave little to be looked for overseas, unless the volume required was so huge that local supplies could not keep pace with demand. One commodity does stand out, however, as something not available locally—silver. Silver was much used by the Indus elite, being made into jewelry such as beads and bangles. Silver objects have been found in major cities, Mohenjo Daro especially, where they include silver vessels and a few seals, and Harappa, but only rarely in other, less important sites—a few pieces at Lothal, pieces in a hoard of jewelry from Allahdino, and in a smaller hoard from Early Indus Kunal. Clearly silver was highly valued and its use was probably restricted to the upper echelons of society.

The Mesopotamians imported silver both from Elam and from Anatolia, but did not much value it for its own sake. It was often used to make rings that acted as a kind of currency, so it was thought useful as a medium of exchange. The texts make it clear that a considerable amount of silver was obtained by the Mesopotamians for trade with the Gulf. So it is quite probable that Mesopotamia was the immediate source of the silver used by the Indus people. There are other sources of silver that were potentially available to the Indus people, in Afghanistan, but these may not have been exploited at the time. Silver was not in use before the Early Indus Period in the subcontinent and ceased to be used after the Indus decline. Here we have a commodity that certainly could have played an important part in the trade between east and west, but hardly important enough to account for the volume of trade from the Indus to the west. We still have an intriguing puzzle about what drove the Indus people to organize such major and long-lasting trade. But we cannot doubt that the justification, whatever it was, was a powerful one.

INDUS ENTREPRENEURS

Evidence of the importance the Indus people attached to trade comes from Turkmenia. The lapis lazuli mines of Badakhshan, the only source of lapis known to the cultures of Western Asia, had been exploited for hundreds of years. A steady flow of this beautiful blue stone found its way through the trading towns of the Iranian plateau to Mesopotamia and even Egypt. Although the Indus people were probably also exploiting the lapis source recently rediscovered in the Chagai Hills of Baluchistan, they seem to have taken over control of the Badakhshan mines, monopolizing their output, which now reached the west only by sea via the Indus. The fact that the Indus people made little use of lapis at home emphasizes the importance they must have been attaching to its trade with the west since, in order to obtain it, the Indus people established a typical Indus town at Shortugai, near the mines and 1,000 km from home.

Such outposts, designed to control the produce of an area, seem to have been one of the hallmarks of the Indus Civilization. Great importance was accorded to obtaining and distributing raw materials. Though not so remote as Shortugai, many of the important Indus towns and cities were located at the borders of the civilization. These areas were physically isolated from other Indus settlements, though linked to them by riverine transport and by the pastoralists whose regular seasonal movements took them between different regions. Such a one was the great city of Harappa in the north, ideally placed to exploit the rich supplies of timber in the Himalayan foothills. Manda and Rupar, on the northeastern periphery of the Indus realms, were similarly isolated, and were important stations supplying teak from the Himalayan foothills.

Another such outpost was Lothal in Gujurat. Lothal lay on the border between the agricultural lands of the Indus Civiliza-tion and the sparsely inhabited North Gujurat plain, home to hunter-gatherer groups, and not far from the sea. A large brick basin constructed along the eastern side of the town was thought by its excavator to have been a dock into which boats would come from the nearby river to unload [Color Plate 13]. Serious objections have been raised to this suggestion. For example, the approach channel turns twice through 90°, which seems excessively awkward, and the positioning of the dock on the opposite side of the town from the river also seems to create needless difficulties of access. The basin could have been a reservoir for drinking water and for irrigation, although some scholars have valid objections: that the water in it would have been contaminated by the town's drains and that the local water supplies were perfectly adequate for agriculture without a special reservoir. The basin, then, remains another Indus mystery. However, there is no doubt that, even without a dock, Lothal was engaged in trade.

A substantial part of this small town was given over to manufacturing various Indus products such as beads and objects of gold, copper, shell, and ivory. The volume of their output was quite out of proportion to the needs of the town's modest resident population and the inhabitants of its hinterland. The greater part of its products, therefore, must have been made for use elsewhere. A substantial warehouse in the citadel area of the town was destroyed by fire at some point in its career. Burnt clay tags from this warehouse bearing the imprint of Indus seals indicate official control of the craft objects produced here. The majority of these were stamped with seals bearing the unicorn image, which I earlier suggested may represent the official authorization of the ruling class [*see* Figure 45]. Some of the goods from Lothal were probably carried by sea to Magan, Dilmun, or Sumer. A circular seal from Dilmun is among the objects found in the town. Some workshops produced goods of local materials for distribution to other parts of the Indus realms. And some products were undoubtedly made for trade with the local non-Indus people.

THE INDUS PEOPLE AND THEIR NEAR NEIGHBORS

Unlike most parts of the world, the development of farming did not end hunting and gathering as a way of life. Within the Indus region, hunter-gatherer groups adapted their self-sufficient lifestyle, moving gradually into mutually beneficial interdependence with settled communities. (Not that the relationship was always peaceful: one later piece of hunter-gatherer rock art shows an episode of highway robbery: a hunter-gatherer armed with a bow and arrow is shown holding up a traveler in a chariot!) Hunter-gatherers could provide the desirable produce of jungle and desert, such as honey, otherwise largely unobtainable by settled groups. They could also act as carriers, transmitting the commodities of one settled region to the inhabitants of another. The hunter-gatherers would

exchange these for both foodstuffs and manufactured goods that were beyond their own technological capabilities.

At the time of the Indus Civilization this relationship was in its infancy but was nevertheless becoming an established pattern. For example, the site of Langnaj was a hunter-gatherer camp that was occupied over a long period. At the time of the Indus Civilization, the bones excavated here show that meat from hunted wild animals was being supplemented by that from domestic animals. Stone tools were joined by Indus beads, a copper knife, and pottery. Langnaj lies in an arid region not far from the Indus settlements of Kutch, but there is a very definite demarcation between the Indus and the hunter-gatherer zones of settlement—to the extent that Possehl and other scholars working in this area have suggested that the Indus people considered it to be in their own interests not to upset the status quo by attempting to settle within the region occupied by these hunter-gatherer communities.

Lothal, therefore, can be seen as an example of a "gateway" settlement, producing goods that were traded with their hunter-gatherer neighbors for local commodities such as ivory and for the products of areas within the hunter-gatherers' annual range of seasonal movement. In addition the hunter-gatherers could have obtained materials from much farther afield, to trade with Lothal. By this means the raw materials of the south and east were also made available to the Indus people through Lothal. Such materials might have included gold from the gold reefs of Karnataka, as well as precious, semiprecious, and other attractive stones for making beads and other jewelry.

The Indus people enjoyed similar trading relations with other peoples on their borders. One example well documented by archaeological evidence was their trade with the people of the Aravallis, known to archaeologists as the Jodhpur-Ganeshwar Culture. Like many of the early inhabitants of northern India, these people gained much of their livelihood from fishing. However, the Aravalli Hills are one of the richest sources of copper in the subcontinent. As early as the Early Indus Period, the days of the first pioneer farmers on the Indus, a relationship had developed between the Indus farmers and the Aravalli fisher folk, giving the Indus people access to the Aravalli copper and perhaps tin. The Jodhpura-Ganeshwar people seem themselves to have mined the copper and exchanged it with the Indus folk, who traveled to the region to trade. In return, the people of the Aravallis obtained manufactured goods and other Indus produce, including some objects made from the copper they had previously supplied.

TRADE AND THE INDUS

At the beginning of the chapter I raised the question of the significance of trade to the Indus people. Could the need to organize the efficient and adequate supply of foreign goods and materials have been the driving force behind the appearance of the Indus Civilization, a major factor behind its prosperity, and the cessation of this trade the reason for the civilization's demise?

The Indus people were deeply involved in overseas trade. They clearly also had an extensive trading network branching out into other regions—into surrounding regions of the Indian subcontinent and to the north and east as far as the Oxus (Amu Darya) River. The materials they obtained in adjacent regions and in parts of their own dominions were widely distributed among the people of the civilization, reaching even minor settlements, and clearly the infrastructure involved in this was significant in the organization of Indus society. But there is a gaping hole in the middle of this picture—there is apparently almost nothing that the Indus people were getting from their trade with Mesopotamia and little from the rest of the Gulf. Until we can solve this puzzle we cannot answer the question fully—but at least at present the answer seems to be a qualified "No": the needs of trade do not seem to have brought the Indus Civilization into being or carried it along. There is reason to suppose, as I shall discuss in Chapter 11, that trade had nothing to do with the Indus Civilization's demise either.

CHAPTER TEN

A PEACEFUL REALM?

WAR AND PEACE

In the previous chapter the affairs of literate ancient Mesopotamia crossed the path of the Indus Civilization. Although Mesopotamia's trade was the main theme, the frequent internal conflicts between its city-states and hostile external relations with its neighbor Elam were also mentioned, because warfare played an important part in the history of this region.

One of the most surprising aspects of the Indus Civilization is that it seems to have been a land without conflict. There are no signs of violence and no depictions of soldiers or warfare in the Indus art. When we look at the other civilizations we can see how unusual and unexpected this is. The texts of contemporary Sumer and Egypt are full of references to warfare and this is underscored by numerous depictions of soldiers, battles, and war captives. The same was true of China, Mycenaean Greece, and many other areas. Mesoamerica from the days of its first civilizations to its collapse at the hands of the Spaniards was the home of bloody conflicts designed to take captives for religious human sacrifices, and a similar situation existed in South America. Many of these societies had periods of peace and strong government, but these were frequently interrupted by fighting between rival groups: city-state against city-state, northerners against southerners, the peoples of the plains against mountain dwellers, dynasty A against dynasty B, the followers of god X against those of god Z.

In particular, the emergence of civilizations was often marked by violence. In Mesopotamia, the later 4th millennium saw the development of city-states, their productive agriculture supporting a priesthood who organized craft workers and foreign trade to ensure the well-being of those within its lands and to glorify the city god or goddess. By the early 3rd millennium, however, population growth within the region was beginning to put pressure on resources and inter-city conflicts developed. It was at this time that war leaders emerged to lead their cities, both in defense against their neighbors' aggression and in attacks on their neighbors. The relationship between the previously dominant priesthood and these emerging kings could be an uneasy one.

Figure 55.

SPEARHEADS

These are copper/bronze spear-heads found at Mohenjo Daro and Harappa. Sir Mortimer Wheeler believed these artifacts and ones like them—arrowheads and daggers—were evidence of Indus militarism. But Wheeler admitted these tools could also be used for other activities, such as hunting.

Figure 56.

MASSACRE

At Mohenjo Daro, Wheeler though he found evidence of a massacre. The skeletons of thirty-seven men, women, and children lay sprawled in clusters in the supposed last-ditch stand of the inhabitants slain in the defense of their homes against invading Aryans. Today physical anthropologists consider they were more likely to have fallen victim to disease.

This period of conflict is vividly reflected in the Sumerian literature about Gilgamesh, the semilegendary hero king of Uruk whose real-life counterpart may have lived around 2700 B.C. Here we see the constantly changing pattern of alliances and conflicts between the city-states and of political struggles within them.

THE INDUS— A PEACEFUL REALM?

When Sir Mortimer Wheeler excavated at Mohenjo Daro and Harappa in the 1940s, he had come straight from the battlefields of the Second World War. Much of his previous archaeological work had been concerned with the Romans, in whose society the army had played a central part. He therefore looked for, and thought he found, evidence of Indus militarism. The massive walls that surrounded the citadels of these two great cities were clearly defensive in Wheeler's eyes. Many Indus artifacts could have been weapons—arrowheads, spearheads, daggers—though to Wheeler's credit he admitted that all of them could equally have been used for other purposes like hunting [Figure 55]. In the streets of Mohenjo Daro, Wheeler found evidence of a massacre [Figure 56]. The skeletons of thirty-seven men, women, and children lay sprawled in untidy clusters in streets and houses in the upper levels of various parts of the city—the supposed last-ditch stand of the unfortunate inhabitants, slain in defense of their homes.

THE MOHENJO DARO "MASSACRE"

The eminent American George Dales, who excavated at Mohenjo Daro in the 1960s, was among the first to call into doubt the supposed massacre here.

"Nothing delights the archaeologist more than excavating the ruins of some ancient disaster—be it flood, earthquake, invasion, or massacre. Evidence was published some 30 years ago suggesting that Mohenjo-daro was destroyed by armed invaders and that the hapless victims—including a large percentage of women and children—were massacred on the spot. The 'massacre' idea immediately ignited and has been used as a torch up to the present day by some historians, linguists, and archaeologists as visible, awful proof of the invasion of the subcontinent by the Aryans. But what is the material evidence to substantiate the supposed invasion and massacre? Where are the burned fortresses, the arrowheads, weapons, pieces of armour, the smashed chariots and bodies of the invaders and defenders?

Despite the extensive excavations at the largest Harappan sites, there is not a single bit of evidence that can be brought forth as unconditional proof of an armed conquest and destruction on the supposed scale of the Aryan invasion. . . ."

The remains of thirty-seven individuals were found within the city, "some . . . in contorted positions and groupings that suggest anything but orderly burials. Many are either disarticulated or incomplete," but as Dales points out, "since there is no conclusive proof that they all even belong to the same period of time, they cannot justifiably be used as proof of a single tragedy."

Furthermore, he notes, "the bulk of the bones were found in contexts suggesting burials of the sloppiest and most irreverent nature" and their examination by the physical anthropologist K.A.R. Kennedy shows that none of the individuals had died by violence [see Figure 56].

Dales, G., 1964, "The Mythical Massacre at Mohenjo Daro" quoted in Possehl 1979, pp. 293–296

In the years since Wheeler's investigations, this evidence has all fallen away. As George Dales, one of the first to reexamine this evidence, pointed out, Wheeler's "massacre victims" were scattered in a number of groups in the lower town, rather than in the citadel where one would expect final resistance by the inhabitants would have taken place. They occurred in deserted buildings and streets of different dates, and none of the individuals appeared to have been killed—physical anthropologists consider that they are more likely to have fallen victim to disease rather than to a human enemy. None of the (admittedly few) burials that have been found show indubitable signs of death by violence either.

Turning to the Indus artifacts, all the objects that could be weapons could equally be tools, such as knives for cutting food, carving wood, or projectiles for hunting [Figure 57]. There are no swords or maces, battle-axes, or catapults. There are no other pieces of military equipment comparable to the helmets, shields, breastplates, chariots, or siege engines used by other cultures, civilized or barbarian, in ancient Eurasia.

Close consideration of the walls around Indus cities has shown that they cannot have been constructed for defense against people (although they could have offered protection against wild animals). In particular, the gateways were not designed to impede the entrance of enemies or give military advantage to defenders. Nothing suggests that the walls ever sustained military attacks or sieges. Instead they provided an outer bulwark supporting the massive platforms on which Indus citadels and towns were often constructed. They were a defense against the constant threat of flooding, although they were also probably intended to impress. The gateways allowed some control over who passed in or out of the settlements and may have been used in collecting customs tolls or taxes.

The only exceptions to this are perhaps in the area along the western border of the Indus realms: here the Indus people may have been threatened by their neighbors and may therefore have needed to defend their settlements against possible attack. The mountainous topography limits access routes from the Makran coast into the interior and these routes were defended by settlements fortified with stone walls and bastions: Sutkagen Dor in the Dasht Kaur Valley and Sotka Koh in that of the Shadi Kaur. Indus relations with the inhabitants of the uplands to their west and north, however, seem generally to have been amicable, and the Indo-Iranian borderlands were probably integrated within the Indus realms. And although it is possible that a major upheaval (marked by burning at several towns) saw the birth of the Indus Civilization, there is no clear evidence of conflict either at this time or later.

SOCIAL CONTROL

The use of force as a sanction was one of the means by which rulers in the early civilizations controlled their realms and ordered society. In the absence of such physical control, what held together the Indus Civilization and ensured cooperation between the members of society? Our evidence is limited but we can make some intelligent guesses. In other civilizations, religion was a powerful force, and rule by religious authorities backed by religious sanctions often preceded that of secular rulers backed by force.

Looking forward in time, we see religion as a major force in Indian life, underlying the whole structure of society through the concepts of rebirth and ritual purity. The caste system, in which every individual has an immutable role in life, complete with rights and duties, is ordained and reinforced by Indian religious belief. In historical times, the smooth running of society, regardless of the people at the top, depended on the caste system and the related jajmani system.

In the jajmani system, everyone within a community, such as a village, has obligations to provide the fruits of their particular labors to meet the needs of others, the potter making pots for all the village, for example, or the priest providing ritual services (such as marriage and funeral rites) for all, supported by food grown by the community's farmers. Many castes also have additional ceremonial or ritual duties at certain times, such as marriages and festivals. Each caste has services to perform for other members of the community and each receives services from others.

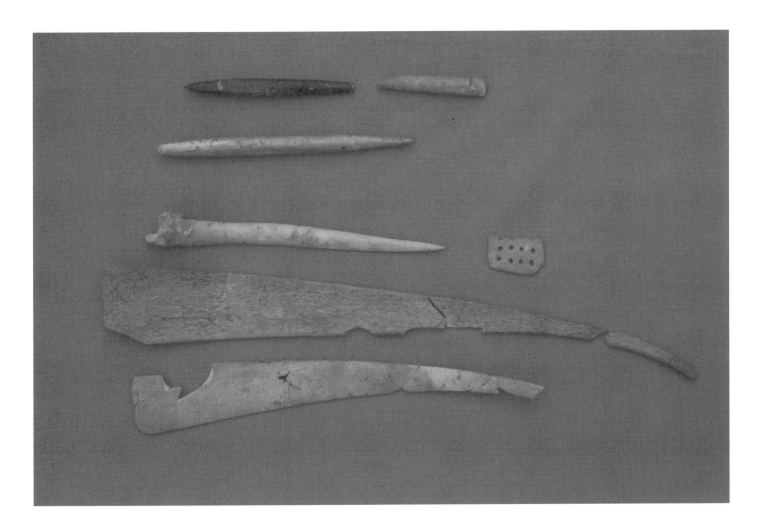

Payment for these services are made in kind and are fixed by tradition.

Crosscutting this system, which operates at the level of the community, is a wider network that links all members of a particular subcaste (jati), wherever they live. All members of a jati (often organized in historical times into guilds) would look after one another's needs while exercising considerable control over the activities of each individual within it. Marriages take place only between members of the same jati.

Can we project such a system back into Indus times? It is speculative to do so, but some of the pieces of evidence discussed in Chapter 7 suggest that it is quite likely.

WHY FIGHT?

This picture of an idyllic Indus society—the first welfare state and the land without an enemy—seems too good to be true. Can we really justify it? History seems to say that warfare and civilization go hand in hand. But we may indeed be wrong to expect evidence of warfare in this society and right to argue that it did not exist.

Figure 57.

BONE TOOLS, HARAPPA

Bone tools found at Harappa from the period of its earliest occupation (3300–2800 B.C.) include projectile points and weaving instruments.

There are two schools of thought on warfare. Many people—archaeologists, anthropologists, historians, and others—look gloomily at the almost unbroken record of human conflict, in societies that range from small independent villages to modern multi-national power blocs, and project it back into the remotest times. To be human is to fight, they believe. There are skeletons to be seen even in the Paleolithic Period where the cause of death is clearly a blow or projectile.

Others, among whom I count myself, are less pessimistic. Explanations can surely be found for the occasional violent deaths attested in the remote past—accidents while out hunting, for instance. People can get along without fighting, we think—they are pushed into conflict by circumstances beyond their control. A major reason for this is a scarcity of resources. Where there are too many people and too little food or other necessities, people may be compelled to compete for these resources, killing each other till the numbers of people and available resources balance. But there are other, alternative ways of dealing with this problem—by emigration, for example.

Resources such as raw materials, water, arable land, and edible plants and animals are unevenly distributed in the landscape, making some regions and locations wealthier or more productive than others. The conflict school of thought points out that the application or threat of armed force has frequently been used by sectors of society to ensure that they have everything they need or want, oppressing their subordinates, who often

have to get by with less than the bare necessities and suffer malnutrition and premature death in the process. But again, this is not the only way to tackle the uneven distribution of resources. Many societies have found ways to even things out, whether through gifts to needy relatives or state redistribution via taxation and benefits.

Looking at the Indus Civilization in this light, perhaps it is not so surprising that we seem to have here a state without conflict. The civilization arose in a highly fertile region where farming communities had been established for less than a thousand years. Nothing in the distribution of settlements suggests that the landscape had yet filled up to the point where there was competition for agricultural land or pasturage. The regions to the south, the Deccan and South India, although not well-suited for growing wheat and barley, offered abundant resources for people herding cattle, sheep, and goats, and during the 3rd millennium B.C., a number of small communities were established in these regions doing just that, at sites like Utnur and Kupgal where "ashmounds" mark the remains of their villages. So emigration provided a means of avoiding population pressure in the Indus Civilization, and the option seems to have been taken up on occasion.

Conflicts could also have arisen between the settlers in the Indus and Saraswati plains and the hunters, gatherers, and fishers who already lived there. Perhaps they did, but all the evidence we actually have of their interactions show them to have been of quite a different nature: the exchange of the raw materials to which the hunter-gatherers had access for the manufactured goods, domestic animals, and cultivated grain of the civilized people. This theory is borne out by the mutually beneficial and symbiotic relationship between settled communities and hunter-gatherers in the Indian subcontinent that existed in historical times and endured into the 20th century.

The distribution of resources within the bounds of the Indus Civilization was certainly uneven. But as I have discussed in previous chapters, Indus society seems to have been organized to minimize these discrepancies and to spread the advantages enjoyed by each region to every other within the Indus realms. Trade and the internal distribution mechanisms of the civilization ensured that most households in the urban settlements at least had access to the full range of goods that were necessary for daily life, and to a more-than-adequate supply of food (as we can see by the analysis of the skeletons from the surviving cemeteries), and to a considerable extent the same seems to be true even of the few village households that have been investigated.

In many parts of the world, conflicts arose between lowland farming communities and their highland, often pastoral nomadic neighbors. Although the same geographical situation existed here, the region's history made the outcome very different during the Indus Period. Far from being competitors and enemies, the people of the Indo-Iranian borderlands were the relatives of the Indus people, from whose communities the Indus region had been settled some centuries before and with whom the people of the plains still enjoyed an intimately interwoven way of life, physically linked by the pastoralists who moved between the two regions, culturally linked by millennia of common development, and almost certainly politically, socially, and economically linked within a single state as well.

So when it comes down to it, whom would the Indus people have needed to fight?

CHAPTER ELEVEN

THE END OF THE INDUS CIVILIZATION

WHAT WENT WRONG?

In previous chapters I have attempted to wring from the limited evidence some picture of the great civilization of the Indus and Saraswati Valleys and concluded tentatively that it was an exceptionally well integrated state, in harmony with its environment, where warfare was absent and everyone led a comfortable existence under the benevolent leadership of a dedicated priesthood. Yet by 1800 B.C., this civilization had fallen apart and the cities had all but vanished, taking with them all the trappings of urban life. What could possibly have effected such an overwhelming change? Invaders from outside? Internal tensions? Natural disasters? Until recently the answer was as speculative as any other of the answers to questions about the enigmatic Indus Civilization—but today it seems we have the evidence to answer with some confidence.

LOSS OF THE URBAN WAY OF LIFE

The collapse of the Indus Civilization was marked by a number of trends that gradually gathered momentum in the first two or three centuries of the 2nd millennium B.C. For a start, there is the general disappearance of those features that distinguished the Indus Civilization from its predecessors: writing, planned settlements, sophisticated public sanitation, monumental architecture, some kind of central control, occupational specialization, and seaborne trade.

In this post-Indus Period local materials were used for objects like stone tools, and the cultural uniformity of the Mature Indus Civilization gave way to at least three regional groupings. The first, in the Punjab and the east, is known as "Cemetery H" after the cemetery of this period at Harappa in which distinctive painted pottery was deposited as grave goods [see Color Plate 21]. The regional group that was spread over Sindh and the Kachi Plain is known

Map 11.

COURSE OF THE SARASWATI RIVER

At the time of the Indus Civilization, two major river systems flowed westward to the Arabian Sea, the Indus and the Saraswati, to its south. By the mid 1st millennium B.C. tectonic up-lift of the Himalayas brought about shifts in the course of the Saraswati. The tributaries that supplied its waters were captured by the Indus and the Yamuna. Where once the Saraswati flowed, its banks dense with settlements, today there remains only desert.

as Jhukar and included Mohenjo Daro, while the third group was concentrated in Gujurat. Many regional styles and traditions of the Early Indus Period now reemerged, having, as it were, lain dormant for many centuries. These included local varieties of pottery and figurines, such as the painted pottery at the important site of Pirak in the Kachi Plain, which harks back to the geometrically decorated pottery of the local "Quetta-Amri" tradition of the early 3rd millennium, along with violin-shaped figurines and geometric, uninscribed circular stamp seals that were also part of the earlier tradition.

Furthermore, many towns were abandoned or occupied by "squatters"—houses were lived in but not maintained and civic amenities such as drains were neglected. At Mohenjo Daro some industrial establishments with unpleasant by-products, such as pottery kilns, had been located within the city during its heyday, rather than being confined to the outskirts of town, but now this was a much more regular occurrence and such industries appeared haphazardly in residential areas and even in the middle of earlier streets, instead of being organized alongside other workshops within a well-planned city. The breakdown of civic life seems particularly marked at Mohenjo Daro, a significant development if, as I have suggested, this was the capital city and center of government. Dead bodies were given perfunctory burial in disused houses or streets here, although extramural cemeteries were still in use elsewhere, like Harappa.

One reason for this urban decay may have been the poor health of the residents. Studies of the skeletons from Mohenjo Daro's upper levels show that many individuals had suffered and often died from malaria and probably other diseases. Ironically the Indus obsession with drainage and water purity may have promoted their ill health, because seepage of wastewater from the drains could easily have contaminated the drinking water within the public wells. An outbreak of cholera in these circumstances could set in motion a vicious circle of contamination and spreading infection, which could seriously have reduced the population of the cities. Although there is no possibility of identifying cholera from the remaining bones, it is a highly plausible and inherently probable scenario.

THE FORCES OF NATURE

Many possible natural disasters have been suggested to account for the collapse of the Indus Civilization, disasters both sudden and dramatic, and long-term and insidious. Has the climate undergone significant changes since Indus times? There is some suggestion that the monsoon winds and the rains that they bring may have shifted slightly southward, decreasing critical rainfall in some areas, causing drought, and increasing rainfall in others, causing flooding. Opinions and evidence on this matter, however, ebb and flow with the years, and we still cannot say for certain whether such a change took place and, if it did, whether it was a contributory factor to the Indus decline. In any case it cannot be anything like the full explanation, and we need to look elsewhere.

For many decades it was argued that the firing of the baked bricks from which the Indus cities were constructed would have entailed massive deforestation. If this were true it would have had a significant impact on the environment. More recently it has been established, however, that the scrubby vegetation of the Indus Valley would have been a sustainable source of fuel adequate for firing even this huge number of bricks. So the construction of the cities did not destroy the environment. Nevertheless the theory of environmental degeneration is still put forward as a partial explanation for the Indus decline. Intensive agriculture over the many centuries of the Indus Civilization, producing crops and animals not only for local consumption but also for export to other Indus regions or even abroad (cotton for example), is likely to have overstrained the environment, and evidence for this exists in some areas such as the Kachi Plain. In lands that had regularly been irrigated, salination would by now have begun to be a problem. Investigators, however, have failed to demonstrate that artificial irrigation was really necessary in the Indus and Saraswati plains. The annual river floods and rainfall combined to maintain a regime that was naturally favorable for agriculture, so this explanation also falls short of accounting for the decline.

What about the rivers themselves? Another suggested cause of the Indus collapse is through major flooding and river course changes in the Indus plains. These were a regular hazard of life in the Indus Valley, but their effect was generally localized, affecting only individual communities. When a section of the river changed its course, the people of a settlement that was left stranded could either move to a new location on the new course of the river or adapt their way of life, for example, putting greater emphasis on pastoralism. If the area of a settlement was flooded over a long period, its inhabitants are also likely to have shifted to a different site. This was part of the way of life to which the Indus people had adapted when they first colonized the region more than a thousand years earlier, and it is improbable that it should now suddenly affect them so adversely.

But if flooding were to have taken place on a much larger scale, the effect could have been disastrous. Environmentalists studying the deposits in and around the city of Mohenjo Daro have suggested that the city experienced a number of very substantial floods, due to more than the normal vagaries of the Indus. Eruptive mud from tectonic activity in the north and west has in recorded times occasionally dammed the Indus, causing massive ponding and flooding that has lasted for several decades, until the river cut a new course around or through the obstruction. If the floods experienced by Mohenjo Daro were of this prolonged nature, it is likely that they would eventually have worn down the city's capacity to cope with the resulting problems—although the city clearly survived a number of such episodes during the major period of the civilization. A long-term, large-scale flood like this would also have seriously affected the regional population, causing a large number of communities to move to a different area. Such floods may also have made the Indus unnavigable for long periods, disrupting the internal and external trade networks. However, although this sounds very plausible, there is yet no proof that Mohenjo Daro really did experience such major floods, and many leading researchers find the suggested evidence unconvincing.

TRADE— THE UNKNOWN QUANTITY

The huge volumes of sediment carried down by the Indus and Saraswati Rivers into the Ranns of Kutch eventually caused this area to silt up, transforming it from the open water that separated Kutch from the mainland in Indus times to the saltwater marshes that exist there today. Indus settlements that operated as ports for trade with the west may have silted up and therefore ceased to operate. It has been suggested that Lothal suffered this fate toward the end of the Indus Period—although it is by no means certain that Lothal was in fact a port. The recently excavated port of Dwarka on the external seacoast of Kutch, however, was apparently founded late in the Indus Period and was still flourishing in the 16th century B.C., so the suggested loss of ports elsewhere in the region seems to have been compensated for.

Perhaps more serious was the decline of the westward trade itself—internal political changes and economic problems in Sumer disrupted the participation of Mesopotamia in the Gulf trade network around the 18th century B.C. This meant that what had been probably the major customer for Indus trade goods was no longer available. As I have already argued, however, the importance of Gulf trade to the Indus people may have been exaggerated, given the wide range of areas from which they were able to obtain the majority of raw materials that they required or wanted. So disruptions to this seaborne trading network cannot provide the explanation for the decline either.

However, the 2nd millennium saw the arrival of Indo-Aryan nomads in the subcontinent, and in the centuries immediately before they entered the plains, they were probably present in the adjacent lands. During this period, the connections between the Indo-Iranian borderlands and the lands to their north were strengthened, partly by the movements of these nomads, who had camels and horses. Likewise the prosperous communities that now existed in Bactria (southern Central Asia) were interested in widening and intensifying their trade networks, and the Indo-Iranian borderlands, with whom they had long enjoyed some trading relations, were ideally placed for greater participation in this growing trade. If the cultures of the borderlands, long an integral part of the Indus cultural and economic system, realigned their trade toward the north and east, this could well have proved a severe economic blow to the Indus people.

RIVERS
AND FARMERS

All these explanations have been skating the surface. Undoubtedly some of the suggested changes took place—but none were sufficient to have caused the complete breakdown of the Indus Civilization. Instead, the fundamental cause lay in a potent combination of agricultural decline and agricultural innovation that between them eventually transformed the way of life not only in the Indus-Saraswati plains but throughout the subcontinent.

In an early chapter I discussed the evidence for a major river system, the "Saraswati," flowing through the region, now desert, that lies to the south of the Indus. In its heyday this river supported the densest settlement and provided the greatest arable yields of any part of the Indus realms. When the Indo-Aryans settled in the region during the 2nd millennium B.C., the "holy Saraswati" was still a considerable river flowing through at least part of this region and was still accorded veneration like that now given to the Ganges. But by 1000 B.C. the Saraswati had dried up, or, more picturesquely, was believed to have retreated to flow underground, joining the Yamuna and Ganges at their confluence at Prayag (Allahabad). Something had taken place in the crucial period from the beginning of the 2nd millennium B.C. that caused this river to decline and then disappear.

The ancient Saraswati drew its waters not only from the rivers and streams that now feed the minor river of this name, but also

from two major tributaries, the Sutlej and the Drishadvati, now known as the Chautang. All originated in the snows and rains that fell in the Himalayas. During the 2nd millennium B.C. both the Sutlej and the Drishadvati changed their course, depriving the Saraswati system of its waters. Various reasons have been suggested for this and all may be valid. Tectonic changes probably occurred in the Siwalik region of the Himalayas, which even today is uplifting, and these could have shifted the course of the major rivers before they descended to the plains. There they joined a number of lesser rivers that rise in the western slopes of the Siwaliks between the Yamuna and the Sutlej and that carry water only seasonally. The flat plains onto which they debouch are very prone to seasonal flooding, resulting in the formation of lakes and the deposition of considerable sediments. Within this area, rivers frequently change their course, cutting new channels where sedimentation has blocked the old. It is possible to trace progressive changes in the course of the rivers, which culminated at some time in the recent past. Some evidence indicates that the Drishadvati shifted its course first, early in the 2nd millennium, becoming a tributary of the Yamuna, which was till then a minor river, and thereby caused a serious decrease in the volume of water carried by the Saraswati. Later the Sutlej also shifted its course to flow into the Indus, causing the Saraswati to dry up. The river Beas, which is now joined by the Sutlej shortly before they jointly flow into the Indus, also followed a different course in Indus times, although it did still join the Indus [Map 11].

This situation is typical of the instability of the river courses in the Indus plains—but in the case of the Saraswati, the effect was not localized but devastating on a major scale. Cities, towns, and villages were abandoned, their inhabitants drifting to other regions of the Indus realms and eastward toward the Ganges, pushing back the centuries-old eastern boundaries of Indus culture and venturing into uncharted territory.

The dwindling of the Saraswati took place over a number of centuries, however, and is unlikely to be the only reason for the Indus collapse. Although the cities are the best-known part of the Indus Civilization, the vast majority of the Indus inhabitants were farmers. City and town dwellers, pastoralists and peasants were bound together by political and religious ties within the complex network of rights and obligations that kept the Indus Civilization functioning as a state. The farmers at the base of the social pyramid were locked into the system by duty and belief, reaping both spiritual and material rewards—but ultimately they were capable of self-sufficiency, whereas the whole infrastructure of urban life was dependent on the supply of produce by the farmers. Disruptions to the agricultural base of the civilization, particularly the gradual decline in the productivity of the vital Saraswati River system, must therefore have had severe repercussions throughout the system. But another major development was also taking place, perhaps not initially appreciated to be significant, but actually of fundamental importance.

Settlement patterns and the agricultural regime within and beyond the Indus realms were now changing. During the heyday of the Indus Civilization, small farming and herding communities existed also in central India, the Deccan, and the south, housing people who probably ultimately had common origins with the Indus folk. In the east, on the middle and lower Ganges, lived unrelated groups of farmers and hunter-gatherers. In the early centuries of the 2nd millennium, two major changes took place in this pattern. Settlement in western India, in Gujurat and adjacent areas, became much denser, the population of the region perhaps being swelled by immigrants from the declining farmlands of the Saraswati Valley or flooded areas of the Indus plain. And farmers and herders began to spread into areas previously sparsely settled or uninhabited, notably the upper reaches of the Ganges and Yamuna. The Indus region was "leaking" its farming population.

The key to this changing pattern was in the new additions to the repertoire of crops and animals on which the Indus people depended. The end of the 3rd millennium saw the adoption of important new crops—rice and various millets in the eastern Indus zone, some introduced from Africa and others perhaps locally domesticated, in Gujurat. This complex of crops requires summer (kharif) cultivation, in contrast to the winter-grown (rabi) wheat, barley, pulses, and other staples of the Indus economy. At the cost of an increase of labor, two crops could now be raised each year in areas where both the old and the new crops could be grown. These included the Kachi Plain where the important town of Pirak replaced the Indus center,

Nausharo, as the major regional settlement around 1700 B.C.—a development that shows that an urban way of life survived to some extent in some pockets, albeit radically altered from Indus times. Rice cultivation here required irrigation, and the importance of the rice crop shows that the people of the region were now investing considerable labor in the creation of permanent irrigation systems. The millets, on the other hand, were tolerant of arid conditions and were therefore well suited for cultivation in the marginal areas that had previously only provided grazing for domestic animals. As well as being eaten by the local people, the millets could also have been used as fodder for the domestic animals of the area, which now included horses that could not thrive on the local rough grazing. Horses and two-humped Bactrian camels, introduced into the subcontinent from Central Asia probably early in the 2nd millennium B.C., were also important in broadening the economy. Camels were able to graze in marginal areas that were previously under-exploited, and both added greatly to the mobility of the pastoral sector of the population, who were also carriers for internal trade, a role enhanced by the utility of the camel as a pack animal.

The new crops were grown in a number of parts of the Indus realms, but were particularly important in the southwest and the east. Gujurat saw a massive increase in population at this time, and the fact that this was possible must reflect the shift to local cultivation of rice and millets, particularly of bulrush millet (bajra). Settlements in the east were relying mainly on rice cultivation.

There is a crucial and fundamental change involved in this, over and above the incorporation of summer cultivation and multicropping within the existing regime, with its concomitant increase in productivity. Wheat and barley, the early staples of South Asian agriculture, are best suited to the northwest and are the major crops in the region still today. Rice and the millets are the crops on which later agriculture in peninsular India depended and depends today. When wheat and barley were the only staple grain crops available to the Indus people, the region in which intensive cultivation could take place was environmentally circumscribed. This constraint was lifted when rice and millet were added to the repertoire of crops, and the temptation to establish new agricultural settlements in the regions to the south and east—the Deccan and the Ganges Valley— where these crops grew well seems to have proved irresistible. Whether this was merely opportunism or whether the farmers were attempting to escape the regimentation of existence within the Indus zone, we shall never know, but the result was the same in either case. The area of distribution of Indus-inspired cultures was steadily increasing, while the ability of the central authorities to control communities at the periphery was ever decreasing.

One of the key factors that archaeologists have identified in the development of civilization in many areas is environmental circumscription: the situation that arises when a culture adapts and develops within a highly productive region surrounded by other far less productive zones—desert, mountains, and the like—that create definite ecological boundaries to the culture's outward expansion as its population grows. The Indus Civilization fit this pattern, developing within the circumscribed region of the Indus-Saraswati plains, which allowed highly productive farming based on the Western Asiatic package of wheat, barley, and pulses. But just at the time when productivity in the circumscribed area was dropping, the boundaries ceased to exist—new crops opened up new vistas. This is a potent explanation for the disintegration of the economic and political entity that was the Indus Civilization.

PIONEERS

We come at the last to the Indo-Aryans, whose role in the collapse of the Indus Civilization seemed so crucial fifty years ago. The arrival of this group in the subcontinent is still the subject of controversy, debate, and considerable acrimony and bigotry. We have a few pieces of concrete information about them. We know that the Indo-Aryan languages, such as Hindi, which are spoken over the northern (and larger) portion of South Asia, belong to the huge Indo-European language family that also includes virtually all the languages of Europe as well as those of Iran and of a number of cultures within the ancient Near East. Attempts to locate the original homeland from which the speakers of these languages spread and the date at which they began to do so are fraught with difficulty, but a substantial proportion of the scholars who have studied the issue favor a

homeland in the steppe zone somewhere between the Caspian and the Black Sea and consider that the Indo-European speakers began to expand outward during the 4th millennium B.C. Aggressive warriors riding horses or fighting from rapid horse-drawn chariots, the Indo-Europeans, despite their small numbers, seem to have ended up defeating and dominating many of the communities with whom they came into contact.

Traditional Indian literature includes a number of books of hymns composed by the early Indo-Aryan settlers—the *Vedas*. From clues in the style of language and the geographical details contained within the Vedic texts, we can date the composition of the earliest book, the *Rigveda*, to around 1500 B.C. and trace the progressive spread of the authors of the Vedic hymns from the northwest into the Ganges Valley, over a number of centuries. These hymns describe the struggles of the Indo-Aryans, aided and abetted by the Vedic gods, particularly Indra the god of war, against the inhabitants of the regions that they moved into. These included the Dasas, a dark-skinned race who dwelt in fortified settlements. Early archaeologists seized upon this description as remarkable evidence of the destruction of the Indus cities by the warlike Aryan invaders. The "massacre" at Mohenjo Daro was attributed to an episode in this conflict. More recently, scholars have cast considerable doubts on every aspect of this scenario. The details of the Dasas' forts in no way match the settlements of the Indus people, and it is possible that these were located well outside the subcontinent, in Iran or Central Asia, and perhaps belonged to an earlier wave of Indo-Aryan migrants. If they existed at all, that is—for perhaps they were an exaggeration of something very small scale. The proposed chronology of the Indo-Aryan arrival in the subcontinent does not fit the neat explanation that the Aryans destroyed the Indus cities, because the Indus decline preceded by several hundred years the arrival of the Indo-Aryans in the same areas.

The Indo-Aryans are extremely difficult to pin down archaeologically—their presence is indicated solely by the odd burial with exotic material, particularly weapons, and by the introduction of the horse, which was present by about 2000 B.C. Nevertheless, we can probably say with some confidence that the Indo-Aryans were among the groups who visited or settled in regions on the periphery of the Indus zone during the very late 3rd millennium and the early centuries of the 2nd millennium, introducing the horse and perhaps the camel and transmitting many elements of general Central Asian culture to the Indo-Iranian borderlands. Linguistic evidence suggests that there were several separate waves of Indo-Aryans who reached the subcontinent and that those who composed the *Rigveda* were not the first. The various groups seem to have settled in different areas,

such as those who were an influential presence in Swat and who were among the individuals buried in the distinctive "Gandhara Graves" of that region. After the Indus Civilization had collapsed and their warlike activities were no longer kept in check, Indo-Aryan groups had a successful time raiding communities in Sindh and Punjab. Interacting in many ways with the local people, they formed an element in the pioneering groups who progressively colonized the Ganges-Yamuna region, adding their pastoral expertise to that of local farmers and cattle-keepers who were spreading the cultivation of rice. The warlike expertise and propensities of the Indo-Aryans eventually saw the triumph of their language over that of the native groups, just as they themselves dominated the local farmers, but the hybrid culture that emerged owed considerably more to the natives than to the invaders.

Indra's triumphant destruction of the ninety-nine forts of the Dasas makes a good story, but it is not the story of the end of the Indus cities. Other factors set the process in motion—but it is certainly possible that the Indo-Aryans encouraged the decline that they encountered. They may not have caused the end of the Indus Civilization, but they sounded its death knell.

CHAPTER TWELVE

THE LEGACY OF THE INDUS CIVILIZATION

THE INCOMPLETE JIGSAW PUZZLE

Identifying the contribution of the Indus Civilization to Indian culture is a little like doing a jigsaw puzzle with many of the pieces missing. When we assemble the puzzle with the pieces that we have, we are able to make out the shape and color of the pieces that are not there and work out how they might complete the picture—but inevitably our image of the missing pieces is rather hazy. Our frustration that we are unable to read the Indus script and see what the Indus people had to say about themselves is compounded by the knowledge that the surviving written texts are so limited that even if we could read them they would not tell us much. We are looking at one of the world's first great civilizations and yet we are compelled to investigate it in the same way as with any nonliterate culture, relying on archaeological evidence alone. This can carry us a long way in reconstructing some aspects of life, such as technology, but leaves us still guessing about so many others.

Fortunately, however, the Indo-Aryans entered the Indian subcontinent not long after the Indus cities declined and became closely involved with the descendants of the Indus people, who, despite their nonurban way of life, were the torch-bearers of the Indus cultural heritage. The Indo-Aryans were illiterate, but they created a wealth of oral literature that was handed down by faithful repetition unchanged over the centuries. This literature is mainly religious, but in passing it chronicles their history and legendary activities in the subcontinent. Read with care and informed experience, these texts can give us a great deal of information about the lifestyle, traditions, and beliefs of the Indo-Aryans from the time they entered the subcontinent until the reemergence of writing during the 1st millennium B.C. when the information available becomes truly historical. Many elements of traditional Indian culture and religion can be traced back to the Indo-Aryans.

But not all. Because they were dominant and gave their language to the greater part of the subcontinent, the Indo-Aryans have tended to obscure the contribution of the pre-Aryan

Figure 58.

MODERN FARMERS, MOHENJO DARO

Although there are modern conveniences, in many ways the life of modern Indus farmers is similar to that of their predecessors more than 4,000 years ago.

SOMA

indigenous peoples. Unraveling the elements of Indian culture, however, it rapidly becomes clear that many aspects of life cannot be traced back to the Indo-Aryans but must have been contributed by their predecessors, the Indus Civilization.

RELIGION

This is particularly true of religion. Learning and reciting *Vedas*, the sacred literature composed more than 3,000 years ago by the Indo-Aryans, is a central part of Indian religion—but when we look into these hymns it is clear that in many ways the religion they describe is very different from that of later times.

The early Indo-Aryans worshipped a number of male deities, particularly Indra, the god of war and thunder, and his assistant, Agni, god of fire and the divine sacrificer. Vishnu, later to become one of the most widely venerated gods in India, was present as only a minor solar deity in the *Rigveda*. The Indo-Aryans sacrificed animals and sometimes people, and their supreme sacrificial animal was the horse. Their rites involved a sacred fire and the consumption of a substance called soma. There has been much speculation about the identification of soma, which was pressed to form a hallucinogenic drink. Magic mushroom is one possibility that has been explored, but a much more widely accepted identification is the creeper *Ephedra*.

The Hindu religion that developed in the 1st millennium B.C. and which gave rise to a number of branches, including Buddhism and Jainism, was very different from the Vedic practices and beliefs [Figure 59]. Rather than being innovations, many of the changes that appeared during that time can be seen as

Figure 59.

HEAD OF
BODHISATTVA
*The serenity of the
mask from Mohenjo
Daro from the about
2500–2200 B.C
depicted in Color
Plate 4 is echoed in
this head of the
Bodhisattva from the
3rd century B.C.*

the reemergence of a number of major elements of Indus religion. Indian religion was heterogeneous, accreting new ways of worshipping as an addition to older ways rather than entirely replacing them, and some elements of the Indo-Aryan rites continued. For example, the ashvamedha, the grand horse sacrifice, closely bound up with territorial aggression, continued to be offered by powerful Indian kings down through the centuries.

But by 500 B.C. there had been a general move away from the sacrifice of animals and the consumption of soma to invoke warlike gods. More emphasis was now placed on the offering of fruit and flowers. Nonviolence and the preservation of life were important

elements in this new synthesis, and the quest for a release from the circle of rebirth played a major part in the philosophy of many sects. Meditation and asceticism were becoming important, and different gods, whose roots can be traced back into Indus and even earlier times, were now coming to prominence.

Goddesses were strikingly unimportant in the Vedic pantheon. But the goddess associated with the tiger who was prominent in Indus art reemerges in many guises in later Indian religion, as the dread goddess of death, the personification of the female principle and wife of the god Shiva, and the eternal mother. Individual aspects of the goddess, particularly as a mother, were well represented in Indus times, as earlier, by figurines, and their worship reappeared in later Hindu folk religion. Many other elements of classical Indian folk religion, including the veneration of trees and animals, have their counterpart in the iconography of the Indus people.

The greater part of our information on Indian religion in the 1st millennium B.C. comes from the areas where the Indo-Aryans were dominant, the north and, more particularly, the Ganges Valley. Much of the subcontinent lay outside these regions, but because they lack the written records and carefully preserved oral traditions of the north, we know far less about the development of religion in the Deccan and South India.

These regions were settled in the 3rd and 2nd millennia B.C. by people related to or descended from those of the Indus Civilization. In this region we might expect to find many elements of traditional Indus life preserved. Here the contribution of Indus religion should be visible without the distracting admixture of Indo-Aryan beliefs and practices that occurred in the north. Although we gain little information on religion from the archaeological evidence of earlier times that survives in the south, by historical times much of the peninsula was a stronghold of the worship of Shiva, one of the two principal Indian deities (the other being Vishnu) up to the present day. As we have seen, there seems strong evidence that Shiva or his prototype was the principal male deity of the Indus people, frequently depicted on Indus seals and represented by phallic objects [Figure 60].

Astronomy and mathematics, which may be intimately linked with Indus religion, appear to have been learned by the Indo-Aryans from the indigenous people they encountered when they entered the Indian subcontinent. The Indian star calendar of twenty-eight constellations is known in Vedic literature by 1000 B.C. Internal evidence, however, such as the place and time of rising of particular stars and constellations, and their interrelationships, shows that this calendar was compiled much earlier—sometime during the period 2400–2200 B.C., when the Indus Civilization was still flourishing. The calendar must therefore have been borrowed by the Indo-Aryans from the descendants of the Indus Civilization.

That this calendar was still extant and could thus be transmitted seems a powerful piece of evidence that the decline of the Indus Civilization did not mean the disappearance of the priesthood and all their accumulated knowledge and wisdom. Writing died out, so this information must have been preserved orally. Although the Indus towns disappeared and the organized state collapsed, there were still settlements of some size and complexity functioning in the 2nd millennium B.C.— such places as Pirak in the Kachi Plain or the prosperous settlements of Gujarat, such as Rangpur. By about 1400 B.C. the villages that had emerged in the Deccan included some, like Inamgaon, that were clearly larger and more important than the others in their regions—the home of chiefs who had some control over lesser villages.

Although the highly stratified society of the Indus Civilization was gone, we have every reason to suppose that some vestige of its broad social divisions remained. Farmers, pastoralists, priests, hunter-gatherers—these still had a place in the less complex society of the 2nd millennium B.C.—and craftsmen and traders may also have survived, even if circumstances made it impossible for them to practice their traditional occupations in the way they had done before. When we add in the newly arrived warriors, we have the makings of the caste system as it is to be seen when literacy begins again in the later 1st millennium B.C. As I argued earlier, the caste system makes much more sense as a legacy of the Indus Civilization than as the novel creation of a handful of warlike barbarian invaders. Very significantly, by the mid–1st millennium, there had been a major shift in the social order. The priest had enjoyed a limited, though important, role in Indo-Aryan society, which was led by warrior kings. But by the time that states began to emerge in the Ganges Valley and adjacent regions, priests were among the leaders of society, rivaling

Figure 60. (opposite)

KRISHNA

Asko Parpola translates a modified version of the Indus fish sign [see Figure 45] as pacu + meen, or "green star." In Tamil, the main Dravidian language spoken today, paccal refers to greenness and to the planet Mercury, which represents the green-hued child Krishna.

ECONOMY

The Indo-Aryans when they entered the subcontinent were pastoral nomads, in contrast to the largely agricultural communities that they encountered there. Although the Indus people and their successors also had a strong pastoral component in their economy and practiced transhumance (seasonal movement between pastures), this was integrated with settled farming. The Indo-Aryans, in contrast, were nomadic and mobile, the horse playing a major role in their lives. They were also warriors, riding their horses or using them to draw impressive war chariots, and delighting to engage in cattle raids. Later they also turned to agriculture, settling in the Ganges Valley along with indigenous colonists of this region. The domestication and cultivation of rice was the key development that permitted the colonization of the Ganges region by farming communities. The Indus people had begun rice cultivation in the closing years of the 3rd millennium B.C. Clearly, therefore, agricultural practices in the subcontinent can owe little to these invaders.

Striking parallels exist, however, between the rural economy of later India and that which we can reconstruct from Indus evidence. The Early Indus field discovered at Kalibangan, for example, was ploughed in exactly the same pattern as is used in the region today [*see* Figure 11]. The tools and equipment used by the Indus farmers, such as ploughs and solid-wheeled carts drawn by bullocks, are also still in use today. The same is true of many other tools and domestic equipment, underlining the antiquity of agricultural practices in the Indian subcontinent and the strong similarities that exist between the daily lives of ordinary people in Indus times and today—4,500 years later [Figure 58].

Although some animals and crops (particularly American domesticates such as tomatoes) have been introduced to the subcontinent in more recent times, virtually all the staples of Indian agriculture were already being raised in Indus times. As we have seen, the crucial transition from the purely West Asian-style farming regime of the Mature Indus Civilization, based on wheat, barley, and pulses, to one that also included rice and millets, the staples of most of the subcontinent, took place within the Indus realms around the end of the 3rd millennium B.C. As far as agriculture is concerned, therefore, the main change between Indus and later times was in its focal area, the center of civilization shifting from the Indus to the Ganges Valley. This is not to say, however, that the Indus region played no role in later Indian prehistory—on the contrary, it was a still major area of settlement, though no longer the leading area.

ARTS AND CRAFTS

Many of the arts and crafts for which the subcontinent is famous cannot be represented by finds from Indus times since they used perishable materials: textile-production, wood-carving, fine painting on cloth or paper, the drawing of lively auspicious designs on house thresholds or,, on festive occasions on human hands and faces. But a few small clues survive. A miraculously preserved scrap of cotton cloth found at Mohenjo Daro and impressions of cloth from a number of sites reveal that many of the techniques involved in their manufacture were similar to those in use today. Although so many colorful aspects of the Indus Valley culture have decayed away, the exuberance of designs on Indus pottery at least hint at the styles of bright and elaborate decoration that were probably present everywhere—on clothing, on houses, on people, and on animals. A figurine from Harappa of an elephant bears faint traces of red and white paint, just like the designs that are painted on elephants, buffaloes, and cattle on festive occasions today [see Color Plate 9].

Timber suitable for various purposes was exported to Sumer and must have been utilized by the Indus people who were familiar with their different qualities. The terracotta models of bullock carts, the few surviving roof beams and door jambs, the depictions of boats on seals, and the pieces of shell inlay used to decorate wooden furniture all emphasize that the Indus people were skilled at carpentry and woodworking. We are surely justified in seeing the Indus Civilization and its predecessors as the source of many if not all the craft skills of later Indian cultures, although there were also undoubtedly some new developments in technology as time went on. Some other arts and crafts that we would expect to have left surviving traces are very poorly represented among those of the Indus people: bronze and stone sculpture in particular. But figurative bronze casting and stone carving were by and large a relatively late development in India, sculpture being until the later centuries B.C. largely confined to exuberant modeling in terracotta. Lively terracotta figurines are a prominent feature of Indus arts and crafts, and in these and many others, such as shell-carving and lapidary work, there is a clear line of development from Indus times (and often earlier) into later times, up to the present day. At a more mundane level, the repertoire of tools and equipment used in historical and modern India for traditional activities includes a great many that had already been developed by the Indus people. And the weight system current in historical India and still used today seems likely to have been based on that originally devised by the Indus people.

Housing is another area in which the pattern set in Indus times has endured. Indus houses were designed to combine privacy with comfort in the extremes of the climate. A central courtyard accommodated the majority of domestic activities for much of the year, providing shade and fresh air protected from the dust of the streets and countryside. Rooms overlooking it provided shelter from the direct sun and from the rains. A bathroom ensured that bathing, almost as important for comfort as it was for ritual purity, was a notable feature of the Indus house. Once house designs suited to the climate and environment of the northwest, and of the subcontinent in general, had been devised by the Indus people, they tended to

BRAHMI

Sometime in the middle of the 2nd millennium B.C., somewhere in the Levant or an adjacent region, an earth-shattering invention was developed—the alphabet. Taking a mere twenty-two Egyptian hieroglyphs and using them to represent individual Semitic consonants, some ancient genius brought into existence a writing system that could in principle be used to write down anything. Of course those who adopted this system, such as the Classical Greeks, made modifications to suit their own requirements— the Greeks, for example, adding signs to represent vowels. Many alphabetic scripts developed in Western Asia, and these found their way by various routes to the Indian subcontinent at some time during the 1st millennium B.C. (the date when this actually took place is controversial). In the northwest, the Aramaic script gave rise to an Indian script, Kharoshti, that did not gain much currency outside its own area. Elsewhere in the subcontinent another, unidentified Western Asiatic script inspired the development of Brahmi.

Although based on an alphabetic script, the Brahmi script was adapted to suit the nature of the local (Indo-Aryan) language, with almost every character representing the combination of a consonant and a following implied vowel—generally a short "a" (giving Ma-ha-bha-ra-ta, for example—the name of a major epic poem). Later, in the early 1st millennium A.D., a modified version was adopted in south India to write the Dravidian Tamil language. From Brahmi are descended more than 200 modern Indian scripts, whose ancestry can be clearly traced.

What cannot be found is a link between the long-vanished Indus script and the Western Asiatic–derived Brahmi script—because there was no connection between them.

be used with little change in later times. This is true of many material features of South Asian life and seems likely to reflect very substantial continuity in the other aspects of life less easily traced from archaeological data.

LANGUAGES AND PEOPLE

In Chapter 8, I considered in some detail the question of what language the Indus people spoke and argued that it is more than probable that it was a language belonging to the Dravidian language family, although there are scholars who would disagree. Although they were submerged in the north by the Indo-Aryan languages, Dravidian languages have survived in southern India up to the present day. The Dravidian languages spoken in the north did not disappear overnight, but survived for many centuries—this is indisputably shown by the fact that they had a profound impact upon the grammar, vocabulary, and syntax of the Indo-Aryan languages. Although the Indo-Aryan languages were introduced by invaders, they were kept alive largely by native South Asians who used their mastery of the intrusive language to attain positions of power or status within the hybrid community dominated by the warlike Indo-Aryans.

What was completely lost, however, was the Indus script. Before writing began in the Indus Valley, other signs were used in a variety of contexts—graffiti on pottery, geometric designs on stamp seals, and the like. After the demise of the Indus Civilization, these started to be used again and graffiti continued to surface in various parts of the subcontinent for several millennia—among the iron-working megalith builders of the south, for example. Despite the best efforts of a number of scholars, however, it has proved impossible to make a valid writing system out of these signs, whose function, though unknown, was clearly different from that of the Indus script or any other full writing systems. There is therefore nothing to link together the Indus script that disappeared in the early centuries of the 2nd millennium B.C. and the Brahmi script that emerged in the later 1st millennium B.C. From the latter spring almost all the later scripts of South Asia, but Brahmi itself is derived from a script used first outside the subcontinent, somewhere in Western Asia. A north Semitic script seems the most likely candidate.

The Indian subcontinent has been invaded many times throughout recorded history. Successful invaders have exercised political dominance and have often made some contribution to the development of Indian culture. Much more obvious, however, is the way that the subcontinent has absorbed and Indianized its invaders. Looking back to the Indus Civilization it is possible to trace there the seeds of Indian culture and the Indian way of life, in its towns and in its rural communities, now beginning to be studied in some detail by archaeologists. One key aspect of Indus society, as I have reconstructed it, is its absence of violence or military activity. Nonviolence and respect for life are major themes running through Indian religion in recorded history: bound up with the concepts of rebirth and ritual purity, they seem fundamental to Indian philosophical approaches to existence. It may be carrying the thesis too far to credit the Indus Civilization with Indian pacifism and nonviolence and place all the blame for violence and warfare upon the waves of later invaders, but there is surely a grain of truth in this suggestion.

CHAPTER THIRTEEN

CIVILIZATION

THE EMERGENCE OF CIVILIZATION

The Indus Civilization is one of the four primary civilizations that developed in the Old World within a relatively short period. The civilizations of Mesopotamia and Egypt emerged around 3000 B.C., a few centuries before the Indus Civilization, while Shang China traditionally dates from 1766 B.C. In Mesopotamia, Sumer and Akkad gave place in time to the Babylonian and Assyrian Empires, while the Nile Valley saw the ebb and flow of Old, Middle, and New Kingdoms in Egypt. In China, the Shang were succeeded by the warring states of Zhou and eventually united into the Qin and then the Han Empire. The factors that had operated in these regions to bring about the birth of civilization continued to nurture it through the ages. In stark contrast, the Indus Civilization had its brief moment of glory and was gone. When civilization reemerged in India, it was in quite a different area, on the Ganges, where civilizations continued to rise and fall for the rest of South Asia's history. In this radical change of geographical focus the Indian subcontinent resembles Mesoamerica, where the focal area of the early civilizations shifted through time.

AGRICULTURAL INTENSIFICATION

What are the factors underlying the emergence of civilization in these regions and their subsequent histories? Various "prime movers" have been suggested that may have pushed societies in a direction that resulted in civilization. One of these suggested catalysts is the development of intensive agriculture in an ecologically circumscribed area. High agricultural productivity, well in excess of individual needs, allowed the population of a region to grow and a portion of society to move away from farming and subsistence activities into full-time specialization in craft production or the exercise of power. In each of these primary civilizations, we are dealing

Figure 61.

Indus River

The Indus River as it is today. Its course at the height of the Indus Civilization is charted in Map 11 on page 184; its modern course is plotted on Map 9 on page 145. On the far banks of the river you can see the temple island of Sadhbela.

with an area where agricultural intensification was made possible by features of the environment. The Mesopotamian, Egyptian, and Indus Civilizations were located in the valleys of major rivers, surrounded by desert, mountains, and sea. Settlement here was only possible when people had developed the techniques of water control and water management that enabled them to cultivate the river lands and cope with the inherent problems, such as a discrepancy between the timing of annual rainfall and flooding and the timing of the crops' requirement for water, but with this knowledge and expertise, yields were high. The inability to expand intensive agriculture beyond the circumscribed region created a self-contained domain within which developments were focused. The situation was similar in Mesoamerica, although the water essential for high agricultural productivity did not come exclusively from rivers but also included hill runoff, shallow wells, swamps, and lakes.

RESOURCE IMBALANCE AND TRADE

Intensive agriculture providing high productivity is not the only factor considered as a prime mover in the development of civilization. Another that is frequently thought critical is the need to obtain desired raw materials. Alluvial river plains are highly fertile but they are often deficient in many of the commodities needed for daily life—wood for constructing vehicles, furniture and boats; stone and metal ore for making tools; ands materials for making luxuries like jewelry. Other areas of high productivity, such as the jungles of lowland Mesoamerica, experienced similar problems of resource imbalance. Life in such an environment, therefore, carries the need to organize trade with areas outside the region where such materials are to be found. In exchange, the people of the agriculturally rich region had much to offer. For a start, there was the surplus of agricultural produce—grain, other plant foods, meat, and perhaps milk products and eggs. Then there were also many goods that could be manufactured from the local agricultural and other resources—pottery from local clay, textiles from wool, cotton, silk or flax, leather goods, baskets, mats from reeds, and so on. The high productivity of the region provided a surplus food supply that could be used to support full-time artisans whose products were both consumed locally and used for trade. In addition, craft specialization encouraged the development of new technology and expertise, so a certain proportion of imported raw materials could be made into quality goods for re-export to the source regions, where their value would be many times that of the original materials. The need to organize and control craft production and trade, as well as the storage and redistribution of surplus agricultural produce stimulated the growth of a managerial class, often the priesthood in the first instance.

The major role of trade in the civilizations we are considering cannot be denied,

and is particularly marked in Mesopotamia and Mesoamerica, regions where intercommunity trade had a long history dating back through millennia. In South Asia, too, trade in highly prized commodities over long distances is known from the days of the first farming villages, when turquoise from Central Asia and shells from the seacoast reached the settlement of Mehrgarh nestled on the Kachi Plain. Trade at this stage was a kin-based, somewhat haphazard affair, moving goods slowly in many small steps. But here as in other parts of the world the existing networks provided the base upon which a more organized system could develop when it became necessary. Indus relations with the fishing communities of the Aravallis well illustrates the pattern of trade that developed as the Indus Civilization emerged: the people of the Aravallis supplied the Indus realms with metal ores, particularly copper but perhaps also tin, receiving in return not only foodstuffs and manufactured goods but even metal objects made from their own ores.

The importance to the Indus people of trade with its immediate neighbors in the hills to the north and the desert to the south is abundantly clear. They also conducted external trade with Mesopotamia and the Gulf region and even established a trading outpost at Shortugai in Afghanistan. Various scholars have argued from this that external trade was the most significant prime mover in the emergence of civilization in the Indus. But the abundance and diversity of resources within their own and neighboring territories makes the Indus people's involvement in long-distance trade hard to understand and it is

therefore hard to justify the idea that it played any part in catalyzing the emergence of the Indus Civilization.

HIGH-RISK LANDS

Although the lands in which the first civilizations grew up were all extremely fertile, many also had unpredictable and unreliable climatic or environmental features. In Mesopotamia, as in the Indus region, the rivers were prone to change their course and ran the gamut over the years between inadequate flow and excessive floods. The Nile also varied in the volume of its life-giving annual inundation and a meter was set up at Elephantine to monitor the river's flood level each year. The unpredictability of the water supply upon which agriculture and life depended encouraged the inhabitants of these regions to rely upon religious leaders whom they credited with the power to placate the gods and control events. This has been put forward as a prime mover in Mesopotamia and seems equally applicable to the Indus region, where serious flooding and changes in the course of rivers could threaten a community's livelihood and even its very existence. A knowledge of the movements of the sun, moon, stars, and planets gave a basis for determining the length of the year and the coming of the seasons, vital information for timing the crucial activities of the agricultural and pastoral year, and in many societies this knowledge was confined to the religious authorities, enhancing their power.

Religion is a feature of most human societies, and has played a major part in the development and organization of civilizations under many different circumstances. In many early civilizations, including those of the Indus and Maya, mathematics and detailed astronomical knowledge seem to have been intimately linked with religion. At present we know much more about Maya astronomy than we do about that of the Indus. The civilizations of Mesoamerica, from the time of the Olmec and their contemporaries up to that of the Aztecs, shared a number of ideological and religious features that determined the pattern of their existence, while providing great scope for variation in the way these features were played out in society. Human sacrifice, the ritual ballgame, a pantheon of ferocious nature gods, and a belief in recurring patterns of existence mapped out by the movements of stars and planets are all features of the religion that underlay Mesoamerican civilization. Here the power of those who mediated between gods and ordinary mortals was just as great as in those societies where an unreliable environment can be invoked as the explanation for the growth and acceptance of priestly power. Perhaps we should not be asking what caused power to come first into the hands of religious authorities, but why some societies moved on to secular leadership while others retained their priest-led social order.

WARFARE AND SOCIAL CONTROL

Population growth is an issue that is constantly under discussion by archaeologists.

Was population increase a constant factor of human existence from the very earliest times, continually driving human societies to devise ways to increase the resources available to them, by making technological changes that increased the carrying capacity of the inhabited area or by migrating into new areas? Or is technological inventiveness the constant factor, continually providing the resources that allow population growth to take place? It is difficult to say which came first, and undoubtedly the two moved along unevenly side by side. Changes that took place in one system could have unforeseen implications in another. Overall human population increase has certainly been a constant feature of the human career, though in individual areas populations might crash or societies deliberately limit their growth. Technology has become ever more complex and essential to human existence through the ages, even though individual areas have seen many advanced technologies of one period lost in subsequent eras.

In the early civilizations that we have been considering, intensive agriculture provided the capacity to support dense and substantial populations, encouraging further population growth regardless of whether the latter was also a prime mover toward the initial intensification of the agricultural system. In many of these civilizations, competition for resources gave rise to warfare between communities. In Mesoamerica there was often a religious aspect to this, warfare being conducted to obtain human sacrificial victims whose blood sustained the gods upon whom society depended. An extreme view of Aztec warfare, not universally accepted, is

Figure 63.

*There is still much
to learn about the
Indus Civilization.
Archaeological work
continues at many
sites in Pakistan and
India. Here a member of the Harappa
Archaeological
Research Project sifts
through a site that
has already yielded
35,000 artifacts.*

into obeying the rules of their society by fear of divine wrath, now the strong arm of the secular law was also there to make individuals toe the line.

The Indus Civilization seems to have been exempt from this move toward conflict and secular rule. Some people argue that its emergence may perhaps have been achieved by force—as we have seen, we have the evidence of burning at several early towns, although it is not clear what this signifies. Many others would argue that the transformation was a peaceful one. But there seems to be general agreement that there is no evidence at all that force was employed to maintain the Indus state. Instead there seems to have been some social mechanism, probably backed by religious beliefs, that ensured cooperation between the people of the Indus Civilization. I have argued that the caste system, strongly rooted in religion and notions of ritual purity, may have already developed in the Indus Civilization, giving every individual a fixed role within society and providing a mechanism that kept society functioning like a well-oiled machine. But to go beyond this and argue, as some scholars do, that the Indus society was without a ruling class and was not a state seems to go too far. The Indus Civilization has no evidence of royal palaces or lavish burials, but the seals with their recurrent animal designs and sophisticated though undeciphered writing demonstrate the existence of statewide organization. The uniformity throughout the Indus lands of many aspects of life underlines the unity of the civilization and contrasts with the diversity shown by the regional groups

that it was directly involved in solving the problem of food scarcity by providing defeated enemies to eat. Less controversial is the view that this cannibalism was ritualistic and ideological in purpose rather than dietary. In some civilizations, religious and secular power rested in the hands of the same individuals—the divine rulers of Egypt, the kings of Mesoamerican states whose supreme duty was to mediate between the material and spiritual worlds. In other states, secular and religious authority were vested in two separate bodies, often at odds or uneasily allied. Where once individuals were coerced that preceded and succeeded the period when the state flourished. And the integration of the complex network of settlements, in which specialized roles (as gateway settlements for trade or as industrial producers of particular goods, for instance) were combined with hierarchical functions as administrative centers providing services, argues the existence of a overarching structure under centralized control.

Societies need leaders, to make decisions, to settle disputes, to cope with disasters, to organize large-scale endeavors, and to sort out problems. Leaders need a hierarchy of lesser authorities who will deputize for them within sectors of society. The greater the number of people within a society, the greater their need to delegate responsibility for its smooth operation and the more need there is for rulers and bureaucrats. The actual Indus rulers and their subordinates have proved elusive, leaving little trace of their own lives. But results of their leadership can be clearly seen. The transformation that took place within the Indus-Saraswati region in the first half of the 3rd millennium B.C.— from individual settlements of pioneering pastoral and farming communities to regionally unified groups to an integrated culture that united the entire Indus-Saraswati realms—must reflect the growth of a highly organized society in which leaders had emerged who were able to ordain and carry out the deliberate construction or reconstruction of massive settlements to a predetermined plan. And once united, the successors to these leaders held the civilization together through 700 years or more, a period in which

the lack of apparent change would seem to reflect the excellence of the state's initial and continued organization.

THE PRESENT'S DEBT TO THE PAST

A number of similar factors seem to have been involved in the development of civilizations in different parts of the world, but each civilization also developed uniquely, setting its own seal upon subsequent developments in the area that it controlled. In many regions, the course of local development has later been changed by the arrival of outsiders with a different cultural background. In most cases, much remains of the indigenous culture, though it may be heavily submerged and therefore difficult to trace. In South Asia, however, despite numerous foreign invasions, indigenous culture has proved strongly resistant and has tended to resurface at the expense of the intrusive culture. Much of the cultural heritage of the Indus Civilization can still be traced today in the Indian subcontinent, despite the change in geographical focus of the later Indian civilizations. Indian ways of life, religious attitudes, and cultural philosophy seem to have crystallized in the Indus Civilization and have shaped the pattern of existence in later ages. Although the present owes a debt to the past worldwide, South Asia and its debt to the Indus Civilization provide a particularly clear example, a model for studying the way in which the past has shaped the present.

BIBLIOGRAPHY

Agrawal, D. P., 1970, "The Metal Technology of the Indian Protohistoric Cultures: Its archaeological Implications," *Puratattva*, Vol. 3, 1969–70, pp. 15–22.

_____. 1982, "The Technology of the Indus Civilization" in ed. R. K. Sharma *Indian Archaeology: New Perspectives*, Agam Kala Prakashan Delhi, pp. 83–112.

_____. 1984, "The metal Technology of the Harappans" in eds. Lal and Gupta, pp. 163–167.

Agrawala, R. C., 1984, "Aravalli, the Major Source of Copper for the Indus and Indus-related Cultures" in eds. Lal and Gupta, pp. 157–162.

Allchin, B. and F. R., 1982, *The Rise of Civilization in India and Pakistan*, Cambridge University Press.

Allchin, B., 1984, "The Harappan Environment" in eds. Lal and Gupta, pp. 445–454.

_____. ed., 1994, *Living Traditions. Studies in the Ethnoarchaeology of South Asia*, Oxford/IBH

_____. 1995, "The Potwar Project 1981 to 1993," *South Asian Studies*, Vol. 11, pp. 149–156.

Allchin, F. R., 1984, "The Northern Limits of the Harappan Culture Zone" in eds. Lal and Gupta, pp. 51–54.

_____. 1996, *The Archaeology of Early Historic India*, Cambridge University Press.

Allchin, R. and B., 1997, *Origins of a Civilization*, Viking Penguin India.

Audouze, F. and C. Jarrige 1979 "A Third Millennium Pottery-firing Structure at Mehrgarh and Its Economic Implications" in ed. Taddei, pp. 213–221.

Bacon, E., ed., 1976, *The Great Archaeologists*, Martin, Secker and Warburg.

Bartelemy de Saizien, B. and A. Bouquillon, 1994, "Steatite Working at Mehrgarh During the Neolithic and Chalcolithic Periods: Quantitative Distribution, Characterization of Material and Manufacturing Processes" in eds. Parpola and Koskikallio, pp. 47–70.

Belcher, W. R., 1994, "Riverine Fisheries and Habitat Exploitation of the Indus Valley Tradition: An Example from Harappa, Pakistan" in eds. Parpola and Koskikallio, pp. 71–80.

Bisht, R. S., 1984, "Structural Remains and Town Planning of Banawali" in eds. Lal and Gupta, pp. 89–97.

_____. 1990, "Excavation at Dholavira, District Kutch," *Indian Archaeology—A Review 1989–90*, pp. 15–20.

_____. 1991, "Excavation at Dholavira, District Kutch," *Indian Archaeology—A Review 1990–91*, pp. 10–12.

_____. 1992, "Excavation at Dholavira, District Kutch," *Indian Archaeology—A Review 1991–92*, pp. 26–35.

_____. 1993, "Excavation at Dholavira, District Kachchh (Earlier Kutch)," *Indian Archaeology—A Review 1992–93*, pp. 27–32.

Bondioli, L., M. Tosi and M. Vidale 1984 "Craft Activity Areas and Surface Survey at Moenjodaro" in eds. Jansen and Urban, pp. 9–37.

Brooks R. R. and V. S. Wakankar, 1976, *Stone Age Painting in India*, Yale University Press.

Bushnell, G., 1968, *The First Americans*, Thames and Hudson.

Campbell, J., 1962, *The Masks of God: Oriental Mythology*, Viking Press.

Chadwick, J., 1987, *Linear B and related scripts*, British Museum.

Chakrabarti, D. K., 1988, *A History of Indian Archaeology*, Munshiram Manoharlal.

_____. 1997, *The Archaeology of Ancient Indian Cities*, Oxford UniversityPress Delhi.

Clarke, D. L., 1979, "Towns in the Development of Early Civilization" in *Analytical Archaeologist: The Collected Papers of David L. Clarke*, Academic Press, pp. 435–443.

Cleuziou, S and M. Tosi, 1994, "Black Boats of Magan: Some Thoughts on Bronze Age Water Transport in Oman and Beyond from the Impressed Bitumen Slabs of Ra's al-Junayz" in eds. Parpola and Koskikallio, pp. 744–761.

Congreve, H., 1844, "Some Observation on a Remarkable Cromlech near Pullicondah in the Carnatic," *Madras Journal of Literature and Science*, Vol. 13, pp. 48–49

Crawford, H., 1998, *Dilmun and its Gulf Neighbours*, Cambridge University Press.

Crystal, D., 1987 *The Cambridge Encyclopedia of Language*, Cambridge University Press.

Culbert, T. P., 1974, *The Lost Civilization: The story of the Classic Maya*, Harper and Row.

Cunningham, A., 1875, "Harappa," *Archaeological Survey of India: Report for the Years 1872–3*, pp. 105–108. Reprinted in ed. Possehl (1979c), pp. 102–104.

Dales, G. F., 1964, "The Mythical Massacre at Mohenjo Daro" in ed. Possehl (1982), pp. 293–296.

_____. 1974 "Excavations at Balakot, Pakistan, 1973," *Journal of Field Archaeology*, Vol. 1, No. 1/2, pp. 3–22.

_____. 1979, "Excavations at Balakot," in ed. Taddei, pp. 241–274.

_____. 1982, "Mohenjodaro Miscellany: Some Unpublished, Forgotten or Misinterpreted Features" in ed. Possehl (1982), pp. 97–106.

Dales, G. F. and J. M. Kenoyer, 1977, "Shellworking at Ancient Balakot, Pakistan," *Expedition*, Vol. 19, No. 2, pp. 13–19.

_____. 1986, *Excavations at Mohenjo Daro, Pakistan: The Pottery*, University of Pennsylvania Museum.

_____. 1993, "The Harappa Project 1986–9: New Investigations at an Ancient Indus City" in ed. Possehl (1993), pp. 469–520.

Dani, A. H., 1992, "Pastoral-Agricultural Tribes of Pakistan in the Post-Indus Period" in eds. Dani and Masson, pp. 395–420.

Dani, A. H. and V. M. Masson, eds., 1992, *History of Civilizations of Central Asia*, Vol. 1, *The Dawn of Civilization: Earliest Times to 700 BC*, UNESCO Publishing.

Dani, A. H. and B. K. Thapar, 1992, "The Indus Civilization" in eds. Dani and Masson, pp. 283–318.

Davies, W. V., 1987, *Egyptian Hieroglyphs*, British Museum.

Dumont, L., 1980, *Homo Hierarchicus*, revised ed., Chicago University Press.

During Caspers, E., 1984, "Sumerian Trading Communities Residing in Harappan Society" in eds. Lal and Gupta, pp. 363–370.

Edens, C., 1993, "Indus-Arabian Interaction during the Bronze Age: a Review of Evidence" in ed. Possehl (1993), pp. 335–363.

Fairservis, W. A., 1982, "Allahdino: An Excavation of a Small Harappan Site" in ed. Possehl (1982), pp. 106–112.

_____. 1983, "Harappan Civilization According to its Writing" in ed. B. Allchin, *South Asian Archaeology* (1981), pp. 155–161.

_____. 1984, "Archaeology in Baluchistan and the Harappan Problem" in eds. Lal and Gupta, pp. 277–287.

Fairservis, W. A. and F. C. Southworth, 1989, "Linguistic Archaeology and the Indus Valley Culture" in ed. Kenoyer (1989b), pp. 133–144.

Fentress, M., 1978, " Winter Rains and Summer Floods," *Recent Advances in Indo-Pacific Prehistory*, Xth ICAES (Poona).

Gadd, C. J., 1932, "Seals of Ancient Indian Style Found at Ur." Reprinted in ed. Possehl (1979c), pp. 115–122.

Gadd, C. J. and S. Smith, 1924, "The New Links between Indian and Babylonian Civilizations." Reprinted in ed. Possehl (1979c), pp. 109–110.

George, A., 1999, *The Epic of Gilgamesh. A New Translation*, Alan Lane, Penguin Press.

Gropp, G., 1992, "A 'Great Bath' in Elam" in ed. C. Jarrige, pp. 113–118.

Guha, S., 1994, "Recognizing 'Harappan': A Critical Review of the Position of Hunter-Gatherers Within Harappan Society," *South Asian Studies*, Vol. 10, pp. 91–97.

Gupta, P. L., 1969, *Coins*, National Book Trust (New Delhi).

Gupta, S. P., 1984, "Internal Trade of the Harappans" in eds. Lal and Gupta, pp. 417–424.

Hammond, N., 1973, *South Asian Archaeology*, Duckworth.

Halim, M. A. and M. Vidale, 1984, "Kilns, Bangles and Coated Vessels" in eds. Jansen & Urban, pp. 63–97.

Hegde, K. T. M., R. V. Karanth and S. P. Sychanthavong, 1982, "On the Composition and Technology of Harappan Microbeads" in ed. Possehl (1982), pp. 239–243.

Houston, S. D., 1989, *Maya Glyphs*, British Museum.

Huntington, S. L., 1995, *The Art of Ancient India*, Weatherhill (New York).

Janaway, R. C. and R. Coningham, 1995, "A Review of Archaeological Textile Evidence from South Asia," *South Asian Studies*, Vol. 11, pp. 157–174.

Jansen, M., 1979, "Architectural Problems of the Harappa Culture" in ed. Taddei, pp. 405–431.

_____. 1981, "Settlement patterns in the Harappa Culture" in ed. Hartel *South Asian Archaeology 1979* (Berlin), pp. 251–269.

_____. 1985, "Mohenjo-daro HR-A, House I, a Temple?—Analysis of an Architectural Structure" in eds. Schotsmans and Taddei, pp. 157–206.

_____. 1987, "Preliminary Results on the 'forma urbis'

Research at Mohenjo-Daro" in eds. Jansen and Urban, pp. 9–22.

———. 1993, *Mohenjo Daro: City of Wells and Drains*, Bergisch Gladbach.

———. 1994, "Mohenjo Daro, Type Site of the Earliest Urbanization Process in South Asia: Ten Years of Research at Mohenjo-Daro, Pakistan and an Attempt at a Synopsis" in eds. Parpola and Koskikallio, pp. 263–274.

Jansen, M. and G. Urban, eds., 1984, *Interim Reports*, Vol. 1., Aachen.

———. 1987, *Interim Reports*, Vol. 2., Aachen.

Jarrige, C., 1992, ed., *South Asian Archaeology 1989*, Madison.

Jarrige, J.-F., 1982, "Excavations at Mehrgarh: Their Significance for Understanding the Background of the Harappan Civilization" in ed. Possehl (1982), pp. 79–84.

———. 1984, "Towns and Villages of Hill and Plain" in eds. Lal and Gupta, pp. 289–300.

Jarrige, J.-F. and M. Santoni, 1979, *Fouilles de Pirak*, Diffusion de Boccard (Paris).

Johnson, G., 1995, *Cultural Atlas of India*, Andromeda.

Kennedy, K. A. R., 1982, "Skulls, Aryans and Flowing Drains: the Interface of Archaeology and Skeletal Biology in the Study of the Harappan Civilization" in ed. Possehl (1982), pp. 289–295.

Kennedy, K. A. R. and G. Possehl, eds., 1984, *Studies in the Archaeology and Paleoanthropology of South Asia*, Oxford University Press.

Kenoyer, J. M., 1984a, "Shell Industries at Moenjodaro, Pakistan" in eds. Jansen and Urban, pp. 99–115.

———. 1984b, "Chipped stones from Mohenjo-Daro" in eds. Lal and Gupta, pp. 117–132

———. 1985, "Shell Working at Moenjo-daro, Pakistan" in eds. Schotsmans and Taddei, pp. 297–344.

———. 1989a, "Socio-Economic Structures in the Indus Civilization as Reflected in Specialized Crafts and the Question of Ritual Segregation" in ed. Kenoyer (1989b), pp. 183–192.

———. ed., 1989b, *Old Problems and New Perspectives in the Archaeology of South Asia*, Wisconsin Archaeological Reports, Vol. 2, Department of Anthropology, University of Wisconsin.

———. ed., 1994a, *From Sumer to Meluhha*, Wisconsin Archaeological Reports, Vol. 3, Department of Anthropology, University of Wisconsin.

———. 1994b, "Experimental Studies of Indus Valley Technology at Harappa" in eds. Parpola and Koskikallio, pp. 345–362.

———. 1998, *Ancient Cities of the Indus Valley Civilization*, Oxford University Press Karachi.

Kesarwani, A., 1984, "Harappan Gateways: A Functional Reassessment" in eds. Lal and Gupta, pp. 63–73.

Knox, R., 1994, "A New Indus Valley Cylinder Seal" in eds. Parpola and Koskikallio, pp. 375–378.

Kocchar, N., R. Kocchar and D. K. Chakrabarti, 1999, "A New Source of Primary Tin Ore in the Indus Civilization," *South Asian Studies*, Vol. 15, pp. 115–118.

Kuz'mina, E. E., 1994, "Horses, Chariots and the Indo-Iranians: An Archaeological Spark in the Historical Dark" in eds. Parpola and Koskikallio, pp. 403–412.

Lal, B. B., 1971, "Perhaps the Earliest Ploughed Field so far Excavated anywhere in the World," *Puratattva*, Vol. 4, pp. 1–3.

———. 1984, "Some Reflections on the Structural Remains at Kalibangan" in eds. Lal and Gupta, pp. 55–62.

———. 1997, *The Earliest Civilization of South Asia: Rise, Maturity and Decline*, Aryan Books International.

Lal, B. B. and S. P. Gupta, eds., 1984, *Frontiers of the Indus Civilization: Sir Mortimer Wheeler Commemoration Volume*, Indian Archaeological Society and Indian History and Culture Society, Books & Books (Delhi).

Lechevallier, M. and G. Quivron, 1985, "Results of the Recent Excavations at the Neolithic Site of Mehrgarh, Pakistan" in eds. Schotsmans and Taddei, pp. 69–90 .

Leshnik, L., 1973, "Land Use and Ecological Factors in Prehistoric North-West India" in ed. Hammond, pp. 67–84.

Lovell, N. C. and K. A. R. Kennedy, 1989, "Society and Disease in Prehistoric South Asia" in ed. Kenoyer (1989b), pp. 89–92.

Lyonnet, B., 1994, "Central Asia, the Indo-Aryans and the Iranians: Some Reassessments from Recent Archaeological Data" in eds. Parpola and Koskikallio, pp. 425–433.

Mackay, E. J. H., 1931, "Further Links between Ancient Sind, Sumer and Elsewhere" in ed. Possehl (1979c), pp. 123–129.

———. 1943, *Chanhu-daro Excavations 1935–36*, Yale University Press.

Maisels, C. K., 1999, *Early Civilizations of the Old World*, Routledge.

Mallory, J. P., 1989, *In Search of the Indo-Europeans: Language, Archaeology and Myth*, Thames and Hudson.

Marshall, J., 1924, "First Light on a Forgotten Civilization," *Illustrated London News*, 20 September 1924, pp. 528–532 and 548. Reprinted in ed. Possehl (1979c), pp. 105–110.

———. 1926a, "Harappa and Mohenjo Daro" *Annual Report of the Archaeological Survey of India, 1923–4*, pp. 47–54. Reprinted in ed. Possehl (1979c), pp. 181–186.

_____. 1926b, "Mohenjo-daro," *Illustrated London News*, 27 February 1926, Reprinted in Bacon , pp. 228–230.

_____. 1931, *Mohenjo Daro and the Indus Civilization*, Probsthain (London).

Meadow, R., 1984, "A Camel Skeleton from Mohenjo-Daro" in eds. Lal and Gupta, pp. 133–139.

_____. 1989, "Continuity and Change in the Agriculture of the Greater Indus Valley: The Paleoethnobotanical and Zooarchaeological Evidence" in ed. Kenoyer (1989b), pp. 61–74.

_____. ed., 1991, *Harappa Excavations 1986–1990*, Prehistory Press (Madison).

_____. 1993, "Animal Domestication in the Middle East: A Revised View from the Eastern Margin" in ed. Possehl (1993), pp. 295–315.

Mehta, D. P. and G. Possehl, 1993, "Excavation at Rojdi, District Rajkot," *Indian Archaeology—A Review, 1992–93*, pp. 31–32.

Mehta, R. N., 1984, "Valabhi—A Station of Harappan Cattle-Breeders" in eds. Lal and Gupta , pp. 227–230.

Mery, S., 1994, "Excavation of an Indus Potter's Workshop at Nausharo (Baluchistan), Period II" in eds. Parpola and Koskikallio, pp. 471–481.

Millar, H. M.-L., 1994, "Metal processing at Harappa and Mohenjo-Daro: Information from Non-metal Remains" in eds. Parpola and Koskikallio, pp. 497–509.

Misra, V. N., 1984, "Climate, a Factor in the Rise and Fall of the Indus Civilization—Evidence from Rajasthan and Beyond" in eds. Lal and Gupta, pp. 461–489.

_____. 1994, "Indus Civilization and Regvedic Sarasvati" in eds. Parpola and Koskikallio, pp. 511–526.

Momin, K. N., 1984, "Village Harappans in Kheda District of Gujurat" in eds. Lal and Gupta, pp. 231–234.

Neumayer, E., 1983, *Prehistoric Indian Rock Paintings*, Oxford University Press Delhi.

O'Flaherty, W., 1975, *Hindu Myths*, Penguin.

Parekh, V. S. and V. H. Sonawane, 1991, "Excavations at Loteshwar, District Mahesana," *Indian Archaeology—A Review, 1990–91*, pp. 12–16.

_____. 1992, "Excavation at Pithad, District Jamnagar," *Indian Archaeology—Areview, 1991–92*, pp. 22–26.

Parpola, A., 1983, "New Correspondences between Harappan and Near Eastern Glyptic Art" in ed. B. Allchin, *South Asian Archaeology 1981*, pp. 176–195.

_____. 1985a, "The Harappan 'Priest-King's' Robe and the Vedic Tarpya Garment: Their Interrelation and Symbolism (Astral and Procreative)" in eds. Schotsmans and Taddei, pp. 385–403.

_____. 1985b "The Sky-Garment. A Study of the Harappan Religion and its Relationship to the Mesopotamian and Later Indian Religions," *Studia Orientalia* (Helsinki), Vol. 57.

_____. 1988 "The Coming of the Aryans to Iran and India and the Cultural and Ethnic Identity of the Dasas," *Studia Orientalia* (Helsinki), Vol. 64, pp. 195–302.

_____. 1992, "The 'Fig-Deity Seal' from Mohenjo-daro: Its Iconography and Inscription" in ed. C. Jarrige, pp. 227–236.

_____. 1994, *Deciphering the Indus Script*, Cambridge University Press.

Parpola, A. and P.Koskikallio, eds., 1994 *South Asian Archaeology 1993* (Helsinki).

Pelegrin, J., 1994, "Lithic Technology in Harappan Times" in eds. Parpola and Koskikallio, pp. 587–598.

Piggott, S., 1950, *Prehistoric India*, Penguin.

Pollack, S., 1999, *Ancient Mesopotamia*, Cambridge University Press.

Possehl, G., 1979a, "Lothal: A Gateway Settlement of the Harappan Civilization" in ed. Possehl (1979c), pp. 212–218.

_____. 1979b, "Pastoral Nomadism in the Indus Civilization" in ed. Taddei, pp. 537–551.

_____. ed., 1979c, *Ancient Cities of the Indus*, Vikras Publishing House (Delhi)

_____. 1980, *The Indus Civilization in Saurashtra*, Indian Archaeological Society, B. R. Publishing (New Delhi).

_____. ed., 1982, *Harappan Civilization*, Oxford University Press Delhi.

_____. 1986 *Kulli: an Exploration of Ancient Civilization in South Asia*, Carolina Academic Press (Durham).

_____. 1990, "Revolution in the Urban Revolution: the Emergence of Indus Urbanization," *Annual Review of Anthropology*, Vol. 19, pp. 261–282.

_____. 1992, "The Harappan Cultural Mosaic: Ecology Revisited" in ed. C. Jarrige, pp. 237–241.

_____. ed., 1993, *Harappan Civilization*, 2nd ed., Oxford University Press Delhi.

_____. 1994 "Govindbhai-no Vadi" in ed. B. Allchin, pp. 193–204.

_____. 1996 *Indus Age: The Writing System*, Oxford University Press Delhi.

_____. 1999, *Indus Age: The Beginnings*, Oxford University Press Delhi.

Possehl, G. and M. H. Raval, 1991, "Excavation at Babar Kot, District Bhavnagar," *Indian Archaeology—A Review, 1990–91*, pp. 6–8.

Postgate, J. N., 1992, *Early Mesopotamia. Society and Economy at the Dawn of History*, Routledge.

Potts, D. T., 1993, "Tell Abraq and the Harappan Tradition in Southeastern Arabia" in ed. Possehl (1993), pp. 323–333.

_____. 1999, *The Archaeology of Elam*, Cambridge University Press.

Pracchia, S. 1987 "Surface Analysis of Pottery Manufacture Areas at Mohenjdaro: the 1984 Season" in eds. Jansen and Urban, pp. 151–167.

Pracchia, S., M. Tosi and M. Vidale 1985 "Craft Industries at Moenjo-Daro" in eds. Schotsmans and Taddei, pp. 207–248 .

Raikes, R. L., 1984, "Mohenjo Daro Environment" in eds. Lal and Gupta, pp. 455–460.

Rao, S. R., 1973, *Lothal and the Indus Civilization*, Asia Publishing House (Bombay).

_____. 1979 (Vol. 1) and 1985 (Vol. 2), *Lothal: A Harappan Town (1955–62)*, Memoirs of the Archaeological Survey of India, No. 78.

Ratnagar, S. 1981, *Encounters: The Westerly Trade of the Harappa Civilization*, Oxford University Press Delhi.

_____. 1991, *Enquiries into the Political Organisation of Harappan Society*, Ravish, Pune.

Roaf, M., 1990, *Cultural Atlas of Mesopotamia and the Ancient Near East*, Facts on File.

Robinson, A., 1995, *The Story of Writing*, Thames and Hudson.

_____. 2001, *Lost Languages*, Peter N. Nevraumont Book, McGraw-Hill.

Roux, G., 1980, *Ancient Iraq*, 2nd ed., Penguin.

Sayce, A. H., 1924, "Remarkable Discoveries in India" in ed. Possehl (1979c), p. 108.

Schele, L. and M. E. Millar, 1992, *The Blood of Kings*, Thames and Hudson.

Schele, L. and D. Freidel, 1990, *A Forest of Kings*, William Morrow.

Schotsmans, J. and M. Taddei, eds., 1985, *South Asian Archaeology 1983*, Naples.

Shaffer, J., 1978, *Prehistoric Baluchistan*, Indian Society for Prehistoric and Quaternary Studies (New Delhi).

_____. 1984, "Bronze Age Iron from Afghanistan: Its Implications for South Asian Protohistory" in eds. Kennedy and Possehl, pp. 41–62.

Sharma, A. K., 1982, "The Harappan Cemetery at Kalibangan: A Study" in ed. Possehl (1982), pp. 297–299.

Shinde, V., 1991, "Excavation at Padri, District Bhavnagar" *Indian Archaeology—A Review*, 1990–91, pp. 8–10.

_____. 1992, "Excavation at Padri, District Bhavnagar," *Indian Archaeology—A Review*, 1991–92, pp. 21–22.

_____. 1998, "Pre-Harappan Padri Culture in Saurashtra: The Recent Discovery," *South Asian Studies*, Vol. 14, pp. 173–182.

Srinivasan, S., 1997, "Present and Past of Southern Indian Crafts for Making Mirrors, Lamps, Bells, Vessels, Cymbals and Gongs: Links with Prehistoric High Tin Bronzes from Mohenjodaro, Taxila, South Indian Megaliths, and Later Finds," *South Asian Studies*, Vol. 13, pp. 209–225.

Steen, A. B., 1986, "The Hindu Jajmani System—Economy or Religion? An Outline of Different Theories and Models" in eds. Parpola, A. and B. Schmidt Hansen, *South Asian Religion and Society*, Scandinavian Institute of Asian Studies, pp. 30–41.

Taddei, M., ed., 1979, *South Asian Archaeology, 1977*, Naples.

Thapar, B.K., 1975, "Kalibangan: A Harappan Metropolis beyond the Indus Valley" in ed. Possehl (1979c), pp. 196–202.

Tosi, M., 1993, "The Harappan Civilization beyond the Indian Subcontinent" in ed. Possehl (1993), pp. 365–377.

Vidale, M. 1987a "Some Aspects of Lapidary Craft at Moenjodaro in the light of the Surface Record of the Moneer South East Area" in eds. Jansen and Urban, pp. 113–149.

_____. 1987b, "More Evidence on a Protohistoric Ceramic Puzzle" in eds. Jansen and Urban, pp. 105–11.

_____. 1989 "Specialized producers and Urban Elites: On the Role of Craft Industries in Mature Harappan Urban Contexts" in ed. Kenoyer (1989b), pp. 170–181.

Walker, C. B. F., 1987, *Cuneiform*, British Museum.

Wanzke, H., 1984, "Axis Systems and Orientation at Mohenjo-Daro" in eds. Jansen and Urban, pp. 33–44.

Wheeler, R. E. M., 1947, "Harappan Chronology and the Rig Veda," *Ancient India*, Vol. 3, pp. 78–82. Reprinted in ed. Possehl (1979c), pp. 288–292.

_____. 1953, *The Indus Civilization*, Cambridge University Press.

_____. 1966, *Civilizations of the Indus Valley and Beyond*, Thames and Hudson.

_____. 1968, *The Indus Civilization*, 3rd ed., Cambridge University Press.

Woolley, L., 1982, *Ur 'of the Chaldees'*, revised and updated by P. R. S. Moorey, Herbert Press.

Wright, R. P., 1989, "The Indus Valley and Mesopotamian Civilizations: A Comparative View of Ceramic Technology" in ed. Kenoyer (1989b), pp. 145–156.

Yash Pal, B. Sahai, R. K. Snood and D. P. Agrawal, 1984, "Remote Sensing of the 'Lost' Saraswati River" in eds. Lal and Gupta, pp. 491–497.

Yule, P. 1988, "A Harappan 'Snarling Iron' from Chanhu daro," *Antiquity*, no. 62, March 1988, pp. 116–118.

ILLUSTRATION CREDITS

BLACK AND WHITE FIGURES

Paolo Biagi: 63
Giraudon / Art Resource: 59, 60
Harappa.com: 3
Harappa Archaeological Research Project: 15
Harappa Archaeological Research Project / Courtesy Department of Archaeology and Museums, Government of Pakistan: 12, 14, 25, 30, 44, 48, 50, 57
Georg Helmes / German Research Project on Mohenjo-daro: 11, 26, 56
Illustrated London News Picture Library: 2
Kenneth A.R. Kennedy: 7, 8
Jonathan M. Kenoyer / Courtesy Department of Archaeology and Museums, Government of Pakistan: 1, 5, 16, 17, 19, 20, 21, 22, 23, 24, 28, 29, 31, 32, 34, 35, 37, 38, 40, 41, 42, 43, 45, 46, 47, 49, 54, 55, 61, 62
Jonathan M. Kenoyer: 6, 9, 58
Munir Khan: 39
Louvre / Art Resource: 53
Richard H. Meadow / Courtesy Department of Archaeology and Museums, Government of Pakistan: 13, 18, 33, 36
Asko Parpola / © Erja Lahdenperä and National Museum of India: 51
Gregory Possehl / Courtesy Archaeological Survey of India: 27
Chris Sloan / Courtesy of Jonathan M. Kenoyer: 4
University of Pennsylvania Museum: 52
Ute Franke Vogt / Courtesy Department of Archaeology and Museums, Government of Pakistan: 10

COLOR PLATES

Shari Clark and Laura Miller / Courtesy Department of Archaeology and Museums, Government of Pakistan: 5
Harappa Archaeological Research Project / Courtesy Department of Archaeology and Museums, Government of Pakistan: 21, 22
Jonathan M. Kenoyer / Courtesy Department of Archaeology and Museums, Government of Pakistan: 2, 3, 4, 7, 9, 10, 11, 12, 14, 15, 16, 17, 18, 19, 20, 23, 25
Scala / Art Resource: 1, 6, 8
Dinesh Skukla: 13
Ute Franke Vogt / Courtesy Department of Archaeology and Museums, Government of Pakistan: 24

MAPS

All maps by Simone Nevraumont

INDEX

tin, 168; source 68; trade 170, 171, 175,
208; weight 125

tool, 9, 21, 35, 102, 124, 126, 138, 159, 163,
179, 201, 206; bone 181; stone 17, 32,
33, 34, 38, 40, 70, 174, 185; flint
blade 66–67

trade, 51, 77, 88, 97, 105, 121, 125, 126, 139,
147, 157–175, 177, 183, 185, 188, 199, 206,
211; Oman (Magan), with, 59, 64

trefoils, 74, 108, 111, 116

Turkestan, 18

Turkmenia, 40, 45, 172

turquoise, 40, 72, 157, 208

Unicorn, 113, 137; figurine 25; seal
109, 136, 138, 174

University of Aachen, 27, 29, 80, 102

University of Pennsylvania, 159

Ur, 16, 19; royal cemetery 7, 111, 161,
162, 164; trade 161, 162, 167

Ur-Nammu, 161, 165

Uralic languages, 147

Uruk, 159, 161, 164, 165, 178

Utnur, 182

Vedas, 16, 20, 108, 128, 147, 192, 196

vegetarianism, 129

Ventris, Michael, 144

Vidale, Massimo, 135

Vishnu, 120, 196, 199

Wahinda River, 54

warfare, 42, 51, 177, 181, 182, 185, 209

water buffalo, 55, 111, 115; tablet 117;
seal 155

weapon, 23, 42, 128, 178, 179, 193

weight, 67, 125, 166, 167, 170, 201

well, 56, 100, 109, 1865

wheat, 37, 38, 39, 43, 56, 182, 190, 191,
192, 200; trade 171

wheel, 78; (sun) sign 154; pottery 63;
spinning 78

Wheeler, (Sir) Mortimer, 20–23, 87,
96, 97, 99, 102, 118, 177; "massacre",
and 120, 178–179

woodworking, 9, 77–78, 201, 206

wool, 55, 80, 163, clothes 134; trade 171,
172, 206

Woolley, (Sir) Leonard, 16, 162

writing, 50, 51, 92, 128, 135, 138, 139, 141,
142, 151, 153, 154, 185, 195, 199, 202,
203, 210; invention of 9, 59, 161;
seal, on 136, 167; vessel, on 137

Yama (god of death), 118

Yamuna River, 54, 88, 189, 190, 193

Yellow River, 7

Yoga, 115, 155

yoni, 108, 116

Zagros Mountains, 38, 39, 161, 164

zebu, 39, 168; figurine 114; seal 138, 129

Zekda, 74

Ziusudra, 159, 165